THE JAPANESE IN THE WESTERN MIND

This fascinating book is an insightful exploration of Western perceptions and representations of Japanese culture and society, drawing on social and cultural psychological ideas around stereotypes and intercultural relations.

Hinton considers how the West views the Japanese as an ideologically different "other", and proposes a cultural theory of stereotypes from which to explore Western observations of the Japanese. The book explores Western socio-cultural representations of the Japanese alongside Edward Said's well-known theory of Orientalism. It examines the West's intercultural relationship with Japan, and how this has changed over time, to show how the Japanese have been represented in the Western mind throughout history, to the present day. Hinton argues that our view of other cultures is based on our own cultural expectations, which involve complex issues of meaning-making and perceived cultural differences. This book foregrounds the research through accounts of Westerners about the Japanese, to reveal how cultural representations can influence the ways in which people from different cultures communicate in interaction, and how intercultural understanding or misunderstanding can arise.

By reflecting on the changing Western representations of the Japanese, and how and why these have emerged, this book will be of interest to students, academics and general readers interested in stereotypes, cultural psychology, intercultural communication, anthropology and Japanese culture and history.

Perry R. Hinton is a cultural psychologist and professor in the Department of Applied Linguistics, at the University of Warwick, UK. His research focuses on stereotypes and intercultural communication, specifically on the cultural formation of stereotypes, and Western media interpretation of Japanese popular culture. His most recent book is *Stereotypes and the Construction of the Social World* (Routledge 2020).

THE JAPANESE IN THE WESTERN MIND

A Psychological History of the Cultural Other

Perry R. Hinton

Routledge
Taylor & Francis Group
LONDON AND NEW YORK

Designed cover image: @ Getty Images

First published 2023
by Routledge
4 Park Square, Milton Park, Abingdon, Oxon OX14 4RN

and by Routledge
605 Third Avenue, New York, NY 10158

Routledge is an imprint of the Taylor & Francis Group, an informa business

British Library Cataloguing-in-Publication Data
A catalogue record for this book is available from the British Library

ISBN: 978-0-367-53469-1 (hbk)
ISBN: 978-0-367-53467-7 (pbk)
ISBN: 978-1-003-08208-8 (ebk)

DOI: 10.4324/9781003082088

Typeset in Bembo
by Apex CoVantage, LLC

To Anna, Anthony and Emma

The actual people who live in Japan are not unlike the general run of English people; that is to say, they are extremely commonplace, and have nothing curious or extraordinary about them. In fact the whole of Japan is a pure invention.

Oscar Wilde (1894, p. 46) *The Decay of Lying*

CONTENTS

PREFACE

This is a book about the Japanese, but its focus is on the different ways that the Japanese have been viewed by Westerners – the people of Europe and North America – from the time when the first Europeans arrived on the shores of Japan in the mid-16th century up to the early 21st century, approaching 500 years of Western-Japanese relations. The motivation to write this book comes from my research interests as a cultural psychologist in the relationship between culture and cognition (making-sense), particularly in the way that our cultural background influences the way we represent people from other cultures. There have been two main strands to my academic research, the psychology of stereotypes and the representation of Japanese popular culture in the British media. This book brings those interests together.

In my work, I have argued that social representations, typically called stereotypes, are not simplistic or fixed images of a social group as a result of some sort of mental error or bias, as proposed in the traditional view of stereotypes, but that stereotypes are social constructions based on the ideology of the cultural group doing the stereotyping. These ideas are described in my book *Stereotypes and the Construction of the Social World* (published by Routledge 2020). Indeed, in my book, I have proposed a cultural theory of stereotypes in contrast to the tradition view that typically has ignored the role of culture in stereotyping. This leads to some interesting questions about people from one culture viewing those from another, such as Westerners observing the Japanese, which are explored in this book. Are these representations simplistic stereotypes or should they be viewed as more complex interpretations? Also, why do these particular representations arise at these particular times? As I shall explore in the book, when Westerners attempt to make sense of the Japanese, they do this in terms of their own cultural expectations, as well as seeking to understand the Japanese in terms of the current state of the relationship between the West and Japan. Indeed, I argue that Western representations of Japan are not either right or wrong, but involve complex issues of meaning-making in the context of perceived cultural differences, in the context of an intercultural relationship.

Yet at the same time, in my research into British media representations of Japanese popular culture, I have shown that the way the Japanese are represented in the British media often tells us more about British cultural expectations, which have been employed to represent the Japanese, than about the Japanese themselves. This is because when people from one cultural background – Westerners – view the behaviour of people from another culture – the Japanese – it is not just the behaviour they report but also their interpretation of it, particularly when the behaviour is unexpected. Hence, the British media interpretation of the Japanese is often more to do with British concerns about – or enjoyment of – their relationship with the Japanese. These interpretations are often very different from the ways the Japanese represent themselves. Indeed, during the last fifty years, the Western perceptions of the Japanese have involved concerns about the Japanese during its economic miracle when Western countries were anxious about their economic performance in contrast to that of the Japanese. Later when the Japanese economy stagnated, the Western economic concerns went away and, for much of the last thirty years, the Japanese have been viewed in terms of the products of their popular culture, such as video games and games consoles, *manga* (comics), *anime* (animated movies) and all the exciting aspects of Japanese design. While my research has focused on the more recent relationship of Westerners with the Japanese, in this book, I am exploring the whole history of that intercultural relationship to illustrate how Western perceptions of the Japanese have changed over nearly 500 years. I will do this by examining the accounts of Westerners about the Japanese during this time. While this approach may not tell us very much about the Japanese, it reveals a very interesting story of the changing ways in which the Japanese have been represented in the Western mind.

I would like to thank all my colleagues and friends who have contributed to my thinking over the years about this topic and have shared my interest in Japanese culture; from the time, many years ago, when I first studied Japanese with a lovely group of people at Kellogg College, University of Oxford, through to all my friends and colleges at the Department of Applied Linguistics at the University of Warwick. In particular, I would like to thank Ema Ushioda, Troy McConarchy and David Fickling for their very helpful discussions about the West and Japan. This has made for some very enjoyable coffee breaks which, although this book is now finished, I hope will continue for a long time to come.

1

THE INTROVERTED SAMURAI

What are the Japanese like?

Since Europeans first encountered the Japanese nearly 500 years ago, there has been speculation about the Japanese character and its relationship to their culture. Are they mild-mannered artisans or hard-hearted warriors? Are they duty-bound and introverted or inventively kooky? With the advent of Western social science (particularly anthropology and psychology), there have been attempts to answer these questions academically. Is there a distinct Japanese character or distinct Japanese culture that can be identified? As we shall see in this chapter, aspects of Japanese character have been described in anthropology and psychology and attempts have been made to distinguish "true" measures of national character from "false" descriptions, called stereotypes. However, this book challenges these ideas. Rather than assuming that there is an enduring Japanese character or Japanese culture to find, this book turns the focus from the people being judged (the Japanese) back on to the people doing the judging (Westerners). It asks a different question: why have Westerners in their engagement with the Japanese represented them in the ways that they have? Crucially, it argues that we cannot separate Western perceptions of the Japanese from the intercultural relationship between the West and Japan. Indeed, Western judgements of the Japanese will tell us just as much – if not more – about the beliefs and assumptions of Westerners than it tells us anything about the Japanese. In consequence, it is argued here that Western perceptions of the Japanese reflect the state of intercultural relations between the Westerners and the Japanese – even for Western social scientists. Hence, after the first chapter, this book examines the changing ways in which Westerners have viewed the Japanese by focusing on the key aspects of the intercultural relationship at different times to identify the reasons why Westerners have made sense of the Japanese in the ways that they have.

DOI: 10.4324/9781003082088-1

More specifically, it examines the ways in which the Japanese have been socially constructed by Westerners in their communication, and the representations of the Japanese that have emerged from it. Rather than revealing enduring aspects of Japanese character, it provides an explanation of the different representations of the Japanese that have been constructed in their accounts by Westerners, which have arisen from the cultural meaning-making of the Western mind. However, before giving this historical account of the ways that Westerners have viewed the Japanese, I am going to begin by considering the attempts to identify the Japanese character in Western academia.

Western anthropology and the character of the Japanese

The Enlightenment set the foundation for Western science, and its fascination with categorizing the world, which produced great advances in knowledge. Carl Linnaeus (1707–1778) produced a systematic analysis of flora and fauna in terms of a hierarchical system, from kingdom at the top to class and genus to species, based on the physical similarities and differences of plants and animals. Despite subsequent changes, the Linnaean system still forms the basis of modern botanical and zoological classification systems. Linnaeus also located people within the animal kingdom with the binomial *homo sapiens*. However, he divided humans into four continental groups, *albescens* (whitish) Europeans, *nigriculus* (blackish) Africans and *rubescens* (reddish) Americans, with Asians as *luridus* (wan, sallow, pale yellow).[1] It is worth mentioning here that the Japanese, who in the Linnaean system were labelled as "yellow" (like other Asians), had been by Linneaus's time viewed by Europeans as "white" during two centuries of intercultural contact (Keevak, 2011; Kowner, 2014, see Chapters 2 and 3). While Linnaeus had not specifically used the term "race" in his classification of people, others did, such as Voltaire, the French philosopher, the British philosopher David Hume, and the German physician Johann Blumenbach (Harris, 1968). Human racial hierarchies were then created (by Europeans) with the "white" and "civilized" Europeans at the top and other "races" below them. Numerous measurements of physical features and social structures were undertaken of other "races" in the guise of scientific investigation but were deliberately interpreted to support a pre-existing racist ideology – which is now appropriately referred to as "pseudoscientific racism" (Pickering, 2001). As Blakey (1999, p. 29) pointed out, the so-called human races were "created by the scientists, not be nature". Particularly in the 19th century, at the height of European imperialism, this scientific racism, or biological essentialism,[2] was employed in Western media representations to justify and normalize European colonialism as the bringing of "civilization" to the other "races" of the world (Pickering, 2001). It is again worth noting here that, before the 19th century, the Japanese had been viewed not only as white but also as civilized by European visitors to Japan for centuries (see Chapter 3). Also, despite at one time or another dominating much of Asia, the European empires failed to colonize Japan (see Chapter 4).

Within anthropology, the German American Franz Boas (1858–1942), and his followers, debunked the idea that human societies can be distinguished in evolutionary terms on a scale from "primitive" to "civilized". Furthermore, societies do not evolve by the "laws of nature", but they change over time, historically, in terms of their culture (Cravens, 2010). Thus, it is to a culture that social scientists should look to distinguish between societies. Anthropologists, such as Ruth Benedict and Margaret Mead, followers of Boas, sought to examine other cultures to understand the rationale of their lives. In her 1934 book, *Patterns of Culture*, Benedict argued that a culture has a distinctive pattern, and this pattern influences the thought and actions of the individual members of it. Just as a psychologist might study the character of an individual, anthropology can study the character of a culture, because "Most people are shaped to the form of their culture because of the enormous malleability of their original endowment. They are plastic to the moulding force of the society into which they are born" (Benedict, 1934/1959, p. 254). Crucially, this is a rejection of the biological determination of a cultural character and the idea of cultural hierarchies. It is the cultural forces that create the specific character or pattern of a culture. National character is a pattern of learnt cultural behaviour. Thus, different cultures, like two different individuals, have different goals. "They are travelling along different roads in pursuit of different ends" (Benedict, 1934/1959, p. 223). For this reason, she argued, one culture cannot be judged in terms of another. Benedict claimed that variations in acceptable behaviour (such as forms of sexual activity) were a result of cultural differences rather than biological prescriptions of "normality". Finally, by a close investigation, cultures can be characterized in terms of cultural character types that are developed through patterns of socialization and institutional practices.

Benedict's later book, *The Chrysanthemum and the Sword*, 1946, sought to explain the Japanese in terms of their cultural character, a book specifically commissioned for the purpose of advising the US government on its strategy of dealing with the Japanese at the end of the Pacific War (in the Second World War). Unable to visit Japan due to the war, she studied documents about Japan and other Asian cultures, examined the available products of Japanese culture, and interviewed Japanese people, and people of Japanese origin, in the United States. At the beginning of her book, she presents the Japanese as a set of binary contradictions, claiming that a "serious observer" who "writes a book about a nation with a popular cult of aestheticism . . . [including] . . . the cultivation of chrysanthemums" has to supplement that book "by another which is devoted to the cult of the sword and the top prestige of the warrior". She goes on: "All these contradictions, however, are the warp and woof of books on Japan. *They are true.* Both the sword and the chrysanthemum are a part of the picture" (Benedict, 1947, p. 1, my italics). Framed by chapters contextualizing the book in terms of the war, Benedict provided ten chapters explaining why the Japanese have the character they do.

In describing the Japanese, Benedict implicitly or explicitly contrasted them with Americans. First, the Japanese are acutely responsive to their position in the social hierarchy, which Benedict referred to as a caste system (although she accepted that the ability to change social class, or caste, is possible). This is followed by a section on the Japanese rigid obedience to a culturally specific pattern of obligations (*on*), and their repayment: either *gimu*, or ongoing dutiful behaviour, and *giri*, the repayment of a debt through an equivalence to that received. She argued that the Japanese live by an "ethics of indebtedness" (Benedict, 1947, p. 103). Crucially, Japan is a shame culture, where shame must be avoided by meeting one's social obligations; unlike the United States, a guilt culture, where moral standards must be met to avoid guilt. The Japanese are not puritans and enjoy pleasure but "Etiquette of all kinds is organized to obviate shame-causing situations" (Benedict, 1947, p. 156). It is not the fear of evil that disturbs the Japanese psyche but the risk of shame. "Shame, they say, is the root of all virtue. A man who is sensitive to it will carry out all the rules of good behaviour. . . . The primacy of shame in Japanese life means . . . that any man watches the judgement of the public upon his deeds" (Benedict, 1947, p. 224). Hence circumspection is required to avoid shame for either party in an interaction and maintain one's self-respect. While the Japanese are loving and indulgent to their children, their upbringing involves the learning of strict self-discipline to follow the obligations of society.

Benedict focused on the concept of *muga*, a state of mind that arises through self-discipline training to achieve a state of expertise. Masters of the tea ceremony, expert fencers and certain painters can perform their roles expertly and seemingly effortlessly in a way that bypasses the "observing self" (or "interfering self"). People in ordinary life seek to bring about this Zen-like state in their own lives, in their approach to work, or indeed any activity. One way to achieve muga without training is to "live as one already dead" (Benedict, 1947, p. 250). Thus, by approaching an activity without the observing self (metaphorically "as if dead"), one can be free to act "expertly", without the burden of fear, obligation or risk of shame (that the dead no longer have). An exhortation to "live as already dead" can be an encouragement for a student before a difficult examination or someone about to undertake an important business deal. Finally, Benedict examined the differences in the American and Japanese views of suicide. For the Japanese, suicide is not an immoral act but a way of restoring one's honour when no other action can achieve it. She highlighted the famous Japanese story of *The Forty-Seven Ronin*[3] to illustrate this point. Their only way to avenge the death of their lord and maintain their honour was to ultimately commit *seppuku* (also known as *hara-kiri*),[4] a ritual form of public disembowelment. As Benedict noted, the forty-seven ronin are held in high regard in Japan as a model of honourable behaviour.

In summary, Benedict argued, "The dualism in their characters creates tensions to which different Japanese respond in different way. . . . But these tensions are a heavy strain upon the individual" (Benedict, 1947, p. 291, 293). This explains why, according to Benedict, the Japanese character is a contradictory combination of "the gentle, obedient, and courteous civilian and the brutal, aggressive soldier" (Cravens, 2010, p. 308). One way to integrate these aspects of the Japanese character, as constructed by Benedict, is the view that on the surface, they appear reserved and polite yet they contain the potential for a callous disregard of the life of another or indeed their own. It is not easy to characterize this representation of the Japanese character, but I would like to suggest (maybe not too seriously) the following: the reserved or *introverted samurai*: determined not to be impolite or rude not only by their behaviour but also when socially required, so duty-bound as to exclude personal feelings. Benedict concluded that this has been achieved at great cost, presenting herself as a compassionate observer: "The Japanese have paid a high price for their way of life. They have denied themselves simple freedoms which Americans count upon unquestioningly as the air that they breathe" (Benedict, 1947, p. 294). Thus, while she may have sympathized with the Japanese, it is clear throughout the book that their culture is *alien*: the Japanese "faith and confidence in hierarchy . . . is alien to equality-loving Americans" (p. 22), "mercy towards the damaged [e.g. wounded or ill soldiers] . . . is certainly alien to the Japanese" (pp. 36–7), their shame of surrender is "alien to our conventions of warfare" (p. 40), their sense of duty and social position is "so alien to arrangements in the United States or England" (p. 81), their ideas about obligations are "so alien to us" (p. 99), a moral code of combatting evil "is alien to the Japanese" (p. 101). Indeed, she had set out her position at the very start of the book: "The Japanese were the most alien enemy the United States had ever fought" (p. 1).

The work of anthropologists such as Benedict stimulated a range of studies in Western social science on national character, seeking to reveal their different cultural personality types (Cravens, 2010). However, there was criticism of this approach. It tended to present the culture in terms of universal categories – such as Japan as a "shame culture" – which led to simplistic contrasts with America as a "guilt culture" (Kato, 1988). In order to do this, ethnographic observations were employed to make broad generalizations about Japanese people, who were assumed to exhibit this national character (Darnell, 1997). This presented an essentialist, fixed view of a national culture that ignored cultural change over time (Lie, 2001). Also, Benedict's book is selective in highlighting the cultural differences that contrast with American culture as "alien", and tends to ignore similarities. Yet hierarchy and obligation are common to many cultures, and honour is viewed as a virtue in Western societies too, with shame as something to be avoided. Also, stories of conflicting loyalties, like the *Tale of the Forty-Seven Ronin*, are not uncommon in the West (Lie, 2001). Furthermore, she ignored aspects of Japanese history, such as its colonialization of its neighbours, at the same time as its industrialization in the 19th and early 20th centuries. Indeed, rather than being a totally alien culture, Japan at the end of the 19th century aspired to be the "Great Britain of the East", a view supported in Britain itself (Conte-Helm, 2013, Hirakawa, 2005, Kublin, 1959). Also, as Lie (2001) pointed out, in focusing on the culture of Japan, Benedict ignores its institutional structures and emphasized its apparent unique and enduring culture.

Within anthropology, Ryang (2004, p. 28) has labelled Benedict's work as the "master narrative" in terms of its influence on perceptions of the Japanese, with its central focus on Japan as a shame culture. However, like Lie (2001), Ryang

(2004, p. 32) questioned Benedict's interpretation: implying that cultures have an "unchanging, fixed structure and nature", suggesting a Japanese cultural essence, and taking little account of the interaction between cultures. Crucially, Benedict's book reflected the specific context of its production, presenting the Japanese as morally inferior to the democratic freedom-loving Americans, from whom they could learn better ways, in the specific context of the Japanese defeat in the Pacific War. Yet, despite this, Benedict's book was very popular in post-war Japan. It had a key impact on the Japanese post-war discussions about themselves and their national character, referred to as *nihonjinron*, with Benedict setting out a basis for it – a fixed idea about a unique culture that could be employed in the ideological construction of Japanese identity (Lie, 2001; Ryang, 2004).

Orientalism and the representation of the Japanese

Benedict had claimed that the Japanese and Americans were cultural opposites (Lie, 2001), but rather than accepting this conclusion, it could be challenged in terms of Edward Said's concept of *Orientalism* (Minear, 1980). Within the history of Western thought, the "Orient" has been represented as a place of difference from Europe (Sanyal, 2019). Said (1978/1995) argued that, throughout Western history, Orientalists – Western experts on the East – had constructed a representation of the Orient in terms of its cultural contrast with the Occident (the West). In Western literature about the Orient, the place and the people are represented as distinct and different – an alien "them" – in contrast to the familiar "us" (Europeans). Said argued that, as a result, the Orient was "known" in Western literature. "These ideas explained the behaviour of the Oriental; they supplied Orientals with a mentality, a genealogy, an atmosphere; more important, they allowed Europeans to deal with and even to see Orientals as a phenomenon possessing regular characteristics" (Said, 1978/1995, p. 42). While Said, a Palestinian, applied his concept to the Islamic countries of the Middle East, others have applied it to the Far East, including Japan (Minear, 1980).

Said argued that the perceived differences between the West and the East, in terms of customs, religion, architecture and so on, have been interpreted in binary terms in an Orientalist framework that represents the East as ancient, mysterious, inscrutable, exotic and erotic – essentially feminine. In contrast, the West is presented as rational, technological and advanced (i.e. modern) – and male. Thus, Western discourse about the Orient has been structured, through the lens of its political and economic interests, to justify its political domination and colonization of Oriental countries (McLeod, 2010). While aspects of the Orient might be represented in positive ways, as an exotic, mysterious place to visit, it is clear that the Western pole of a binary contrast is presented more favourably, with European cultures represented as superior. Minear (1980) noted that within the writings of a number of key Western commentators on 19th- and early 20th-century Japan, the superiority of Western culture is assumed either implicitly or explicitly; suggesting that the Japanese had a lot to learn from the modern West, which has little to learn from them. In judging the Japanese against Western values, these authors – despite their positive views of the Japanese and fascination with Japanese cultural products from the wood-block prints and pottery to kimono and lacquerware – can be seen as exhibiting an Orientalism that Said identified in his book. Fifty years after these 19th-century authors, it is clear within Benedict's account that the "equality-loving Americans" with their "simple freedoms" are considered to have a superior culture to the obligation-ridden, shame culture of Japan, which is to be pitied, rather than emulated. The Orientalism criticism of Benedict's analysis of Japanese culture challenges her interpretation of the Japanese character (Lie, 2001). While she had stated that the contradictions about the Japanese character were true (see earlier), they could now be seen as Western interpretations of Japanese culture through its own Orientalist cultural lens, and hence reveal more about a Western interpretive framework than anything genuine about Japanese national character. Fifty years on from Benedict, there was a trend in anthropology to focus on the modern products of the Japanese popular culture, such as toys, video games and comics, which also risked Japan (and the Japanese) being viewed as different and exotic (Ryang, 2004, see also Chapter 7). In consequence, "the problem inherent in Japan anthropology has been over-exoticization and romanticization of Japan" (Ryang, 2004, p. 199). While Ryang argued that it was unhelpful to call this Orientalism, anthropologists have sought to avoid this criticism.

Robertson (2005) argued that, unlike Benedict, Western anthropologists studying the Japanese are now fluent in speaking and reading the language and hence avoid the linguistic misinterpretations of Benedict. Hendry (2015) has described the benefits of long-term working in Japan to gain a deep understanding of Japanese interpersonal relationships, and of working with Japanese colleagues in the research process. Ryang (2004, 2020) has sought to decouple the culture of Japan from a study of the Japanese nation state, to bring about a more complex, detailed and richer understanding of the diverse aspects of Japanese culture. Hence, modern anthropology has sought to go beyond Benedict's view of the Japanese, rejecting the concepts of cultural essence and national character, while still acknowledging the historical influence she had on the discipline, in "the attempts of non-Japanese anthropologists, among others, to unmask, unwrap, and to otherwise reveal the presumptive authentic core or essence of Japanese society" (Robertson, 2005, p. 7). Indeed, Benedict's Janus-like image of the polite, modest and quiet – introverted – Japanese alternating with the fanatic warrior – a samurai – has resonated in Western accounts of the Japanese since its proposal (see Chapters 6 and 7).

Western psychology and the character of the Japanese

While Western anthropologists focused on culture in their explanations of behaviour, American social psychologists deliberately did not. Floyd Allport (1924), one of the founders of experimental social psychology, claimed that behavioural causation lies in the individual, with group explanations being merely descriptive. As a result, there was a schism between anthropology and psychology for most of the twentieth century: a lack of communication that later both psychologists such as Jerome Bruner (1990) and anthropologists such as Bradd Shore (1996) viewed as detrimental to the disciplines. The dominant individualistic approach of academic psychology argued that there are correct judgements of the character of a social group (such as nationality), which Allport (1954) referred to as "group traits" and inaccurate "stereotypical" judgements of the character of the group: the label "stereotype" being a term invented by the journalist and political commentator Walter Lippmann (1922) for a fixed idea about a group of people.[5] Lippmann (1922, p. 89) argued that stereotypes were cognitively efficient, in that, on labelling a person as an agitator or a foreigner (two of his examples), or the Japanese (my example) "we fill in the rest of the picture by means of the stereotypes we carry about in our heads". Importantly, he made the point that these stereotypes are learnt from the culture, that is, culturally specific, a point that was often ignored in the later psychological research that was predominantly undertaken in the United States (Hinton, 2020a).

In a seminal psychological study on stereotypes, Katz and Braly (1933) asked 100 Princeton University students to select words from a list of personality characteristics "which seem to you typical of [*the nation under study*]" (p. 282). A number of nationalities were examined, including the Japanese. The responses were then aggregated across the participants. The top selected characteristics for the Japanese were intelligent and industrious, picked by over 40 percent of the students, followed by progressive, shrewd, sly and quiet (ranging from 20 to 25 percent). Katz and Braly claimed that these results revealed the stereotype of the Japanese. Furthermore, they claimed that the "stereotype" was the result of a fallacy on behalf of the participants – a mistaken belief about the group. This is an extraordinary conclusion, given that the participants had little choice in what they did when following the experimental instructions. Crucially, no claims about the participants' actual beliefs could be made using this methodology. In order to perform the task, the participants may simply have been reporting what they had picked up from the media, independent of their own beliefs. This is most likely the case, given that Katz and Braly observed that the results matched American media representations of the nationality, and they explicitly stated that the Japanese "stereotype" indicated "some recognition of the westernization of Japan" (p. 287). However, rather than examining the role a specific representation, such as this Japanese "stereotype", serves within American culture, the mainstream psychological research focused on the idea of stereotypes as fallacies (mistaken or erroneous beliefs) in the minds of their participants (Hinton, 2020a).

Concerned about racism and anti-Semitism in the United States, Gordon W. Allport (1954) – the brother of Floyd – in a very influential book on prejudice claimed that stereotypes arose from the "faulty" – rigid and simplistic – thinking of prejudiced individuals (as a consequence of a strict, conservative upbringing[6]). He contrasted this "prejudiced personality" with the liberal-minded "tolerant personality" who, he claimed, did not use stereotypes. This offered a rather idealistic psychological solution to prejudice in American society: eradicate stereotypes from the American mind (and the media) and bring up children to be liberal-minded democratic individuals, who do not use stereotypes.[7] Unfortunately, there are numerous methodological problems with this model of stereotypes, which simply does not adequately explain the psychological evidence (Perkins, 1979, Hinton, 2020a). Crucially, everyone employs generalizations about social groups ("stereotypes") – not just prejudiced individuals – regardless of their upbringing. It is just that people holding different ideological positions, such as conservative or liberal, employ different stereotypes, which reflect their different political viewpoints, such as "bleeding-heart liberal" or "hard-hearted conservative" (Ahler, 2018, Hinton, 2020a). Furthermore, there are stereotypical generalizations for all the known social groups in a society from anthropologists and Japanese-Americans to librarians and psychologists, and to yacht-owners and zoologists, so stereotypes are not uniquely related to groups subject to societal discrimination. Billig (1978) also showed that prejudiced people were not engaging in an inferior thinking process, but used complex arguments to support and maintain their prejudiced views. While they hold views that are generally agreed to be abhorrent, Billig (1985) argued that racists are not simplistic in their thinking – they are simply racists (Hinton, 2020a). Finally, the "faulty thinking" explanation of stereotypes ignored the cultural, sociological and institutional factors that influence the relationship between groups in a society (Hinton, 2020a). However, the vast amount of experimental research did produce a range of stereotypes employed within American culture, revealing the shared representations of social groups – including the Japanese – present in their society (Hinton, 2020b). In rejecting Allport's model of stereotypes, we can ask a different question about the stereotypes present in a culture: why has this particular set of characteristics been attributed to this particular social group in this particular culture? And the answer lies in the relationship between the groups.

From the work of the social psychologist Fritz Heider (1958), we can see that we may not be able to know what comprises the "true" characteristics of any group of people – if indeed we can make a claim that such characteristics exist. However, we can avoid this philosophical problem by seeking to determine why one group of people view another in the way that they do. Hence, from this perspective, we can examine the role of generalizations ("stereotypes") about social groups in the ideological construction of difference by members of one group about another group, as argued by anthropologist McDonald (1993), communication and media theorist Pickering (2001), and myself (Hinton, 2020a). This approach to stereotypes makes no claim about the "accuracy" or "inaccuracy" of stereotypical characterizations but argues that they involve the social construction of a social group, related to perceived aspects of social reality. As Van den Berghe (1997, p. 3) put it:

> Fictions abound in social life, but pure fictions do not fly. For example, the notion that the Japanese emperor is the father of the Japanese nation is a fiction which no one takes literally, but which, considering the history of Japan and its monarchy, is nevertheless credible at some level, and therefore was effective in the cultivation of Japanese nationalism.

Stereotypes serve an explanatory function for the members of a cultural group: the people doing the stereotyping. Allport (1954, p. 192) was well-founded in his view that stereotypes serve as a "justificatory device", to provide an explanation of a group and justify action towards them. By attributing the characteristics of intelligence and industriousness to the Japanese (as found by Katz and Braly, 1933), the stereotype provided a shared explanation by people in the United States for the rapid technological development of Japan during the previous seventy years (see Chapter 5). However, the American stereotype of the Japanese is not simple or fixed but is sensitive to changing intercultural American-Japanese relations. For example, Seago (1947) employed the same methodology as Katz and Braly (1933) during the years 1941 to 1945, specifically examining the stereotype change after the Japanese attack on Pearl Harbor in December 1941. She noted that, before the attack in 1941, the positive stereotype of the Japanese was similar to the findings of Katz and Braly. However, in 1942 (and in the subsequent years), the stereotype of the Japanese became highly negative. The Japanese were now stereotypically cruel, deceitful, treacherous, sly and shrewd. The American stereotype of the Japanese had radically changed as a result of the attack on Pearl Harbor. For the shocked Americans, only a cruel and treacherous people could possibly have undertaken such a deceitful attack before a declaration of war. Thus, it was right to wage an all-out war against them. The Japanese stereotype had changed to provide an explanation of their actions in the American mind and to justify the American response.

Barely a year after Allport (1954) produced his influential book on the faulty thinking model of stereotypes, psychologists Prothro and Melikian (1955) proposed a counter-view (which I support, Hinton, 2020a). They argued that stereotypes – and particularly their specific characteristics – reflect "the state of politico-economic relations between groups" (p. 3). Unfortunately, this approach, showing that stereotypes concerned intergroup relations, remained undeveloped within academic psychology during the second half of the 20th century (Hinton, 2020a). However, this idea was supported by anthropologist Margaret Mead (1956), who brought out the important cross-cultural aspect of stereotypes, in that stereotypes can be understood as providing explanations of the behaviour of one group by another group in an intercultural context. Indeed, further replications of the Katz and Braly study have supported the link between stereotypes and intercultural relations. The replication of Gilbert (1951) matched Seago's 1945 stereotype, showing that the American view of the Japanese was still strongly influenced by the wartime experience. Yet, over twenty-five years later, Karlins et al. (1969) found that the Japanese stereotype had changed. Now, industrious and ambitious were the top two characteristics of the stereotype, with efficient and intelligent in the top seven. This is not surprising, given the highly successful Japanese economic reconstruction after the war, with Japan becoming the second-largest economy in the world, where it remained for over forty years. Hence, it was again not surprising when, at the turn of the century, Madon et al.'s (2001) replication showed that intelligent and industrious were the top two characteristics of the Japanese stereotype, followed by scientifically minded, loyal to family ties and ambitious. Their stereotype of the Japanese in the second half of the twentieth century provided Americans with an explanation for Japan's late 20th century "economic miracle" (see Chapter 7).

I have argued that stereotypes are social constructions, forming a folk psychology within a culture concerning the meaningful social groups within it, reflecting the ideological structure of the society and the intergroup relations within it (Hinton, 2020a). Hence, in examining how people in the West have viewed the Japanese over nearly 500 years, the present book will describe the changing cultural context that led Westerners to construct different representations of the Japanese at different historical times. As Bruner (1990) has made clear, everyday thinking is not about a philosophical search for truth but concerns cultural meaning-making and, in order to make meaning, "we" (members of one culture) tell stories about "them" (another culture). In doing so, "we" represent "them" in particular ways that reflect the intercultural context. These Western generalizations or representations of the Japanese may be referred to as "stereotypes", but they are not simple, fixed or "inaccurate" (or "accurate"), but reveal the intercultural relationship between the West and Japan from a Western perspective.

The national character of the Japanese

In Western academia, following in the Allport tradition that there are "false" stereotypes and "true" personality characteristics, social scientists, both psychologists and sociologists, have sought to distinguish between "true" national character and "false" national character stereotypes (Peabody, 1985; Inkeles, 1997/2017). Inkeles was well aware that these studies were in a controversial territory as any proposed measure of national character could be criticized, especially in American academic psychology, as simply reinforcing a (false) stereotype in a different methodological guise, with any conclusions risking the allegation of perpetuating discriminatory views of nationalities. While acknowledging the many methodological problems of studying national character, Inkeles proposed a measure of a national character called the modal personality. As a way of examining national character, it draws out the commonalities from individual personality assessments to produce an aggregated, or modal personality for the cultural group members. Inkeles (1997/2017, p. 11) stated that "national character refers to characteristics that are *common* or standardized in a given society". However, he acknowledged that modal personality is related to the sociocultural system, in a reciprocal process of two-way influence. In this way, the term personality could remain reasonably uncontroversial at the level of the individual (as employed in mainstream Western psychology), yet still allow for a national character to be investigated by examining the aggregated data. Thus, individual standardized personality tests developed in Western academic psychology could be used – in their aggregated form – as a "valid" measure of national character.

Crucial for this methodology is the standardized personality test, to be given to the members of a cultural group to produce their national character. One of the most famous of these tests is the Eysenck Personality Questionnaire (EPQ). Using an early version of this test, Iwawaki et al. (1977) compared English and Japanese university students, psychotic individuals and children, producing the average scores for each of the groups to compare the English and the Japanese character. Iwawaki et al. found that up to grade four, the young Japanese children were more extravert than their English contemporaries, but after that age all Japanese groups (children, psychotics and university students) were more introverted than the English, suggesting a cultural influence on Japanese introversion. There were some minor variations in the neuroticism scores for the children but the researchers concluded that the results "seem to be that Japanese children are higher on N [*neuroticism*] at all ages" (Iwawaki et al., 1977, pp. 31–2). The Japanese university students and psychotics scored higher on the neuroticism scale than their English contemporaries. Finally, all the Japanese groups scored higher on psychoticism (when aggregated) than their English comparison groups. The researchers concluded that "for both adults and children Japanese have higher scores on N [*neuroticism*] and P [*psychoticism*] and lower scores (at least from secondary school onwards) on E [*extraversion – i.e. they are more introverted*]".

In a follow-up study, using the standard version of the EPQ, Iwawaki et al. (1980) compared Japanese and English adults (both male and female). The results confirmed the earlier findings that the Japanese were more introverted than the English, and also scored higher on the psychoticism scale. A minor variation was that Japanese males scored higher on neuroticism than the English, but not the Japanese women. In a much larger study comparing twenty-five different nations on the EPQ, Barrett and Eysenck (1984) showed that Japanese men were the third most introverted, the second most neurotic and the eleventh most psychotic. Japanese women were the seventh most introverted, the seventh most neurotic and the eleventh most psychotic. In an even larger study by Lynn and Martin (1995) with thirty-seven countries, not separated by gender, the Japanese were the fifth highest on introversion, fourth highest on neuroticism and thirteenth highest on psychoticism. The high levels of introversion and neuroticism held up across the studies for the Japanese character, but the level of psychoticism was unexceptional in comparison to a large number of other countries. In addition, Lynn and Hampson (1975) argued that a high level of neuroticism and introversion (as exhibited by the Japanese) should predict a high level of suicide in a country. Indeed, Japan does have one of the highest rates of suicide in the developed world (Kawashima et al., 2019). And Russell et al. (2017) have argued that in Japan, there is "a tradition of honorable suicide as well as permissive attitudes towards suicide that remain in modern times".

Thus, it was argued that the aggregated personality tests revealed a combination of neuroticism and introversion that creates a picture of the Japanese character as reserved (introversion), anxious about the world, that is, concerned about doing the right thing (neuroticism) and when things go wrong, a willingness to commit suicide to take the honourable way out: a character we can sum up (maybe not too seriously) as the *introverted samurai* once again. This appears all very neat, as the psychological research, employing personality tests, appears to give similar results to the anthropological work of Benedict (superficially at least). The aggregated personality tests appear to show a "true" measure of the Japanese character as introverted and neurotic that resonates with Benedict's view of the Japanese Janus-like national character. However, just as I challenged the faulty thinking of stereotypes, in favour of an intergroup (intercultural) explanation, I am also challenging the use of Western standardized personality tests as a measure of "national character".

Cultural norms and intercultural relations

Terracciano et al. (2005) sought to distinguish "false" stereotypes from "true" personality by giving a standardized personality test in forty-nine countries, which showed that the Japanese were in the top five for neuroticism and the bottom five for extraversion (i.e. in the top five for introversion). At the same time, they administered a second survey where respondents were asked to fill in a thirty-item questionnaire describing a typical member of their culture, as a perception of national character measure (PNC). They then compared the personality scores with the PNC scores, which showed little correlation. They concluded that the standardized personality scores were producing an accurate ("true") measure of national character, and therefore the PNC scores (expectations of national character) must be revealing "false" national character stereotypes.

While this appeared to resolve the issue, the cultural psychologists Heine et al. (2008) expressed their surprise at this conclusion. They argued that people are aware of the cultural differences between their own and other cultures, and these perceptions can be accurate, as members of a culture can make meaningful judgements about their own culture. Hence, they argued, the PNC scores might be an accurate representation of the culture and it is the personality test results that are inaccurate. They tested this by comparing the scores on "conscientiousness" from the Terraciano et al. study against measures of conscientiousness from specific behaviours in a culture (walking speed, postal workers' speed, the accuracy of clocks in public banks, per capita GDP and longevity). They found that these criterion measures correlated negatively with the personality questionnaire employed by Terracciano et al. In contrast, the average PNC scores from Terraciano et al. correlated highly with the actual behaviour in the culture. Heine et al. (2008, p. 312) argued:

> Participating in a world where the clocks are on time and people work effectively and earn a good income leads people to adopt conscientious habits, and these habits continue to shape and reinforce the surrounding culture. . . . Participation in a cultural world comes to shape the cultural norms[8] that people perceive as reflecting general conscientiousness. These norms are apparent when people evaluate their own culture.

The perceptions of national character (PNC) matched actual behaviour in the culture but the aggregated personality tests did not. So why do the Japanese appear introverted and neurotic on personality tests?

Hofstede (1980) argued that different cultures have different orientations, with individualistic cultures, such as those of North America and Europe, emphasizing personal autonomy and individual responsibility for behaviour. However, collectivistic cultures, such as those in India and East Asia (such as Japan), tend to focus more on the group, and its goals and responsibilities. Whereas an individualistic society promotes the independence of the person, collectivistic cultures emphasize the interdependence of its members. In an individualistic society, self-expression and personal goal seeking are encouraged in contrast to a collectivistic society which values respectfulness, social harmony and collaborative goal seeking. Furthermore, Hall (1959) argued that "context" is also a distinguishing feature between individualistic and collectivistic cultures. In low-context (individualistic) cultures, personal identity is considered separate from the group, with straight-forward, plain speaking, veering on bluntness, being positively valued as "honest" self-expression by the individual (Kim and Sherman, 2007). However, in high-context (collectivistic) cultures, identity is more integrated into the family and the community, and communication is more indirect, with the implicit aspects of the context determining the appropriate forms of expression. Circumspection is more important than directness of speech, as the latter can sound disrespectful and rude. Thus, while a Westerner might give a blunt "no" or "no way" to an idea in a business meeting that they disapprove of, a Japanese person might say "that would be difficult", as a culturally more polite and respectful way of indicating disagreement.

Now, if we examine the personality tests, we see that they include questions such as "are you a talkative person?" or "do you enjoy meeting new people" (typical questions related to the introversion-extraversion measure), which may have different meanings when answered by people from different cultures. Within an individualistic culture, speaking one's mind and networking are positively valued, so we would expect the aggregated data to show positive responses to these questions. However, in a collectivistic culture, unrestrained self-expression risks being impolite and disrespectful. Meeting unknown people, which requires careful consideration to maintain the proper respect for all the people involved in an interaction, is unlikely to be viewed as enjoyable, so we would expect the aggregated data to show negative responses to these questions. Hence, the questions do not have the same meaning in the two cultures. Negative answers to these questions are inferred to indicate introversion, *if the respondents are Western*, as the cultural norm is more positive. However, a negative response to these questions, *by Japanese respondents*, is normative, suggesting that, in terms of their own culture, an aggregated negative response is not indicative of introversion. As I have argued (Hinton, 2020b), the Japanese as a group are only "introverted" to Westerners, not within the context of their own culture. Despite its "standardization", the personality test, devised in an individualistic culture, contains cultural assumptions within it. When applied to a collectivistic culture, with different cultural norms, the results are misinterpreted in terms of Western personality assumptions – ignoring a cultural explanation. Hence, we can argue that the aggregated personality tests are not revealing an enduring aspect of Japanese character, but a different cultural norm.

To elaborate: in a Western culture, being talkative is viewed as a positive characteristic (i.e. normative). Talking in a group environment is viewed as *participation*, and is positively valued as *student engagement* in a Western classroom (Christenson et al., 2012). A student who does not speak in the class is viewed in a Western culture as either disengaged or, if clearly interested in the topic, introverted. This cultural norm exists in the education system, where students are expected to engage (i.e. express their views). Hence, in the construction of the questions in a personality test, not being talkative, combined with other answers, is taken as a sign of introversion. This shows that the tests are ethnocentrically Western (e.g. Heine et al., 2008). The Japanese responses make them appear introverted in terms of Western cultural expectations enshrined in the test analysis. However, talkativeness is not traditionally the cultural norm in Japanese culture. In 1938, the Englishman John Morris went to Japan to teach university students at Keio University. He noted: "Rather than take the risk of appearing rude, they would sit stiffly silent, perched on the edge of their chairs" (Morris, 1945, p. 48). Morris was well aware that the silence was not an indication that his Japanese students were introverted, simply that they were following the cultural norm of not wanting to risk appearing rude. However, for many Westerners, the Japanese (cultural) reticence in talking in class is interpreted (erroneously) as introversion. In support of this, psychological studies on stereotypes show that Westerners commonly attribute the personality characteristic of introversion to the Japanese (Sue and Kitano, 1973). Everett and Stening (1983) found that while British managers perceived their Japanese colleagues to be introverted, their colleagues, the Japanese managers, did not see themselves as introverted at all. We can conclude that both Western personality tests and Westerners interpreting their Japanese students or colleagues as introverted are making inferences based on their own cultural assumptions, rather than detecting aspects of Japanese character (Hinton, 2020b).

This criticism, that a difference in cultural norms is misinterpreted as a difference in personality, can also be applied to Benedict's view of the Japanese national character "as personality writ large" (LeVine, 2001, p. 810). Benedict provided a description of the Japanese national character, within the context of the ferocious conflict between the United States and Japan during the Pacific War. She then sought to explain this Japanese character in terms of antecedent aspects of Japanese culture. In her attempts to summarize the large and complex society of Japan, while located in the United States, she did the opposite to the ethnographic fieldwork and the long-term engagement with a small face-to-face community, such as that of John Embree's study of the Japanese village of Suye during 1935–6 (Embree, 1939), more typical of anthropological research. Consequently, other anthropologists were highly critical of her analysis of the Japanese character "from a distance". In particular, despite her detailed analysis, Benedict may have interpreted changeable cultural norms as aspects of "national character". It is quite likely that this is the case, as Levine (2001, p. 813) points out: "More recent evaluations of the book by specialists on Japan indicate its accuracy as an account of Japanese normative ideals prevalent in the past".

Why is it that Westerners favour personality explanations by claiming that the Japanese are introverted rather than explaining their behaviour in terms of different cultural norms? The answer appears to lie in their individualistic culture, where dispositional explanations of behaviour are enshrined in their thinking. Ross (1977, p. 184) called this the *fundamental attribution error*: a "general tendency to overestimate the importance of personal or dispositional factors relative to environmental influences". Ross went on to argue that this error was affecting professional psychologists as well. He noted the research evidence demonstrating low levels of cross-situation consistency in behaviour "making personality scales very poor predictors of behaviour", and wondered why such findings were "so controversial and prompted energetic rebuttal research" by Western psychologists. His answer was "the deep conviction that personal dispositions control and are reflected in everyday social behaviour" (Ross, 1977, p. 187), a conviction that has pervaded Western social psychology since its foundation at the time of Floyd Allport. Crucially, research across cultures shows that people in collective cultures tend not to make the fundamental attribution error, and consider both personal and cultural factors when deciding on an explanation of behaviour (Miller, 1984; Morris and Peng, 1994; Miyamoto and Kitayama, 2002). Hence, the distinction between so-called true personality tests of national character and false stereotypes is a specious one. It is not that the Japanese are introverted as a cultural group, but that Westerners *think they are* because the behaviour of the Japanese is interpreted through the lens of Western cultural norms, and the Western emphasis on individualistic (character-based) explanations of behaviour (Hinton, 2020b).

The idea that Western social psychology could find the "truth" about the Japanese character was further undermined by the research of anthropologist Joseph Henrich and his colleagues (Henrich et al., 2010). They showed that most of the academic psychological research had been undertaken with Western participants, in particular American undergraduate students, which comprise only 12 percent of the world's population – and they are a WEIRD group of people at that: where WEIRD is an acronym for people from Western, Educated, Industrialized, Rich, and Democratic cultures. Thus, the vast majority of psychological theory has an inbuilt Western cultural bias within it. What is more, Henrich (2020, p. 21) argued:

> Unlike much of the world today, and most people who have ever lived, we WEIRD people are highly individualistic, self-obsessed, control-oriented, nonconformist, and analytical. We focus on ourselves – our attributes, accomplishments, and aspirations – over our relationships and social roles. We aim to be "ourselves" across contexts and see inconsistencies in others as hypocrisy rather than flexibility.

Henrich's work showed that Western academic "psychological science" was not the objective discipline it claimed to be. Psychological theory based on Western cultural assumptions and expectations can lead to a misinterpretation of other cultures, such as the Japanese. The advent of cultural psychology (Stigler et al., 1990) has sought to deal with this issue by acknowledging the importance of culture in human psychological – cognitive – functioning. We all have learnt our culture's folk psychology (or indigenous psychology): the pattern of norms, cultural assumptions and expectations present within it (Bruner, 1990). This has been referred to as "culture in mind" by the anthropologist Bradd Shore (1996) and I have employed the concept in psychology (Hinton, 2017, 2020a). I have even argued that what is referred to as "psychological science" (especially experimental social psychology) is actually a Western or (given the volume of their research output) an American cultural psychology rather than a psychology of general applicability (Hinton, 2020b). As Benedict (1934/1959) proposed, and Spencer-Oatey and Kádár (2021) have integrated into their analysis of intercultural relations, we are all influenced by our cultural patterning. Our culture provides us with a normative understanding of the world (Bruner, 1990). Within a culture, most behaviour is normative and therefore expected and understood. As Semin (1980) pointed out, we only need to seek explanations of unexpected behaviour, as we have a "ready-made" set of cultural explanations for any expected behaviour. The problem is that people from other cultures do not always behave as expected – according to Western cultural norms – and individualistic Westerners have a tendency to attribute these cultural differences to dispositional factors (national character or national character stereotypes) that may be used to claim an ideological superiority of their own culture (or nation) over that of a "cultural other",[9] a different cultural group (Shi-xu, 1995). Cultural differences, such as those observed by Westerners when encountering the Japanese, may be viewed as exotic, appealing, interesting, surprising or shocking, with the unexpected ways of another culture often interpreted through Western cultural values as immoral and inferior, especially if they conflict with Western ideological and religious norms (Shi-xu, 1995). Making a stereotypical claim about the character of the cultural other can be considered "a denial of history" (Pickering, 2001, p. 48), as it constructs the cultural other as essentially "fixed" in character, different to one's own cultural group, and ignores the changes in their culture and behaviour over time. Hence, cultural psychology seeks to examine the ways in which the members of one culture discursively construct, and represent, in their communication the members of another culture (e.g. Shi-xu and Feng-Bing, 2013).

The cultural psychological approach of this book argues that judgements of the cultural other take place within the context of intercultural relations. Western perceptions of the Japanese have always taken place in terms of the purpose and meaning of the relationship between the West and Japan at the time of the judgement. Often the assumption is made that the character and customs of the Japanese as determined by Westerners at one particular time are assumed to be enduring. Yet cultures are not fixed and unchanging, neither that of the West nor Japan, so at different times throughout the history of the Western-Japanese relationship, the Westerners have viewed the Japanese in a variety of different ways, indeed some that are diametrically opposed to each other. This book seeks to counter the "denial of history" by examining the Western construction and representation of the Japanese across the history of their intercultural relations. And, as we shall see, these Western interpretations of the Japanese often tell us more about the cultural understandings of the West, and its culturally based perception of the Japanese, at a particular time in history, rather than anything about any enduring characteristics of the Japanese.

This book broadly follows a chronological path to plot out some of the dominant ways that Westerners have described the Japanese during the history of Western-Japanese relations. Chapter 2 examines Western perceptions of the Far East, and in particular Japan, prior to and at the time Europeans arrived on the shores of Japan in 1543. Chapter 3 examines the so-called Christian century in Japan, when the Jesuits accompanied the Portuguese merchants, with a mission to convert the Japanese to Catholic Christianity: a century that ended with the expulsion of all Europeans from Japan except a small Dutch trading station in Nagasaki harbour. Viewing Japan as a "closed country" (Chapter 4) for over 200 years, from the 17th to the 19th century, Europeans had only the imported Japanese luxury goods and accounts from the employees of the Dutch East India company (*Vereenigde Oost Indische Compagnie* or VOC) to learn about Japan. This all changed in 1853 when US Commodore Perry and his gunboats arrived in Edo (Tokyo) Bay, demanding Japan open to trade. Victorian Westerners now flocked to Japan to see this strange but fascinating country with its delightful people, which was now "open" to them. It was not only viewed as a place of art and artisans but also inhabited by a people keen to learn Western ways (Chapter 5). However, Westerners were shocked when Japan "suddenly" emerged as a major world power and was viewed a threat (a "yellow peril") to the West that culminated in the Japanese surrender in 1945, in the Pacific War (the Second World War) (Chapter 6). Post-war Japanese reconstruction progressed rapidly, to Western surprise, which turned to anxiety when the Japanese "economic miracle" threatened to dominate world trade – at the expense of Western companies – only to flounder in the early 1990s. As Western anxiety dissipated, Japan's economic woes could be looked on with schadenfreude, while at the same time the cultural products of Japan – such as manga, anime, and video games – enthralled Western youth (Chapter 7). The final chapter will reflect on how Western representations of the Japanese have changed over time, in the context of the changing intercultural relationship between the West and Japan, and how these inform our academic understanding of the role of the perceiver's culture in representations of the cultural other (Chapter 8).

Notes

1 He originally described Asians as fuscus ("brown, swarthy") but changed it to luridus in a later edition.
2 The view that differences in people of different "races" are the result of biological differences.
3 Ronin refers to a masterless samurai.
4 Seppuku is translated as "cutting the belly" and hara-kiri as "stomach cutting".
5 Lippmann used the name of a metal plate used in the printing process, a stereotype, for his term.

6 In Freudian terms, they had developed repressed anxiety which they redirected onto out-groups.
7 Gordon Allport was himself a mid-20th-century American liberal, and his idealistic beliefs can be clearly determined within his book (Hinton, 2020a).
8 Sherif (1936, p. 3) defined a norm as "the customs, traditions, standards, rules, values, fashions, and all the other criteria of conduct which are standardized as a consequence of the contact of individuals". Norms involve not only what people typically do (descriptive norms) but also what they should and should not do (injunctive or prescriptive norms) in the culture (Cialdini, 2012).
9 Pickering (2001, p. 69) points out: "The concept of the Other takes us some way beyond the limitations of the stereotype by bringing more closely into the frame both those involved in the process of othering as well as the object of this process".

2

FINDING THE JAPANESE IN THE FAR EAST

Japan in the Far East

It is only from Europe that there exists a place called the *Far East*. Westerners hardly give a thought to locating Japan in it. Yet on a globe, there is no Far East – the far east is the same as the far west or more precisely the *far side* of the world from a fixed point on the globe. Descriptions of East or West only make sense when a specific location is highlighted. Yet, in the European (and North American) consciousness, the East is a real place called *The Orient* (Said, 1978/1995) which is constructed in comparison to the West (i.e. itself). The Near East was often used as a label for Anatolia and the Levant. The term Middle East later encompassed the Levant, Mesopotamia, Egypt and the Islamic states in North Africa and Western Asia. India lay between the Middle East and the Far East, with the Far East employed as a label for Eastern Asia. However, the region east of the Indian subcontinent (sometimes as far as Japan) was referred to by the term "the East Indies". Often the European-centric East-West distinction has been a way of differentiating "us", Europeans, from "them", the Orientals (Said, 1978/1995). Throughout the Middle Ages, Europeans looked with fascination to the Far East, where lay the powerful empire of China, and beyond that the mysterious "island" of Japan, lying at the end of the world. Indeed, the Japanese archipelago is the farthest land to the east from a location in southern Europe, especially Portugal (whose sailors were the first Europeans to arrive in Japan in the 16th century). If you travel due east from Lisbon (latitude 38.7°N longitude 9.1°W), the farthest land you encounter is Honshu, the main island of Japan, specifically in the northern region of Tohoku (whose largest modern city of Sendai lies at 38.3°N and 140.9°E). Further east and you encounter the North Pacific Ocean until arriving at 180° from Lisbon, and after that you are travelling back round the other side of the world. From Portugal (or southern Europe more generally), the islands of Japan are

DOI: 10.4324/9781003082088-2

indeed the farthest large landmass to the east before crossing the half-way point at the opposite side of the Earth. Thus, *the Orient*, at times divided into the Near East, the Middle East, India and the Far East, was a construction of the imagination of the people of Europe, as a way of describing Asia, which has nevertheless become very real to them.

The mythical Orient in the European mind

Christian Europe in the Middle Ages was well aware that it was bounded by the Muslims of the Near East (referred to as "Saracens"), in control of the holy city of Jerusalem, and the Muslims of North Africa (referred to as "Moors") and in al-Andalus in the South. In fact, any route to the Far East from Europe had to go beyond these Islamic powers and, if they were to be bypassed, then this route had to be by the sea. Muslims were often characterized in crude, negative ways in medieval European texts: with misrepresentations presenting Islam as an opposite to the virtues of Christianity (Southern, 1962). Tales of Christian knights vanquishing their evil and malevolent enemies circulated in Europe, generated by the concerns about the threat posed by the Islamic states to Christendom (Vitkus, 1999). The crusades had brought European Christians together in a fight against that perceived threat which had ultimately failed. This was further exacerbated by an awareness of "the cultural superiority of the Muslims, especially those of al-Andalus" (Watt, 1991, p. 88). In reality, the Christian-Muslim relationship was much more complex, such as when Christian and Muslim armies united against a common foe, especially on the Iberian Peninsula[1] and, for example, in European tales of the loyal and noble Saracen (Kangas, 2013).

However, Edward Said (1978/1995) saw the medieval period in Europe as the beginnings of *Orientalism*, a Western characterization of the Orient, particularly the Middle East, that was structured by its Christian world view and which supported its political aims. As Said (1978/1995, p. 1) argued, Orientalism is "a way of coming to terms with the Orient that is based on the Orient's special place in European Western experience". Drawing on the work of Southern (1962), he argued that, during the medieval period, a body of European texts – from the Venerable Bede in the early 8th century CE to Martin Luther in the early 16th century CE – was employed to represent the Orient, or as Said (1978/1995, p. 63) put it, to "stage" the Orient in an academic way to provide a coherent "explanation" of the "problem of Islam" that sought to establish and maintain the European world view of the superiority of Christianity, and position Islam as a "misguided" form of Christianity. Thus, Orientalism, according to Said, is often the outcome of scholarship – a knowledge of Western texts about the Orient – rather than mere ignorance of the East. As Southern (1962, p. 92) pointed out: "The scholars who labored at the problem of Islam in the Middle Ages failed to find the solution they sought and desired", yet he argued that, as a result of their academic endeavour, the "statement of the problem became more complex, more rational and more related to experience".

Said (1978/1995) argued that Orientalism has been a feature of Western thought that has dominated Western views of the East for over 500 years. The Orient was given a definition as a "real" place, with distinct people, such that "the Orient, and in particular the Near Orient became known in the West as its great complementary opposite" (Said, 1978/1995, p. 58). Consequently, a range of polar concepts were employed in the characterization of the Orient and Oriental people. Western religion (Christianity) was represented as superior and Eastern religions as inferior, and the morality of the people of the West was positioned in contrast to the "degeneracy" of the Oriental. As Said (1978/1995, p. 63) claimed: "An Orientalist is but the particular specialist in knowledge for which Europe at large is responsible". By establishing in their culture a place called "the Orient", with the representations constructed by Orientalism, when the Europeans ventured further East, into the unknown Orient, they would have their framework of interpretation already established in their minds.

The Christian kings of the distant Oriental lands

Ideas of the Orient and its people have played an important role in the culture of Europe throughout its history. At the heart of the Christian story is the account of the Magi, who came from the East to worship "the child who was born King of the Jews" according to chapter two of the Gospel of Matthew in the Christian Bible. The Magi – priests or magicians in Greek but later translated as "wise men" – with their rich gifts of gold, frankincense and myrrh, gained a central role in the nativity, who acknowledged the status of the new-born Jesus. Furthermore, their gifts were the highly prized and eagerly sought products of the East. Powell (2000) suggests that they would not originally have been viewed as royal visitors, but rather as astrologers. However, subsequent Christian writers embellished the story, identifying their number as three, naming them (Balthasar, Melchior, and Gaspar), promoting them to kings and giving them countries of origin, so that, from Matthew's brief account, the Magi evolved into the Three Kings of the Orient of Christian tradition – wealthy pro-Christian rulers from countries in the East. Numerous art works were produced depicting the *Adoration of the Magi*, from the early studies in the 4th century BCE, where they wore ordinary Persian garb, through to the 10th century when they gained crowns and finer clothes. By the Middle Ages, they acquired even more magnificent regal status, with large retinues and rich adornment. For example, Botticelli painted the scene about 1475, Leonardo Da Vinci in 1481, and Fra Angelico in 1492. These images established the idea of Oriental Christian kingdoms in the European imagination.

By the Middle Ages, stories of a contemporary Christian king of the East emerged in Europe: a wealthy and powerful monarch called Prester John (John the Priest), a saintly character who ruled over an abundant and civilized realm, and who might assist the Europeans in their time of need (Brewer, 2015). Supported by the Pope, in 1096, Western European Princes set out on the First Crusade to expel the "Saracens" (Turkic Muslims) from the holy city of Jerusalem. On route to war, the Europeans saw the wondrous products of the Orient first hand in the markets of Constantinople (modern-day Istanbul), the capital of the Byzantium Empire: the silks from China and the spices from the East Indies, sold by Muslim traders. Marching from Constantinople, the crusaders arrived at Jerusalem in 1099. After a bloody battle, and the massacre of its citizens, the city was captured by the Europeans, who then established four Christian Kingdoms in the Levant. However, these were under constant threat and when the first of them, Edessa, fell in 1144, the Pope announced the Second Crusade (1147), whose armies were comprehensively beaten by the Seljuq Turks. The remnants of the European forces were again soundly defeated at the siege of Damascus (1148). It was during this crusade that rumours began to circulate amongst the Europeans that Prester John and his army were marching to their rescue (Venning, 2015). But he did not appear.

European Christians had known of Christians in the East since the accounts of Thomas the Apostle travelling to India and possibly even as far as China (Vadakkekara, 1995). The presence of Christians in the East was confirmed by European contact with the Nestorian Christians of Persia and Syria. However, this intercourse was often difficult as first the Persian Empire and then the Turkic Muslim Empires made overland communication between Europe and the East difficult. It was in this knowledge vacuum that speculations about the mysterious Orient filled the void in European texts of the medieval period (the years prior to 1500 CE). As well as fantastic tales of men with heads of dogs, living beyond the known world, the stories of Prester John fascinated Christian Europe, as an ideal Christian king, pious and true, incredibly wealthy, and ruler of a civilized people somewhere in the East. He was a descendant of the Magi and would help Christian Europe in a time of need. In 1165, a letter purportedly from Prester John was apparently sent to the Byzantine Emperor. The letter circulated around Europe, detailing the wonders of Prester John and his kingdom: a fabulous empire of Eastern Christians that fascinated its readers (Brewer, 2015). Indeed, it was so-well accepted that Pope Alexander III sent a reply in 1177 (to no avail). While later textual analysis showed the letter to be a fake, with a European origin, the myth of a Christian empire in the East was now an established feature of the imagination of Europeans, who keenly wished to find its location.

Marco Polo's Far East, and his account of Japan

In the 13th century, despite the immediate threat to Europe of the Mongol Empire under Genghis Khan, the Mongol victories in the East offered the possibility of travel to the Far East under the *Pax Mongolica* stretching from Europe to China. One of the European travellers who made the tortuous journey to China, and returned, was the Venetian Marco Polo (1254–1324), who travelled along the Silk Road in 1271, returning a very wealthy man nearly twenty-five years later in 1295. During that time, Polo had met with Kublai Khan, the grandson of Genghis Khan, and became his foreign emissary. On behalf of the Great Khan, Polo had travelled to

South Asia, including India, Burma (Myanmar) and Indonesia. Crucially, he identified and described the spice-growing regions of South East Asia. On his return, he took part in the Venice-Genoa war, and was captured by the Genoese in 1296 and imprisoned for three years. It was during this time he dictated his adventures to a fellow prisoner, Rustichella da Pisa. When published, this manuscript became known as *The Travels of Marco Polo* (Polo, 1958). The book opened up the Far East to a European readership, detailing the fabulous wealth in spices, silks, gold and silver, with descriptions of lands and people that were "steeped in hyperbole" in a European tradition of exotic descriptions of the unknown lands of Asia (McOmie, 2005, p. 6). Polo claimed that Prester John had been killed in a war with the Mongols, but that the Mongols respected Christianity. However, most importantly Polo described the richness of the lands and the wealth of their rulers. Indeed, Polo gained the nickname of "millions" for his constant depiction of the Great Khan's wealth (Komroff, 1926). Polo not only reported on what he had seen personally but also described the Eastern lands that he had been told about. Despite not visiting it, Polo provided the first account for Europeans of the "island" of Japan, across the sea from China in the far east of Asia.

> Japan [*which Polo referred to as Zipangu or Chipangu*[2]] is an island far out at sea to the eastward, some 1,500 miles from the mainland. It is a very big island. The people are fair-complexioned, good-looking, and well-mannered. They are idolaters, wholly independent and exercising no authority over any nation but themselves. They have gold in great abundance, because it is found there in measureless quantities. . . . I can report to you in sober truth a veritable marvel concerning a certain palace of the ruler of the island. You may take it for a fact that he has a very large palace entirely roofed with fine gold. Just as we roof our houses or churches with lead, so this palace is roofed with fine gold. And the value of it is almost beyond computation. Moreover all the chambers, of which there are many, are likewise paved with fine gold to a depth of more than two fingers' breadth. And the halls and the windows and every other part of the palace are likewise adorned with gold. All in all I can tell you that the palace is of such incalculable richness that any attempt to estimate its value would pass the bounds of marvelous. They have pearls in abundance, red in colour, very beautiful, large and round. They are as worth as much as the white ones, indeed more.
>
> *(Polo 1958, pp. 243–4)*

In his overblown description, Polo "greatly exaggerated the abundance of gold and other precious metals in Japan and created an image of Japan as a fabulously wealthy insular kingdom" (McOmie, 2005, p. 6). Not only were these fair-skinned[3] and well-mannered people so wealthy that they could cover their roofs with gold but, as Polo also writes, they had resisted Kubali Khan's attempts to invade their country. Unlike many of the other people described by Polo, the

Japanese appeared to have admirable qualities to the European readers. More importantly, this image of Japan definitely made it a desirable place for Europeans to find, and visit.

Perceiving the cultural other on the journey to Japan

The Europeans realized that if they could find a way to trade directly with the source of the expensive products – pepper and spices from India, nutmeg, mace and cloves from the "Spice Islands" (the Maluku Islands), the silk of China and the gold and silver of Japan – then huge fortunes could be made by bypassing the intermediaries along the Silk Road. However, this required finding a sea route to the East Indies, with good maps, in ships that could make the journey. At the beginning of the 15th century, this possibility started to become real. For the early European map makers, there were large areas of the world that were unknown, surrounded by seas where imaginary exotic creatures and sea monsters were placed. Furthermore, a medieval European map was not a map in the modern sense of creating an accurate representation of the physical geography of a place, but a representation of their Christian world view with Jerusalem placed in the centre, such as the Beatus Mappa Mundi, produced in France around 1050 CE. Indeed, the Mappa Mundi in Hereford Cathedral, England, produced around 1300 CE, not only is the largest surviving such medieval map but also includes the island of paradise, at a location approximately where Japan would be (Ayabe, 2007). By the 15th century, maps had begun to be more geographical but they were often wildly inaccurate. For example, the first European map to explicitly show the "island" of Japan ("Isola de Cimpagu") in Asia is that of Fra Mauro, a monk living near Venice in 1459, but not at its true location (Falchetta, 2006). Along with the developments in map-making, the prospect of ocean-going travel began to be possible with the construction of the caravel, developed from Portuguese fishing boats with the support of Prince Henry the Navigator (1394–1460), the fourth son of King John I of Portugal. The caravel was a faster and lighter sailing ship than traditional European vessels, which could sail into the wind making it much more manoeuvrable, regardless of the prevailing winds. The invention of the caravel was combined with Henry's enthusiasm for exploration, which was partly driven by his fascination with the tales of the Christian king Prester John, whose lands he wished to find (Russell, 1997), and his avid reading of Polo's account of the fabulous wealth of Asia (McOmie, 2005).

Importantly, the Portuguese explorers had the support of the Pope in their engagement with the non-Christians (or infidels) they would meet. Church law had established that the Pope, as Vicar of Christ, had jurisdiction over all people (as God made them all), so he could sanction a Christian army against infidels who were violating natural law, such as the worship of idols (as it flouted the truth of the one creator) or engaging in perverse practices (as the destruction of Sodom and Gomorrah had demonstrated God's will in this matter). He also had a duty to send out missionaries to preach the word of God to them, and for Christian armies to protect the missionaries if they were in danger. This expanded in the 15th century with the justification for European conquest of infidel lands in terms of bringing civilization and order to primitive people, who otherwise might threaten missionary activity (Muldoon, 1979). It was with this religious sanction in their minds that the Portuguese (and also the Spanish) captains set out.

Taking the sea route east to Asia

An eastern sea passage to the Far East would be a long journey, requiring friendly ports on the route. The Portuguese knew that travelling round Africa and India was necessary, but it had not yet been achieved. Under the initiatives of Prince Henry and supported by young King Alfonso V, his nephew, the sea-going caravels, sailed by the skills of the Portuguese seamen, gradually explored the west coast of Africa, claiming the islands of São Tomé, Principe and the Cape Verde archipelago for the Portuguese crown – islands that were turned into sugar plantations and centres of the slave trade (Caldeira, 2011). Thus began what is often referred to as the Age of Discovery, the period of European exploration and expansion between the mid-15th and 18th centuries.

In the 1440s, as the caravels made their way down the east coast of Africa, Portugal began its involvement in the Sub-Saharan African slave trade with royal approval. The views of the 13th-century theologian Thomas Aquinas that "slavery was a divine punishment for man's original sin" underlay the Portuguese justification for slavery (Russell-Wood, 1978, p. 33). Furthermore, they claimed it was the duty of all Catholics to turn unbelievers into Christians, a duty which gave papal sanction to Portuguese slave traders on condition that the slaves were converted to Christianity. Indeed, the papal bull *Dum Diversas* of Pope Nicholas V in 1452 explicitly allowed the Portuguese to enslave "Saracens, pagans and any other unbelievers", a right that was confirmed and developed in the papal bull *Romanus Pontifex* of 1455 (Ajala, 2013). A further justification, along with converting the heathen to Christianity, was to "civilize" all the "uncivilized" peoples they encountered who would otherwise remain in a perceived state of "degeneracy" (Russell-Wood, 1978). Yet, Russell-Wood (1978, p. 34) argued, the primary reason for this inhumane treatment of people was its economic value: "the slave was a marketable item to be sold, traded, and purchased like any other commodity". With the dearth of agricultural labourers in Portugal at the time, bringing slaves from Africa was a highly profitable trade. As the Portuguese continued to journey east, their enslavement of local people persisted all the way to – and including – Japan (de Sousa, 2019; Nelson, 2004).

John II succeeded his father Alfonso in 1481, and seeing the benefits to the royal treasury of trade (and colonization), encouraged the "expansion" east. In 1482, Portugal built a fortified trading station on mainland Africa, the Castelo de São Jorge da Mina, in the Gulf of Guinea (in what is now Ghana), which was later to become one of the most important centres of the transatlantic slave trade (Boscariol, 2021). This set a pattern of the Portuguese approaches to establishing trading stations. Initially, they sought to negotiate the land for a "factory" (the name for a trading station) by gift-giving to local leaders but, if and when this faltered, they had military force to get what they wanted (Hair, 1994). However, the success of São Jorge da Mina depended on its trading links with the African merchants from further inland. Hence, some accommodation was necessary with local rulers to maintain the trade (Boscariol, 2021). Huge profits began to be made from slavery, the gold of Guinea, and the ivory of the Congo. By 1487, the Portuguese ships had reached the southernmost tip of Africa, and in 1488, Bartolomeu Dias rounded the Cape of Good Hope, opening the eastern coast of Africa, particularly Mozambique, to the Portuguese ships. With their African factories, the Portuguese now had a supply chain to India.

The route west

Meanwhile, the Spanish were developing their own sea-borne exploration in their caravels, but looking west. There was the possibility that they could beat the Portuguese to Japan (and China) by travelling westward across the Atlantic to find the lands of the Far East. This was the plan of Christopher Columbus when he set out on his Atlantic voyage in 1492, supported by the monarchs Ferdinand of Aragon and Isabella of Castile, who in the same year completed their conquest of Muslim Granada, defeating the last of al-Andalus, making the whole Iberian Peninsula Christian, and creating what was to become the kingdom of Spain. Columbus hoped that he could reach Japan (Zipangu or Cipangu), about which he had learnt from the *Travels of Marco Polo*. It is argued that Columbus underestimated the distance westwards to Japan, assuming that it was only a quarter of the actual distance (Cummins, 1992). Contemporary maps located the island of Japan between the mainland of Asia and Europe with, of course, no mention of the Americas. One possibility is that Columbus may have seen the globe of Martin Behaim, who had been in Portugal at that time, which showed the large island of Cipangu (Japan) quite prominently (Flint, 1992; Cummins, 1992). On this globe, the distance across the ocean between Europe and Asia is 4,500 miles, with the island of Cipangu 3,000 miles east of the Canary Islands (Siebold, 2015). In comparing this globe with a modern one (and ignoring actual distances), it located Cipangu somewhere around Central America. This explains why, when he landed on a small island in the Bahama Archipelago on 12 October 1492, he insisted that he had found the Indies and landed on an island near Japan ("Cipango") (Bergreen, 2011; Flint, 1992). And, in his journal of 23 October 1492, he confused Cuba with Japan declaring: "I desired to set out to-day for the island of Cuba, which I think must be Cipango" (Columbus, 1893, p. 56).

During the next few months, he explored various islands in the search for gold, trading glass beads and tiny bells for gold ornaments with the local "Indians" (Bergreen, 2011). Like the Portuguese in Africa, the Columbus expedition combined a search for riches with a belief that they were undertaking God's work, and hence they felt no compunction in enslaving members of the local population, who were treated as inferior beings (Bergreen, 2011) This view was echoed by the later Spanish conquistadors, who declared their intention "to conquer and govern" the lands of the Americas (Mantovani, 2000, p. 34).

Columbus (1893) described the indigenous people as docile, "guileless and unwarlike" (p. 71), with "no religion" (p. 90), and, on 11 November 1492, he reported to Ferdinand and Isabella:

> If devout religious persons were here, knowing the language, they would all turn Christians. I trust in our Lord that your Highnesses will resolve upon this with much diligence, to bring so many great nations within the Church, and to convert them; as you have destroyed those who would not confess the Father, the Son, and the Holy Ghost.
>
> *(Columbus, 1893, pp. 71–2)*

In December, he was still questioning the indigenous people about Cipango where he believed there were vast amounts of gold (Columbus, 1893). Finally, in March 1493, he arrived back in Europe from his first Atlantic voyage to the "Indies". As is well-known, the arrival of Columbus in the Americas was not the European encounter with Japan that he had hoped for. The European discovery of the American continent and later the Pacific Ocean beyond delayed the Spanish search for a western route to Japan, as they journeyed back to the Americas, searching for gold, and enslaving the indigenous people (Stone, 2021).

Despite the thrust of the Spanish to the west and the Portuguese to the east, there remained the risk of a serious clash between the two powerful Christian nations. In 1494, in the Treaty of Tordesillas, under the aegis of the Pope, the world of the "unbelievers" was divided into two, at a meridian to the west of the previously uninhabited, but now Portuguese, Cape Verde islands passing north-south through the Atlantic. Spain was given the Western hemisphere and Portugal the Eastern hemisphere to conquer and Christianize. Consequently, Spain "acquired" most of the newly discovered Americas, and Portugal could claim Africa and Asia. In the west, the meridian line placed the portion of South America that jutting into the Atlantic ocean (part of Brazil) in the Portugal half of the globe, which meant that they now had a right to take over that part of the Americas, as it was in their hemisphere (Waisberg, 2017).

Continuing the route east

The Portuguese had "acquired" India by the Treaty of Tordesillas, and with their recent access to the Indian Ocean, it was now available to their vessels. In 1497, Vasco da Gama, with four ships, left Lisbon to take the sea route to India. According to a report of their journey, in Mozambique, they were told that the land of Prester John lay in the African interior, a place only accessible by camels (Ravenstein, 1898, p. 24). This led to the idea of Ethiopia[4] as the location of

Prester John's kingdom, although the prospect that it might lie farther in the east remained a possibility (Manning, 1922). Finally, in 1498, da Gama's ships arrived near Calicut (Kozhikode) on the Indian Malabar coast (Kerala). There, when traders asked why they had come, they replied "in search of Christians and spices" (Ravenstein, 1898, p. 48). While unable to gain trading concessions at this time, da Gama still returned to Portugal with spices of great wealth. He was followed to India by Pedro Álvares Cabral, with a larger fleet, who was able to set up a factory in Calicut. He sought to have the Muslim traders expelled from the region and seized a Muslim ship. In retaliation, the Portuguese factory was attacked and the Portuguese inside it were killed. Cabral began attacking and destroying Muslim ships in the harbour, killing and plundering, before retreating from India when faced by a large Calicut fleet (Cliff, 2011). In 1502, da Gama returned to Calicut, this time as "Admiral of India" with 15 ships and 800 men. In the northern Indian Ocean (the Arabian Sea), he attacked and destroyed Muslim trading ships. Finding a pilgrim ship *Meri* returning from Mecca to Calicut, da Gama captured it and destroyed it by fire, killing the nearly 300 men, women and children aboard (Ghazanfar, 2018). Da Gama ruthlessly sought to have his demands met: that the Indian rulers expel all Muslim traders and offer generous trading terms to the Portuguese. He bombarded Calicut almost to destruction and agreed terms with neighbouring states. He was delighted to find Christian communities in India but did not discover Prester John (Cliff, 2011). In 1505, with the growing presence of the Portuguese in India, King Manuel I appointed Francisco de Almeida as the first Portuguese Viceroy of India, to set up four forts on the Indian coast. In 1509, Almeida with a fleet of 23 ships faced the combined ships of the Mamluk Egyptians, the Ottoman Turks, and the forces of Calicut and Gujarat, off of Diu on the north east coast of India. The decisive Portuguese victory in the Battle of Diu ended the Muslim spice trade in the Indian Ocean and gave the Portuguese a monopoly in the region (Pombo and Cardoso, 2020). The Portuguese expansion now continued into the East Indies.

Alfonso de Albuquerque was appointed the second Portuguese Viceroy of India in 1509. In 1510, Albuquerque captured the city of Old Goa, which was to become the centre of the *Estado da Índia*, the Portuguese empire in India. King Manuel I wanted to keep up the expansion east, in his rivalry with the Spanish. In 1511, Albuquerque took a fleet across the Indian Ocean to capture the city port of Malacca, on the Malay Peninsula, which controlled the Straits of Malacca, through which all the sea trade between India and China passed. After a bombardment, and having received support from the Hindu and Chinese trading communities, the city was attacked. With the subsequent Portuguese victory, the Sultan fled, and Albuquerque began building a fortress. Now the Portuguese had a permanent base from which to trade directly with the Spice Islands (the Moluccas), although not the power to conquer them. Soon after, in 1513, the Portuguese captain Jorge Álvares sailed into the South China Sea, arriving in China, near Guangzhou (also known as Canton)

(Zurndorfer, 2018). While the Chinese administration rejected his request for a trading station, the Portuguese now joined the unofficial ("pirate") traders in the South China Sea, which also included the Japanese.

Further west, into the Pacific

Back in Portugal, Ferdinand Magellan, who had been with the Portuguese fleet in India and Malacca, offered to find a westward route to the Spice Islands, but King Manuel turned him down. Magellan then turned to King Charles I of Spain, offering to act for the Spanish crown. In 1519, Magellan, now of Spanish allegiance, set off with five ships. Only three of the ships survived the passage through the Straits of Magellan, entering the Pacific Ocean in November 1520. Like Columbus before him, Magellan expected to reach Japan or China in a matter of days. However, it was March 1521 when Magellan arrived in the Philippines, where he began to trade with the people there and sought to make them Christians. However, arriving at Mactan Island with a small force, Magellan was killed by the islanders in April 1521. The one remaining Spanish ship sailed westwards, finding the Spice Islands and finally arriving back in Spain in September 1522, the first European ship to circumnavigate the world. While it would be forty years before the Spanish forces returned to colonize the Philippines (in 1565), they now knew of the route to the East Indies across the Pacific from their growing empire in the Americas. From their future base in the Philippines, the Spanish would later be able to reach Japan by sailing directly north.

Both the Spanish and Portuguese were now in a sailing distance of Japan (despite not knowing exactly where it was). However, extending the agreed meridian line around the world from the 1494 Treaty of Tordesillas now meant that the Portuguese possessions, such as Malacca, in the region of the Spice Islands were in the Spanish half of the world. At the Treaty of Zaragoza in 1524, the anti-meridian line was moved to the east of the Moluccas and Portugal paid Spain a large sum in compensation. The treaty held quite well between the two countries, despite Portugal's expansion across Brazil and the Spanish claiming the Philippines. The new meridian line cut through the sparsely populated island of Hokkaido, placing the Empire of Japan in the Portuguese half of the globe, requiring that the Spanish leave it to them to conquer and Christianize, if they could find it.

Converting the unbelievers

A major impetus of the Portuguese and the Spanish expansion was the Papal sanction for their actions. The sailors would receive religious blessings before their journeys and the cross adorned their sails and garb. Their work was not simply to conquer but to Christianize. As a result, the Catholic mendicant orders – such as the Franciscans – accompanied the Spanish *conquistadores* to the Americas. A new religious order, the Jesuits, sometimes rival to the mendicant orders, was established in 1540, specifically to convert the unbelievers, as a result of the Protestant schism from the "universal" church in the first half of the 16th century. After Martin Luther listed his complaints against the Catholic Church in 1517, many people, especially in northern Europe, guided by theologians such as John Calvin, who himself left the Catholic Church in 1530, joined the Protestant Christians in a movement known as the Protestant Reformation. In 1534, after the Pope refused to grant him a divorce, King Henry VIII broke from Rome and declared that he was now head of the English Church. For the rest of the 16th century, Europe was ravaged by a series of bitter Wars of Religion that continued well into the 17th century, as Protestant countries emerged from the once universal European Christendom. In the Counter Reformation, the Catholic Church sought ways to reverse the Protestant tide. In 1537, Pope Paul III approved of a new order within the Church, and, in 1540, issued the bull *Regimini Militantis Ecclesiae* (To the Government of the Church Militant), the foundation document of what became the Society of Jesus, with its members referred to as Jesuits. Their role, in the words of their head, Ignatius of Loyola, was to "serve as a soldier of God beneath the banner of the cross in our Society" (O'Malley, 2013, p. 40); that is, take up the religious life obedient to the Pope. Honouring their vows of chastity and poverty, their mission was to propagate the Catholic faith, stem the spread of Protestantism and bring the souls of the unbelievers into the Catholic Church. With the support of King John II of Portugal, the trade routes to the East provided the means to do the latter.

From now on, the Jesuits accompanied the Portuguese traders to convert the indigenous people to Christianity. In 1542, with the encouragement of King John III, a thirty-six-year-old Basque Francis Xavier, a founding member of the Jesuits, arrived in Goa, India, the heart of the Portuguese *Estado da Índia*, to begin his mission in Asia. His headquarters became St Paul's College, a seminary, to which he was appointed head. Over the next three years, he travelled around mainland India seeking converts, but it was clearly hard work, for reasons he expressed in a later letter to Ignatius.

> The whole race of the Indians, as far as I have been able to see, is very barbarous. . . . Most of the Indians are of a vicious disposition, and averse to virtue. Their instability, levity, and inconstancy of mind are incredible; they have hardly any honesty, so inveterate are their habits of sin and cheating.
>
> *(Coleridge, 1872b, p. 67)*

He decided he would travel further east in the hope of greater success.

Meeting the Japanese

Unable to get an agreement with the Chinese government to set up a factory on Chinese territory, the Portuguese traders began to operate illegally in the South China Sea and were viewed, like the other traders, as pirates by the Chinese authorities, with various unsuccessful attempts made to remove them from the Chinese ports. In the early 1520s, the Portuguese established an illegal entrepôt at Ningbo (on the island of Shuangyu) near Guangzhou in the Zhejiang region, from which they raided nearby ports and captured slaves. The Portuguese had established themselves within the pirate trading community, with access now to the East China Sea. In September 1543, a Chinese trading junk, carrying three Portuguese men, was caught in a storm and blown off course in the East China Sea. It arrived in a damaged condition on the coast of Tanegashima, a small island off of the south of Kyushu, one of the main islands of Japan (see the Appendix). The first Europeans had arrived on Japanese soil.

The first meeting of the Portuguese with the Japanese in their own country is briefly described by António Galvano in his *Discovery of the World*, originally published in Portuguese in 1563 (Bethune, 1862), and in detail by Fernão Mendes Pinto in his *Peregrinaçao* (pilgrimage), published in 1614, an account of his travels in Asia (Pinto, 1989). There are also accounts of it in the Japanese sources (Lidin, 2002). However, it is only Pinto who describes the Japanese. Unfortunately, *Peregrinaçao* is not a reliable historical document, as the heroically portrayed adventurer Pinto of the book doesn't always match the documented evidence about the author. For example, Pinto claims he was one of the three Portuguese who landed at Tanegashima, while the other sources give different names, and there is good evidence that Pinto was elsewhere at the time (Lidin, 2002). Yet this does not mean that his account should be dismissed. He certainly did visit Japan more than once as one of the earliest European travellers, with corroborating evidence in a number of instances, so his descriptions have a valuable contribution to make about the first encounter. It is just that, like a modern autobiographical dramatization, he tended to present himself at the centre of the important action which may overemphasize his involvement. Furthermore, his account also involved a satirical critique of the politics and religion of his times rather than an attempt to make an accurate historical record (Pinto, 1989).

The arrival of the junk was met with great interest by the Japanese, who treated the visitors well. Diogo do Corto, the historian of Portuguese India, wrote in 1597:

> From the land, small boats at once put out to meet them, in which came men whiter than the Chinese, but with small eyes and short beards. From them, they learned that these islands were called Nipongi, the one which we commonly term Japan. And finding that these people were kind, they mingled with them, by whom they were very hospitably received.
>
> *(Boxer, 1951/1967, p. 25)*[5]

The goods onboard the ship were traded with the Japanese for silver at a great profit, and the Japanese provided assistance in making the junk seaworthy once more. Finally, after a number of weeks or, as Pinto claims, months, the ship and its company left the shores of Japan (Lidin, 2002). However, this encounter now presented the opportunity for the Portuguese traders in Ningbo to begin trade with

Japan, particularly for its precious metals. Indeed, here at the end of the world, was another country for the Portuguese to extend their global influence in accord with the Treaty of Zaragoza.

Pinto's favourable account of the Japanese supported Marco Polo's view that the Japanese were fair-skinned and civilized. And they were curious and clever. Pinto discussed the young lord of Tanegashima buying a musket from the Portuguese traders and learning how to use it. Crucially, the Japanese reverse engineered the weapon and within a year were able to produce their own, an ingeniousness that the Portuguese had not observed in other indigenous people. The Japanese sources support this time as the introduction of the gun into Japan, which gained the name of *tanegashima* after the location of their first production (Pinto, 1989; Lidin, 2002). According to Pinto, the Portuguese travellers enjoyed their time as "the Japanese are by nature a very friendly and sociable people" (Pinto, 1989, p. 277) and the Japanese fascination with the gun indicated "how naturally they take to military exercise" (Pinto, 1989, p. 278). Pinto also discussed visiting the province of Bungo (on the east of Kyushu) where the lord's son injured himself when trying to use a musket. Fortunately, so Pinto wrote, the young man recovered from his cut head and damaged thumb under Pinto's ministrations (which saved Pinto from the Japanese retribution).

In describing a second trip to Japan under merchant captain Jorge Álvares, Pinto noted that "the Japanese are much more zealous about their honor than any other nation in the world" (Pinto, 1989, p. 448). It was on the return from this second trip that Pinto claimed that a Japanese man called Anjiro[6] joined their ship to escape from a chasing group of men claiming he was a traitor. Pinto states that he accompanied Anjiro on the return trip to Malacca, to meet the Jesuit Francis Xavier. There is evidence that Pinto did meet Xavier and, having become wealthy from his mercantile endeavours, contributed money to Xavier's Jesuit mission (Pinto, 1989). In 1545, Xavier had arrived in the Indonesian archipelago, where he continued his mission, before returning to Goa in 1548. Yet he was not enamoured by the people there either, as he expressed to Loyola.

> The natives themselves are so enormously addicted to vice as to be little adapted to receive the Christian religion. They so dislike it . . . they think it like death to be asked to become a Christian.
>
> *(Coleridge, 1872b, p. 70)*

However, there had been one event on the trip that had created a different impression. He had learnt about Japan. Near the end of 1547, in Malacca, Xavier met Anjiro, who had learnt some Portuguese, and knew something of the Christian faith. About their meeting, Xavier wrote: "If the rest of the Japanese have the same ardour for gaining knowledge that Anger [*Anjiro*] has, then they surpass in genius all nations anywhere found" (Coleridge, 1872a, p. 417). Xavier asked Anjiro about the possibility of converting the Japanese, and he replied that they would listen to argument and, if convinced, would become Christians: "the King, the nobility, and all other grown up men would certainly join the flock of Christ – for theirs is a nation which follows the guidance of reason" (Coleridge, 1872a, p. 418); a view supported by Captain Álvares who told Xavier "the whole nation in Japan surpasses others in its desire for knowledge" (Coleridge, 1872a, p. 417).

Indeed, in 1547, Álvares provided Xavier with a report on Japan – one of the most reliable accounts of the Japanese at that time. He described their cultivated land, the cornucopia of their natural produce, their well-made wooden houses with large gardens, and the life of these well-ordered communities in a bucolic landscape, such that Boxer (1951/1967, p. 33) commented: "he gives a distinctly idyllic picture of rural life and contentment". Álvares also provided a description of the people: "In the main the Japanese are of medium and stocky build. They are sturdy, they are white people, and they have good features. . . . They are not given to greed", and, while eating three times a day, they only have small portions, with very little meat, which they eat with chopsticks. They drink *sake* (rice wine), and "another beverage" (presumably tea) "which everyone in general drinks, both adults and children". They are welcoming, "and, indeed, are very friendly" (Willis, 2012, pp. 395–6). The people are proud, hate theft (with thieves killed when caught); there are no prisons, and they respect their lords and their priests. The men have only a single wife: the women are "pale and well-proportioned", noble women respect their husbands, with good women revered by their husbands (Willis, 2012, p. 399). But he notes that not all women are like this. Álvares described Japanese clothing, in terms of a long shirt and a tunic, with long and baggy breeches, with the women wearing long gowns and petticoats. And he clearly implied their lack of European prudery in a number of references to the frequency of bathing by the Japanese. "The Japanese bathe twice a day and quite immodestly. They do not care whether others see their private parts" (Willis, 2012, p. 398), a point he repeated about Japanese women. He noted that people bathe in rivers, hot springs, and that the *bonzes*[7] (Buddhist priests) have baths with heated water.

Álvares stated that the Japanese "devoutly worship their idols" (Willis, 2012, p. 398), that they pray daily, and the women are also very devout. He described in detail the dress and behaviour of the bonzes when conducting their religious activities. He also noted that they are not allowed to have sexual intercourse with a woman "on pain of death", but then stated: "So they resort to sodomy with the youths whom they teach and are not censured for doing so" (Willis, 2012, p. 399). Boxer (1951/1967, p. 35) claimed that Álvares was "horrified at this", maybe an inference from the European view of sodomy at the time, where it could lead to being burned at the stake in Catholic Europe. However, Willis (2012) points outs Álvares does not explicitly say this, rather only noting that it appeared to go unpunished in Japan.[8]

For Francis Xavier, he was sure he had found a people who would embrace his religion, despite currently being idolaters. He returned to Goa in 1548 and immediately began to plan a voyage to Japan. "All the Portuguese merchants who come back from Japan assure me, that if I make this voyage, I shall spend my labour much better than in India, inasmuch as I shall have to do with a nation that is governed by reason" (Coleridge, 1872a, p. 418). He was clearly very enthusiastic about the mission.

> I have determined to go thither as soon as I can. I undertake this voyage with great happiness in my soul, and with still greater hope, because I feel quite confident that the labour we may spend on that nation will produce solid and lasting fruit.
>
> *(Coleridge, 1872b, p. 71)*

In Goa, Anjiro and his two Japanese companions became Christians and studied Portuguese. Encouraged by Anjiro, Xavier developed an extremely optimistic view of the mission, believing that the Japanese were already somewhat like Christians: "The whole nation pray on beads as we do. . . . The religious make profession and vows of chastity, poverty, and obedience, and practise this in humility before they are received into religion" (Coleridge, 1872b, pp. 213–4). He even went so far as to write, presumably based on what he had been told by Anjiro: "It is said that some of the great people in Japan are thinking of sending an embassy to the King of Portugal, to ask him to send them some priests who may preach to them the law of Christ" (Coleridge, 1872b, p. 168).

The white and well-mannered Japanese

In 1557, the Chinese authorities agreed to a Portuguese factory being set up in Macau. With the Japanese still banned from trading with China,[9] the Portuguese could now "officially" make large profits as middlemen, trading Chinese silk for Japanese silver, and a range of other products that could be brought back to Europe, along the trade route of factories, forts and colonies, of the Portuguese Empire. Among these "commodities" were Japanese slaves, some of whom may have been the first Japanese to visit Europe (de Sousa, 2019). The Portuguese merchants, despite the risk of losses at sea, had become wealthy from their African and Asian trade (like Pinto had apparently done). In many cases, the trading agreements had been ruthlessly won through military violence bringing death and destruction until concessions were made. The enslavement of the peoples along the route indicated that they were viewed as inferior – as Muslim enemies, pagans (i.e. Sub-Saharan Africans) or idolaters (Asians) – to the Christian conquerors. At the end of the long trade route, in the Spice Islands, China and Japan, it was harder to bring overwhelming force, and trade negotiations were necessary with local rulers. Yet with the trade route now set up, it was easier to transport goods and supplies across the world. Now the "devout religious persons" (as Columbus described them) could follow the Spanish and Portuguese sailors, to convert the indigenous people to Christianity. For the Portuguese, this meant the Jesuits. For Francis Xavier, he had seen the different people of Africa and India, noting: "For as there is so great a variety of colour among men, and the Indians being black themselves, consider their own colour the best, they believe that their gods are black" (Coleridge, 1872a, p. 160). He had also found the Indians and Indonesians unreceptive to Christianity (as noted earlier). Yet he felt the Japanese were very different to all these other "unbelievers", and more like Europeans than any other people so far encountered.

Marco Polo had identified the Japanese as white and well-mannered, a view that Álvares and Pinto concurred with. Xavier had even met some Japanese people, Anjiro and his companions, who had confirmed these opinions – and they had converted to Christianity. What is more Xavier had learnt from Álvares that the Japanese lived in well-organized communities, in a society that gave every indication of being civilized, as viewed from a European perspective, with houses, towns, farms and commerce. These were not the "primitive" people that the Iberians had encountered elsewhere. Indeed, Álvares presented Japan as a sophisticated, bucolic society resonant of the idyllic kingdom ruled over by Prester John. The Japanese were honourable and welcoming. And, crucially, they were governed by "reason", a point that Xavier makes many times in his letters (Coleridge, 1872a, 1872b), a quality not always attributed to non-Europeans in the 16th century (e.g. Delgado, 2016). For Xavier, as a university man, he relished the idea of debating religion with reasonable, civilized, knowledge-seeking people, who would clearly be convinced of the truth of the Christian faith. While it was obvious that the Empire of Japan was not the land of Prester John, everything he had learnt about it suggested that, as the outcome of a Jesuit mission, it could become a Christian empire in the East.

Notes

1 For example, the famous Castillian knight Rodrigo Díaz de Vivar (c. 1043–1099), known as El Cid, fought both with and against Muslim armies.
2 See the Appendix.
3 In the translation by Nigel Cliff, in 2015, the translation is given as "white" rather than "fair-skinned".
4 Ethiopia was often used to indicate somewhere in Africa.
5 The sailor Pero Diez, who visited Japan in the following year, 1544, also described the Japanese as white (blanca) (Ellis, 2003, pp. 165–6).
6 Also called Yajiro by some sources.
7 From the Japanese bonsō – an ordinary (bon) priest (sō).
8 The Japanese did not have such a positive impression of the Portuguese sailors and merchants, as the ordinary Japanese had on Pinto and Álvares (Lidin, 2002). They were friendly towards them – interested in them and their technology – and Álvares noted their curiosity about the African slaves of the Portuguese (Willis, 2012). However, the Europeans wore beards with curly hair, giving them a wilder hairier appearance than the Japanese. They had thicker features, with long noses, with a distinct smell. One reason for the latter was that the Europeans did not bathe with the frequency of the Japanese, as we see from Álvares's account. Combined with the European preference for eating meat, which they ate with their hands unlike the Japanese who ate with chopsticks, this gave the impression, as Pinto notes, of uncouthness and brutishness in the minds of the Japanese (Boxer, 1951/1967, p. 39). As the Portuguese had come from the south, through the East China Sea to Kyushu, the term that was coined in Japan as a name for these foreigners was *nanban* or southern barbarians.
9 The Ming dynasty had banned trade with Japan in an attempt to stop the activity of the *wokou*, Japanese pirates, and the ban was still in force.

3

THE CHRISTIAN CENTURY IN JAPAN

Xavier's dream of a Christian Japan

In August 1549, Xavier and his companions arrived at Kagoshima – on the southwestern tip of Kyushu – the home town of Anjiro. According to the historian Charles Boxer (Boxer, 1951/1967), this began "the Christian Century in Japan". The travellers were received hospitably due to the offices of Anjiro and were the subject of great interest by the community. Xavier was favourably received by the local *daimyo* – the lord of the domain – who believed that he could gain an advantage from the growing (and profitable) Portuguese trade by welcoming the Jesuits. Meeting the Japanese in their own lands only added to Xavier's enthusiasm for their character:

> I really think that among barbarous nations there can be none that has more natural goodness than the Japanese. They are of a kindly disposition. . . . They are wonderfully inclined to all that is good and honest, and have an extreme eagerness to learn. They listen with great avidity to discourse about God and Divine things, especially when they can well understand what you say.
>
> *(Coleridge, 1872b, p. 238)*

Xavier endeavoured – although with great difficulty – to learn some Japanese, with not much success, so he relied on the translation of the Catechism by Anjiro. Initially, through Anjiro's ambiguous translations and the Jesuits arriving from India, the Buddhist monks viewed Christianity as some form of exotic Indian Buddhist sect. However, on realizing that Xavier's religion was not a version of Buddhism, they turned against him. The mission also lost the support of the daimyo, possibly as Portuguese traders did not come to his domain (López-Gay, 2003).

DOI: 10.4324/9781003082088-3

From Kagoshima, Xavier sailed north to Hirado, an island off the northwest coast of Kyushu, which was developing into an important centre for Portuguese trade. He was allowed to engage in public preaching by the local daimyo and, although only staying briefly, Japan's first church was built there a few months later. Xavier's plan was that he should "go to the King of all Japan himself, wherever he may be, and lay before him the message which I have for him from the Supreme Emperor of all nations, our Lord Jesus Christ" (Coleridge, 1872b, p. 179). Unfortunately, Xavier, unaware of the dynamics of power in *sengoku* Japan,[1] at a time of civil war, set out to see the powerless Emperor, rather than the Ashikaga *shogun*,[2] the military ruler, who he misunderstood to be the King of all Japan (see the Appendix). He set out for Kyoto, the seat of the imperial court. On arrival, Xavier realized his mistake. He saw the damage to the city due to the civil war and learnt of the straitened circumstances of the Emperor Go-Nara, who had no interest in seeing the foreigners, especially as these poorly dressed strangers had not brought any gifts, which was expected of an audience (Boxer, 1951/1967).

The experience of the journey to Kyoto led to a change of strategy in Xavier's approach to the mission. In Yamaguchi, wearing richer clothing, he presented himself to the daimyo as the ambassador of the Viceroy of Portuguese India and of the Bishop of Goa, and gave him a number of expensive gifts, including a clock, a telescope and a musket. It had the desired effect and the missionaries were given a place to stay and were allowed to preach, which they did for the next four months. However, a document allowing the missionaries to use an old temple in Yamaguchi stated: "The sō [*a term for Buddhist priests*] who have come from the West, in order to preach the Law of Buddha are hereby authorised to build that temple" (Cieslik, 1954a, p. 86), indicating that the mission was not well understood. Xavier then set out for Funai in Bungo Province, in the east of Kyushu, another port that had attracted Portuguese trade, and received a warm welcome from the daimyo, Sorin Otomo.[3] Finding no letters from Goa on the Portuguese ship docked there, Xavier decided to return to India, and soon after left Japan on the same ship, promising to return, but, unfortunately, he died of an illness on a visit to China in December 1552.

While Xavier's visit to Japan established a small Christian presence in Japan, it was uncertain what the converts actually believed. Also, the mission had been welcomed primarily by daimyo who had received, or expected to receive, a material benefit; a welcome that was swiftly removed when the prospect of Portuguese trade disappeared. Yet Xavier's image of the Japanese was unshaken, claiming that they were "the best thus far discovered" (Ellis, 2003, p. 156). They were white, civilized, and rational – all traits that allied them to Europeans – and because of that, he believed that it would only be a matter of time before they embraced the Catholic faith. He wrote: "Such a prudent and talented people, eager for knowledge, obedient to reason, endowed with many other good qualities cannot fail to yield much fruit" (Elisonas, 2000, p. 3). To a Catholic Church reeling at the rise of Protestantism in Europe, Xavier's image of the Japanese, embracing all the potential of a Christian empire of the East (that would support the Catholic West) was to dominate the view of the Japanese in Europe during the following decades, as the Jesuit reports from Japan were disseminated.

The image of the Japanese in the Jesuit reports

As Portuguese trade with Japan expanded, especially after the establishment of their factory in Macau, China, in 1557, the Jesuits accompanied the traders from Lisbon via India to Kyushu in Japan. Indeed, they had royal and papal support to do so. For the next fifty years, until the arrival of the Dutch, the Portuguese monopoly in Japan meant that the European image of the Japanese was dominated by Jesuit communication. As well as letters by individual Jesuits, there was the *carta annua de Japão* (the annual letter) reporting on the events in Japan during the previous year. However, it is important to note that the annual letter – or indeed any Jesuit letter – was a highly selective account of the Japanese. Letters, while informing the Europeans about Japan, presented a positive account of the mission detailing successes rather than failures, and often were structured to gain financial and other support from European rulers, nobles and wealthy traders to fund the mission (Sindemann, 2001). These letters served a public relations purpose of promoting the mission, and propagating the Jesuit image of Japan across Europe. Letters were copied and copied again as they passed through ports on the journey back to Europe, and then copied in Europe to be sent out amongst Jesuit communities. They were also edited in their transmission: passages were removed or added, and the meaning was altered or emphasized, to meet the needs of the Jesuit community (Schwemmer, 2022; Loureiro, 2004). As Schwemmer (2022, pp. 35–6) put it, the Jesuit "story machine" was designed to "inspire the whole world with tales of conversion, devotion and martyrdom". Or, more bluntly, as Domínguez (2012, pp. 294) expressed it: "the information on these letters used to be selfishly distorted by the missionaries, who exaggerated their achievements and used an exemplary tone".

Xavier himself was well aware of the importance of these letters. He had written:

> In your report you have to exclude what could be offensive to others because of unpopular comments and the image must be one of a certain religious serenity, so that it can be published immediately when it arrives in Europe and be told to externals as well. Such news . . . is much appreciated and read with great interest in Spain, Italy and other countries. So we have to take great care in writing these letters, and that they please everyone . . . [*as*] they will find their way to the hands of unpleasant persons or even enemies. We must keep an eye on the objective of these letters, they should encourage the praise of God and the Holy Church, but none should find a reason to be offended or to unrightfully interpret them.
>
> *(Sindemann, 2001, p. 127)*

As a result, Boxer (1951/1967, p. 39) pointed out that the report of Jorge Álvares was "the last report [*on Japan*] available by a layman, for after the arrival of

Francis Xavier Japan is seen only through missionary spectacles until the coming of the heretic Hollanders half a century later". One key theme within these letters was the battle to undermine the Buddhist priests (referred to as bonzes) in the minds of the Japanese, both by disputing the Buddhist doctrine and by personal attacks on the character of the Buddhist priests. A second was to report back to Europe on the attempts to convert as many Japanese as possible but particularly the nobles (especially the daimyo). Finally, there was an ongoing discussion amongst the Jesuits about the best way to engage with the Japanese.

Them and us: perceived differences between the Japanese and Europeans

Both Xavier and the later Jesuit visitor (a powerful inspector of the mission) Alessandro Valignano, who arrived in 1579, had a very positive view of the Japanese, and proposed a strategy of integration into Japanese culture to promote the mission. They had noted that the Japanese were proud of their culture and civilization, and did not accept European superiority. Furthermore, these Jesuits had distinguished the Japanese from other Asians as "like us" (white and civilized) but with a different language and culture, which the Jesuits should learn as a part of their conversion strategy. However, not all the Jesuits shared this view. For example, the leader of the Jesuit mission from 1570 to 1581, Francisco Cabral, while encouraging converts with success, maintained a view of Japanese inferiority, discouraged the learning of Japanese and denied the elevation of the Japanese to the priesthood – until he left his post under pressure from Valignano (Hoey, 2010).

The problem for the Jesuit view of the Japanese as "like us" was that there were many differences between Europeans and the Japanese. Indeed, in 1585, the Jesuit Luis Frois, who had lived in Japan for twenty-two years and spoke the language fluently, put together a list of over 600 differences in a treatise, the *Tratado*[4] (Willis, 2012). Amongst the physical differences, he noted that European men are for the most part taller than Japanese men, with longer noses. Unlike European women, Japanese women attach no importance to their virginity, may leave their house without their husband's permission, and, unlike in Europe, divorce him. Frois lists over 100 differences between Western and Japanese clothing, before describing the differences between child-rearing in the two cultures. He then described over seventy differences concerning priests and religious practices, with various negative comments about the bonzes (see next section). Differences in food and eating practices are then listed, often in minute detail, including that the Japanese cut melons crosswise (unlike the European lengthwise!) and that "we" (Europeans) chill wine, whereas the Japanese warm it. This is followed by differences in weapons and warfare. "To us it is a great sin for a man to kill himself; whereas in Japan, when in battle they are unable to go on, deem it an act of great valour to disembowel themselves" (Willis, 2012, p. 422). A whole range of other differences are described covering topics from horses and houses to writing and ships. This is followed by differences in entertainment. Frois not only noted that the Japanese find European musical instruments "harsh and unpleasant" but also criticized Japanese singing as "the most horrendous noise that one could make" (Willis, 2012, p. 432). Finally, in a list of extraordinary things, he contrasts European acceptance of the killing of animals and shock at the killing of men, with the opposite view in Japan, where he says that the punishment for the theft of even trivial amounts, or of servants, is usually death.

It is very clear that the Jesuits living amongst the Japanese appreciated the differences between Europeans and the Japanese. However, the Jesuit letters, from Xavier onwards, sought to establish an equivalence between the Japanese and the Europeans that was absent in their views of other people of the East Indies (Kowner, 2014); and therefore made them ripe for conversion. However, the Jesuits could not avoid the wide range of cultural differences identified by Jorge Álvares and Lois Frois. Indeed, Frois specifically wrote his *Tratado* as a long list of binary cultural opposites, which clearly made the Japanese a distinct cultural other. Yet there was a solution to this issue in the Jesuit imagination. Many of the cultural differences were not problematic, such as differences in clothing, eating habits, language and social mores. Indeed, Valignano's strategy required a willingness to adapt to Japanese customs (Hoey, 2010). However, there were many aspects of Japanese life that disturbed and offended Jesuit morality. These they attributed to a religious cause – a Japanese failure to recognize the one true creator. At first, Xavier had misunderstood the Japanese religion to have a single god, and assumed a similarity to Christianity, but he soon learnt that it did not and was not. This meant that the conversion of the Japanese to Christianity was crucial to bring about a Japan with a Christian morality, which would make "them" more like "us", with new Christian names and new identities (Ellis, 2003), such as Anjiro being baptized by Xavier as Paul, when he converted.

The devil's work and the "perversion" of the bonzes

In presenting the Japanese as the best of people – civilized and rational – the Jesuits had created a perplexing issue for themselves: why were the Japanese idolaters and why had they not discovered the one true God? This problem was expressed in a letter back to Europe, in 1557, by the Jesuit Gasper Vilela. He wondered how it was that: "people who are white, and prudent in their worldly customs, [*are*] yet so bereft of the knowledge of their creator" (Elisonas, 2000, p. 3). Having posed the question, the answer was obvious to the Jesuits: it was a result of the devil, working through the Buddhists and their vile practices. Xavier, who eulogized the Japanese in general, was particularly condemning of the bonzes who he accused of sodomy, sexual activities with nuns, and of being avaricious, hypocritical parasites. Here the accusation of sodomy, being unrelated to reproduction, was particularly damning as a mortal sin (Ellis, 2003). Hence, the Jesuit mission was especially important, as only by its success would the natural order would be restored and such practices disappear (Ellis, 2003). Xavier wrote in 1549:

> The laity live better in their state than the Bonzes in theirs; and withal this is so manifest, it is astonishing in what esteem the former hold the latter. There are many other errors and evils among these Bonzes, and the more learned are the worse sinners
>
> *(Boxer, 1951/1967, p. 402)*

Thirty-five years later, Frois claimed that the bonzes "have an inner filthiness and commit every abominable sin of the flesh". They take on the religious life "to lead a life of pleasure and idleness", "are very acquisitive", "spiritually abominable", "often found in a state of drunkenness in the streets", "revere and worship" the devil (Willis, 2012, p. 413–5). Buddhist nuns fare no better in Frois's view: their convents "are little better than a street full of whores" (Willis, 2012, p. 410). Hence, throughout the mission, in the letters back to Europe, the Jesuits "emerged as the rescuers of the [*Japanese*] people in danger [*of damnation*] . . . [*and*] depicted as an instrument of the will and grace [*of God*] . . . with truly miraculous abilities" (Domínguez, 2012, p. 304).

However, the Jesuits had a problem. In order to fight against the "errors" of Buddhism, they needed to learn about it. From Xavier onwards, the study of Buddhist texts became a key aspect of Jesuit activity. In 1556, for example, they produced a *Summario*, a "Summary of the errors in which the heathen of Japan live and of some heathen sects on which they principally rely" (Elisonas, 2000, p. 4) in which they described what they had learnt about Shinto and Buddhism for their colleagues – in order to attack it. As well as having to learn about Japanese religions, the Jesuits to some extent had to imitate the bonzes in order to be acknowledged – and respected – as religious teachers by the Japanese people. For the Jesuit visitor, Alessandro Valignano, this meant dressing in Japanese clothes, eating Japanese food (with chopsticks), speaking the language and following Japanese customs (Hoey, 2010). The irony of this approach was that the Jesuits, in order to challenge the Buddhist priests, had to learn their religion and mimic their behaviour.

The romance of Christian kings in the Orient

The Jesuit strategy to convert the Japanese leaders began to achieve some success. Yet the daimyo varied from minor nobles – clan members with little wealth and landholding – to the powerful warlords who dominated the country. Furthermore, people in Europe would not know what a "daimyo" meant. Thus, the Jesuits in their letters, not by chance, referred to any landowning noble as a king. To present themselves back in Europe as having the favour of a king sounded impressive. Indeed, Xavier had set an example of this in a letter from 1552.

> The King of Bungo commands numerous and very war like troops, and as things go with Japanese kings, has vast dominions to govern. He has a great liking for

> the Portuguese. No sooner was he informed of the power and character of the King of Portugal than he wrote to him asking to be admitted into the number of his friends, and sending him a rich suit of armor as a token of friendship.
>
> *(Coleridge, 1872b, p. 344)*

This gives the illusion of some sort of equivalence of the "king" of Bungo with that of Portugal. However, Bungo was one of the nine provinces of Kyushu,[5] roughly the size of Norfolk in England or Delaware in the United States (not normally considered "vast" in the West), and relatively minor amongst the sixty-six provinces of Japan, especially in terms of the powerful warlords emerging in Honshu. Yet the image of Christian "kings" of Japan resonated with the European idea of a Christian king of the East, such as the Magi or Prester John.

The Christian "kings" of Japan

The majority of daimyo favourable to the Portuguese – and who welcomed the Jesuits – were located in Kyushu, and benefitted financially from Portuguese trade, which supported their political aspirations in a time of uncertainty. Of these, three featured prominently in the Jesuit story-telling about Japan. First amongst these was Sumitada Omura, in the west of Kyushu, in competition for the Portuguese trade with the Matsuda clan in Hirado to the north. He attracted the Portuguese to his domain by offering them access to the port of Yokoseura. And, in 1563, Omura converted, with the Christian name of Bartholomew. This was a major coup for the Jesuits – to convert the "king" of Omura. Yet Omura's lands were so small, even relative to Bungo that he was sometimes referred to as the "Prince of Omura" (although in later texts, he is labelled a king: for example, Crasset, 1705; see Chapter 4). When Omura converted, his retainers followed suit, and he began actively destroying the Buddhist temples in his domain. He also offered the Jesuits access to a small fishing village, which was to expand into the port of Nagasaki. Omura became the major beneficiary of Portuguese trade in Kyushu. In 1568, Don[6] Bartholomew (as he was now referred to in the Jesuit letters) offered the Jesuit Gaspar Vilela a pagoda for his base in Nagasaki. Within a year, Vilela had allegedly converted the entire community, earning himself the appellation of "the Apostle of Nagasaki" (Cieslik, 1954b). The pagoda was soon demolished and the Church of All Saints was constructed in its place. In 1570, Omura opened Nagasaki's protected harbour to Portuguese ships, and Vilela continued to convert the growing population. In 1571, the first Portuguese ship from Macau arrived in Nagasaki, beginning its development as a major Portuguese trading centre. By filling up a large carrack (called *nau* in Portuguese) of up to 1,600 tons, the regular trade of these black ships (because their hulls were painted with pitch) between China and Japan made huge profits for the Portuguese and the Omura clan (Boxer, 1985).

With Portuguese support – including military – the Bungo daimyo, Sorin Otomo, the second and more justifiable "king" of the Jesuit letters and stories, was able to expand his influence to more than half of Kyushu, and, in 1578, he too converted to

Christianity, with the Christian name Francis, and was referenced in numerous Jesuit reports as the "King of Bungo". However, at the time of his conversion, he handed over many of his responsibilities to his son and planned to "retire" to Tsuchimochi in Hyuga (in Kyushu) to form a Christian community. This explains why Elisonas (2007) argued that while it may have been a moot point whether Otomo deserved the title of "king" or not, more importantly, he was no longer even acting as the daimyo of Bungo at this time.

In Shimabara, in Hizen Province to the west of Bungo, the daimyo, Harunobu Arima, had initially persecuted Christians but, under threat from a neighbouring daimyo, he had turned to the Portuguese for aid. In 1579, he too became a Christian, taking the name Protasius, the third of the Christian "kings" highlighted in the Jesuit letters. However, his domain was a very small "kingdom", being only a small part of Hizen, and not even the whole of the Shimabara peninsula (Elisonas, 2007). While not the only daimyo who converted to Christianity, these three "kings" of Omura, Bungo and Arima (or Hizen) would feature prominently in the Jesuit mythology of Japan, despite these domains being half the size of Wales – or less than that of Connecticut. Furthermore, these daimyo had, on conversion, required their subjects to convert as well. Hence, it allowed the Jesuits, in their letters back to Europe, to suggest that they had converted whole kingdoms in the Japanese Empire to Christianity. In 1580, "Don Bartholomew" gave Nagasaki to the Jesuits, which now effectively became a Portuguese colony in Japan with its population now promoted as wholly Christian. Nagasaki was to become known as a Christian city which, along with Goa, Mangalore and Manila, was at times referred to as "the Rome of the East" (Domínguez, 2012).

A number of other daimyo converted to Christianity but the vast majority did not. Also, the Jesuits were well aware of the real power in Japan. They were given audiences with the dominant Japanese warlords, the "unifiers" Nobunaga Oda (1534–1582) and Hideyoshi Toyotomi (1534–1598) – see the Appendix – who treated the Jesuits cordially whilst they did not pose a threat to their authority. However, tales of Christian "kings" in the East prepared the way for Valignano's propaganda strategy of sending an embassy of young Japanese Christian boys to Europe.

The "Magi" in Europe: the Tensho Boys Embassy

Valignano's embassy had three goals: to gain support from European nobles and the Church, to have impressionable young Japanese travellers observe the grandeur of Europe (which they could report back to Japan), and to maintain papal support for the Jesuit monopoly in Japan – and stop a Franciscan mission to Japan from the Philippines threatening their influence in Japan (Cooper, 2005). Essentially, this meant selecting appropriate Japanese Christian boys who could be schooled to perform their roles. The "ambassadors" would be representatives of the "kings", Francis (the most powerful), Bartholomew and Protasius. It was intended that Francis's (Otomo's) nephew, the son of the "king" of Hyuga (the province south of Bungo), would be the senior member of the party but he was in Kyoto and unable to arrive before the designated ship departed. So, thirteen-year-old Mancio Ito, the lord of Hyuga's grandson and a more distant relative of Otomo, took up the role. The second boy and Omura's nephew, fifteen-year-old Michael Chijiwa, was also a second cousin of Arima, so represented both Omura and Arima. Two additional boys, both fourteen years old, Martin Hara and Julian Nakamura, young nobles linked to the Omura family went as their companions. All four boys were studying in a Jesuit school in Kyushu (Cooper, 2005).

Valignano schooled them so they could act as exemplary Christian Japanese to King Phillip II of Spain (since 1580 united with Portugal) and the Pope to enhance their support. As Christians, they were familiar with the devotional practice, had learnt about European dress and social mores, had been taught Latin and were as familiar as possible with what they were going to face. They were also young and personable. Thus, they combined both the familiar and the different that was most likely to have a positive impact on the powerful Europeans they met. The Jesuit historian Michael Cooper claimed that the embassy was only a "legation" and argued that Valignano only claimed that the boys were "noble youths", yet he also acknowledged that once in Europe, they were treated (and referred to) as "Japanese kings or princes" (Cooper, 2005, p. 14). Indeed, regardless of the alleged modest claims about the boys, this was a clever public relations exercise by Valignano – "a publicity stunt" according to Elisonas (2007, p. 27) – that was to have a major impact on European perceptions of the Japanese (Cortazzi, 2007), due to the fantastic success of the embassy.

The embassy left Japan in February 1582. Valignano had to remain in India, but the boys and their tutor arrived in Lisbon in August 1584. There they visited Cardinal Albert, the Archduke of Austria and the Viceroy of Portugal three times, who showed them "every sign of friendship and affection" (Cooper, 2005, p. 48) and gave them 300 crowns for their journey. On route to Madrid, they visited the Duke of Braganza where they were royally entertained and given many gifts. On the outskirts of Madrid, they were met by a procession of mounted nobles, and travelled into Madrid in coaches drawn by white horses. Phillip II – the most powerful monarch in Europe – gave them an audience where he was presented with letters from the three sponsoring Japanese "kings". Again the boys were treated as honoured ambassadors and princes, and given 500 crowns as expenses. From Madrid, they progressed to Rome to meet the Pope. In Belmonte Cathedral, they were saluted by cannon fire, and large crowds turned out to see them, as they were in Murcia. From there, they sailed to Italy. At Pisa, they were entertained by the Archduke of Tuscany, where Mancio danced with the archduchess. The royal treatment continued in Florence, before they continued to Rome. Here, a large military escort guarded them through the cheering crowds into the city (Cooper, 2005). The fact that they had come from the East was not lost on the crowds and, with Julien unwell and unable to attend, their procession through the city provided a spectacle of three kings of the Orient that resonated with images of the Magi[7] for both the humble people lining the streets, and the cardinals and nobles in the parade. Indeed, Guido Gualtieri (1586) explicitly made this association between the boys and the Magi in his account of the embassy.

Their audience with Pope Gregory XIII was a huge public spectacle. Led by Swiss guards and the papal household, trumpeters and drummers, the boys, mounted on horses provided by the Duke of Sora, and accompanied by bishops on either side, passed through the watching crowds, as they were saluted by cannon and musket volleys. In the Vatican, the Sala Regia was packed with cardinals and nobles. When the boys arrived, each was embraced by the Pope. In a welcome speech, it was stated that "Francis King of Bungo, Protasius King of the Arimans, and Bartholomew, Prince of Omur, hath sent you their kinsmen to him from the remote Japonian Islands" (Cooper, 2005, p. 90). Also, the Jesuit Gaspar Gonçalves eulogized the people of Japan, claiming that the Japanese Isles had now replaced the (Protestant) British Isles as a centre of the Catholic faith. Just to make the point, the excommunication of Protestant Queen Elizabeth I of England was reissued (Screech, 2012).

While in Rome, the boys were feted by cardinals and ambassadors and visited the Pope a number of times. Even when Gregory XIII died, the new Pope Sixtus V gave them a prominent role in his coronation, and later he made them Knights of St Peter. Sixtus promised a generous increase in the annual donation to the mission in Japan, and after two months they left Rome. They were feted in Bologna, and in Venice, and the boys' portraits were painted by Tintoretto.[8] Sadly, these paintings were lost until that of Mancio was rediscovered. The painting has the title: "Don Mancio, Nephew of the King of Hizen" (Massarella, 2014). Finally, the boys returned to Spain where they had another audience with King Phillip II, before returning to Lisbon, where in April 1586, they boarded the ship to return home. In Goa, Valignano joined them once again, and they finally arrived back in Nagasaki in July 1590.

The publicity stunt had been enormously successful, and achieved all of Valignano's goals. The boys had been royally treated as ambassadors of kings. Switching between Japanese and European dress, to the Europeans they had been exotically different yet comfortingly familiar. In fact, they had been charming. One description did note that "they are rather short, of swarthy colour, small eyes, thick eyelids, a rather wide nose", but crucially, it concluded that they had "a naïve and refined appearance with nothing which resembles a barbarian" (Cooper, 2005, p. 110). In Catholic Europe, the boys had not only been living proof of Christian kingdoms in the East, with their embassy echoing the Magi, but here at a time of religious upheaval in Europe, was further proof of the true God operating in the farthest East of the world.

The unravelling of the illusion of a Christian Japan

Yet, when the boys returned,[9] the image of a Christian Japan that was so carefully constructed in the European mind collapsed completely in the face of the reality of Japan. The warlord Hideyoshi Toyotomi was now master of all Japan. And his opinion of the Jesuits changed as a result of his campaign in Kyushu where he defeated the Shimazu clan in June 1587. He had learnt the extent of the Portuguese (and

Jesuit) influence in the politics of Kyushu, discovered that Nagasaki was now under the sole control of the Jesuits, and that Japanese slaves were being traded by the Portuguese slave traders. He wrote to the head of the Jesuit mission:

> It has come to our attention that Portuguese, Siamese, and Cambodians who come to our shores to trade are buying many people, taking them captive to their kingdoms, ripping Japanese away from their homeland, families, children, and friends. This is insufferable.
>
> *(Nelson, 2004, p. 465)*

He demanded their freedom and their return (Nelson, 2004). Furthermore, with the Portuguese (based in Macau) and the Spanish (from the Philippines) now meeting to trade in the Jesuit port of Nagasaki, the combined Catholic powers appeared to be a threat to Japan (Boxer, 1985). As a result, in 1587, Hideyoshi issued two edicts, one limiting the propagation of Christianity and the second expelling the missionaries. In the first, while an individual could still choose to be a Christian, they could not demand it of their retainers. Furthermore, fief-holders would require permission before they could become a Christian. In the second, it was stated that "the false teaching from Christian countries" could no longer be tolerated. The destruction of temples, by Christians, and the giving of land to the Church was now illegal. The missionaries were to leave Japan, although the Portuguese trade could continue (Boxer, 1951/1967). Nagasaki was taken from the Jesuits into Hideyoshi's personal control. The Jesuit historian Hubert Cieslik referred to Hideyoshi's edicts of July as happening "like a bolt from the blue" and a "notorious decree" (Cieslik, 1954c) – a view of the edicts as an inexplicable shock which has persisted in the Western (Christian) mind. Yet Cieslik, as a good historian, had noted the developing signs: even from his own writing it can be seen that Hideyoshi, as the dominant warlord, at the end of long years of civil war – who knew of the Iberian conquests across the world – followed a predictable path in his actions to ward off a perceived threat to his power. Even though Hideyoshi did not assiduously follow up the edict, the mission was left to manage its retrenchment.

Then came the incident of the *San Felipe* in 1596. In 1593, Franciscan friars had arrived on a diplomatic mission from the Philippines for the Spanish government. However, they had remained in Kyoto allegedly preaching with missionary zeal, in contrast to the Portuguese Jesuits who had kept a low profile after Hideyoshi's edicts. In 1596, the Spanish galleon *San Felipe* from the Philippines on its way to Mexico was typhoon-damaged and ran ashore on the Japanese island of Shikoku. There was a dispute about what should happen to the cargo and the ship's Pilot-Major

> in an ill-judged effort to impress . . . with the power of the Spanish King, incautiously admitted . . . that the Spanish overseas conquests had been greatly facilitated by the Christian "fifth column" (to use modern jargon) formed by the missionary friars before the arrival of the conquistadores themselves.
>
> *(Boxer, 1951/1967, p. 166)*

This supported a view propagated by the bonzes (Buddhist priests) that the Jesuits were doing the same in Japan (Boxer, 1951/1967). In consequence, twenty-six Christians were executed: six Franciscans, three Jesuits and seventeen Christian Japanese in February 1597. The following month, another decree repeated Hideyoshi's order for the Jesuits to leave Japan. Over the next year, they closed their schools and began to leave. However, in 1598, Hideyoshi died. There was a brief hope that the third and final unifier of Japan, Ieyasu Tokugawa (1543–1616) the new master of Japan, might be persuaded to revoke the edicts, particularly as he accepted Hideyoshi's Portuguese translator, the Jesuit João Rodrigues, a fluent Japanese speaker, as his own interpreter (Cooper, 1974). Yet, just as the Jesuit story of a Christian Japan was unravelling, their representation of a unified Catholic Europe – the image they had sought to plant in the Japanese mind – was also about to be shattered with the arrival in Japan of Protestant Europeans.

An English outlook: William Adams, pilot and samurai

Since 1568, the Dutch had been fighting to gain their independence from Spain and, in 1581, the Northern provinces created a Dutch Republic (the Republic of the Seven United Netherlands). The Portuguese, united with Spain in 1580, were now also subject to Dutch enmity. The English, a long-term ally of Portugal and an enemy of Spain, had suffered from the union of the two kingdoms, as their spice supplies from the Portuguese had dried up under Spanish influence. Now the Dutch and the English had sea-going ships, they threatened the Iberian hegemony in the East Indies. In 1598, five well-armed trading ships left Rotterdam for the Far East, their probable destination being the Spice Islands, via the Magellan Straits and across the Pacific. Their weaponry enabled them to engage any Spanish or Portuguese vessels on route. Unfortunately, it was an ill-omened adventure and only one vessel survived the Pacific crossing. When the *De Liefde* (Love) made landfall – at Bungo in Kyushu – on 19 April 1600, only 24 out of the original 111 crew were still alive, and 6 more died soon after (Boxer, 1951/1967).

The Portuguese Jesuits, knowing that the arrival of the Protestant Dutch would destroy the Japanese belief in a universal Catholic Europe, wanted the sailors executed as pirates, but Ieyasu Tokugawa imprisoned them while he decided what to do. Famously amongst them was the first known Englishman in Japan, the pilot of the *De Liefde*, William Adams.[10] From the age of twelve, he had worked as an apprentice in a shipyard in Deptford, London, learning shipbuilding, astronomy and navigation. He joined the Royal Navy and served under Sir Francis Drake and fought against the Spanish armada in 1588 (Massarella and Farrington, 2000). By the time he joined the five Dutch vessels as a pilot, he had considerable seamanship experience. Ieyasu spoke to Adams three times between May and June 1600, and Adams felt these meetings went well: "Coming before the king, he viewed me well, and seemed to be wonderfull favourable" (Rundall, 1850, p. 39). At first, Adams was concerned that Jesuit interpreters were doing the translation: "which was not to our good, our mortal ennemies being our Truchmen [*interpreters*]" (Rundall, 1850, p. 24). However, it is clear that Ieyasu had learnt a lot about Europe from Adams who noted:

> He demanded of me, of what countrey we were; so I answered him in all points; for there was nothing that he demanded not, both conserning warre and peace betweene countrey and country . . . also as conserning the warres betweene the Spaniard or Portingall and our countrey, and the reasons; the which I gave him to understand of all things, which he was glad to heare, as it seemed to me.
>
> *(Rundall, 1850, pp. 24–5)*

It was obvious to Ieyasu that Adams, though a Christian, was not like the Jesuits and had no desire to proselytize. His interests were focused on the mundane world, which had practical value to Ieyasu. Adams was able to demonstrate his shipbuilding skills when Ieyasu ordered him to work with Shogen Mukai, the naval commander, and the carpenters of the city of Ito, to build a Western-style sailing ship. Initially, an 80-ton vessel was built. It was clearly a success, as Adams wrote that Ieyasu "comming aboard to see it, liked it very well" (House, 2021, p. 106). A second vessel of 120 tons was built the following year. Adams wrote that he learnt Japanese and, as well as demonstrating his shipbuilding skills, he gave advice to the shogun (Ieyasu)[11] – teaching him amongst other things, aspects of geometry and mathematics. Adams wrote:

> I pleased him so, that what I said he would not contrarie. At which my former ennemies did wonder; and at this time must intreat me to do them a friendship, which to both Spaniards and Portingals have I doen: recompencing them good for evill.
>
> *(Rundall, 1850, p. 28)*

Now the situation was reversed with his Jesuit interpreters. Adams was given the two swords to elevate him to the rank of samurai and also given a Japanese name, Anjin Miura (the Muira pilot). He was further generously rewarded with the rank of *hatamoto* (a bannerman or samurai directly responsible to the shogun) and a fief in Hemi of about 250 *koku*, indicating an estate with a yearly yield able to feed 250 people in rice for a year. In 1610, Ieyasu's Portuguese Jesuit advisor and interpreter, João Rodrigues, was banished from Japan (after thirty-three years) and was replaced by Adams as his foreign interpreter and trade negotiator (Cooper, 1974).

The Dutch had formed the VOC in 1602 and established a factory in Pattani on the Malay Peninsula. With access to the East China Sea, in 1603, the Dutch attacked the Portuguese ship for Japan, out of Macau, and stole the entire cargo. The Dutch now began to dominate the East Indies. Things got worse for the Portuguese when Adams obtained letters from Ieyasu encouraging Dutch trade, which were dispatched with most of the *De Liefde* crew, who were allowed to leave Japan in 1605, and delivered to Pattani. In 1609, Dutch ships arrived in Japan to set up a VOC factory in Hirado. And, in 1613, an English ship, the *Clove*, captained by John Saris, arrived in Japan. A factory for the English East India Company (EIC) was also set up in Hirado, with Richard Cocks as its chief factor.

Screech (2012) argues that the Japanese restriction of the Catholic priests resonated with the English, who had expelled them from their own country in 1585. The failed Catholic plot to blow up King James and his Parliament (the "gunpowder plot") of 1605 had further strengthened anti-Catholic animosity in England. Rather than siding with their fellow Europeans, the English acknowledged, and encouraged, the Japanese right to expel the Catholic priests in defence against a "perceived Catholic menace" (Screech, 2012, p. 13). Indeed, in 1614, English gunpowder and ordnance was employed by Ieyesau in his successful taking of Osaka Castle from his Toyotomi enemies, who had Catholic support. The English sought to position themselves as sympathetic to Ieyasu in wanting to avoid a Spanish invasion – something that they themselves had only just avoided with the failed Spanish Armada of 1588. Cocks wrote "the King of Spain usurpeth Portingall by force . . . , as he does the like in other parts of the world, and would do the like in Japon, if he could, and the padres are fit instruments to stir the people to rebellion" (Screech, 2012, p. 20). In 1614, an edict was issued banning all evangelism and requiring the remaining Jesuit priests to leave. As Cocks wrote in his diary "The Emperour of Japan hath banished all Jesuites, pristes, friers, and nuns out of all his domynions" (Cooper, 1974, p. 268). The only missionaries remaining in Japan were now those in hiding, at risk of persecution from the authorities.

The EIC factory was a failure; and Cocks, who remained in charge for its decade in existence, has often been blamed, yet fundamentally the EIC had little to trade that the Japanese wanted to buy. For example, English cloth did not compare to silk and was useful only for padding armour (Corr, 1995). Also, the Chinese, Dutch and Portuguese had more experience and better networks for meeting the Japanese trading demands. Adams worked for the EIC and through local knowledge produced some successful trades. But his influence waned in 1616 when Ieyasu died, and he himself passed away in 1620. The EIC interests had turned to India, and there was no desire to persist with the Japanese loss-making factory. In 1623, the factory closed, and in December, onboard the company ship *Bull*, Cocks and his English colleagues left Hirado for good.

Adams, not surprisingly, had had a very positive view of the Japanese:

> The people of this Iland of Iapon are good of nature, curteous above measure, and valiant in warre: their justice is severely excecuted without any partialitie upon transgressors of the law. They are governed in great civilitie. I meane, not a land better governed in the world by civill policie.
>
> *(Rundall, 1850, p. 32)*

Cocks also noted the severity of their justice on a number of occasions, including the case of a sixteen-year-old boy who was executed for stealing a small boat, despite Cocks' plea for clemency (Cooper, 1965, p. 160). However, whilst noting such cultural differences, they also saw an association between themselves and the Japanese in their material interests and anti-Catholic sentiments. Subsequently, the image of Adams, an Englishman landing in an exotic country but adapting to life within Japan, and making a name for himself, has offered a fascinating story in the West of an English samurai (see Chapter 7).

Dutch merchants in Japan

The arrival of the Dutch in Japan occurred at the beginning of what has been referred to as the Dutch Golden Age (see Chapter 4), when they sought to supplant the Portuguese in the East Indies. During this time, the VOC was able to act as a sovereign state in the East with dozens of ships and thousands of men at its disposal. However, at the end of their supply chain, in Japan, the Dutch had to adopt a different strategy to avoid the fate of other Europeans and avoid expulsion from the country. To maintain the existence of the Japanese factory, as Clulow (2014, p. 17) put it, the Dutch had "to refashion themselves – from subjects of a fictive king[12] to loyal vassals of the shogun". Their initially very large profits made this strategy financially successful.

After the death of Ieyasu in 1616, Western traders were restricted only to Hirado and Nagasaki. With the Spanish expelled from Japan in 1624, there only remained the Portuguese and the Dutch. However, in 1637, as a result of high taxation by the Shimabara daimyo Katsuie Matsukura and his persecution of Christian converts, nearly 40,000 Catholic peasants revolted. They held out in Hara Castle against a force of over 100,000 soldiers sent by the Tokugawa shogunate. The Dutch were asked to support the action by supplying cannon fire. Whilst reluctant to do so, the Chief Factor (the *Opperhoofd*) Nicholaes Koeckebacker sent the *De Rijp* ("hoarfrost") with twenty guns, which shelled the besieged Hara Castle. At the end of the siege, 37,000 Christian peasants were executed. For many Portuguese, the action of the Dutch was heinous, in supporting an attack on fellow Christians. However, for the shogunate, it was the Portuguese who were assumed to have clandestinely helped the rebels (Keith, 2006). In 1636, a man-made island had been built in Nagasaki harbour, called Dejima, to confine the Portuguese traders. In 1637, no Westerners were allowed to travel within Japan, primarily to stop the Portuguese, who might seek to portray themselves as Dutch. In 1639, children of European-Japanese parentage were expelled from the country, and, in the same year, as a result of the *sakoku* ("seclusion") edicts, the Portuguese were expelled from the country. Now any Portuguese ship arriving in Japan was, by law, to be burnt and the crew executed. In 1641, in the same year that the Dutch took Malacca from the Portuguese to dominate the East Indies, the Dutch factory was required to move to Dejima Island – where they were restricted – as the only Western traders in Japan for the next 200 years.

Embracing martyrdom

When Valignano died in Macau in 1606, the Jesuits celebrated his role in Japan in his panegyric, calling him "the Apostle of Japan" (Valignano and Braga, 1942, p. 530), yet his legacy was collapsing. By 1612, the last of the three Christian "kings" who had sponsored the Tensho Boys Embassy was dead, and his sons had all rejected Christianity. From 1614 onwards, Catholic priests were living on borrowed time. In 1620, the senior Jesuit and secretary of the Society in Japan, Christovao Ferreira wrote:

> As the persecution becomes increasingly violent, the Society and the Christian community are pressed harder than ever. We are particularly distressed by the reasons the shogun gives for the persecution, namely, the interests of state. He imagines that we intend to rob him of his kingdom by our preaching of the Gospel. He has had this kind of fear for some time and it is constantly being confirmed by the Dutch heretics.
>
> *(Cieslik, 1974, p. 7)*

After 150 of civil war, for the Tokugawa shogunate, social control and loyalty was paramount. The daimyo demonstrated their loyalty by the *Edo sanpo*, where they had to journey to the city of Edo[13] every year to pay homage to the shogun. When they were allowed to return to their own domains, family members remained in Edo as hostages. For the populace, loyalty to the shogun had to predominate. Having decided that the Christian faith represented a loyalty to a foreign religion associated with foreign powers – and not to the shogun – it had to be stamped out. In 1626, the *fumi-e* (the "stepping on picture") was introduced, a brass or woodblock image of Christ or the Virgin Mary that had to be trodden on to indicate a rejection of Christianity. Thousands of Christians – the vast majority – many of whom had converted at the behest of their lord, apostatized and adopted an acceptable Buddhist sect. Yet many devout Catholics were willing to die – and embrace martyrdom – rather than deny their religion. And hundreds did. But it was not the death of Christians that was sought by the shogunate, but their public rejection of it – apostasy. In consequence, various tortures were employed to encourage apostasy, including the offer of stopping the torture of others by one's own by apostasy. In 1633, the Jesuit Christovao Ferreira faced this dilemma and he apostatized (Cieslik, 1974). He was given a Japanese name, the wife and family of an executed man and, now as a Buddhist, was required to write criticisms of Christianity. He featured in the 1966 novel *Silence* by Shusaku Endo, a story that sought to offer a Christian justification for such an apostasy (Endo, 1969). The book was made into a Hollywood movie, directed by Martin Scorcese in 2016.

However, in 1633, Ferreira's apostasy was a great shock to a Church that embraced the martyr as a true witness of the faith, and who died for Christ in an imitation of his suffering. The martyr was honoured but the apostate had committed a great sin. By 1640, the Japanese trade with Portugal had ended, most Christians had renounced their faith, and during the next ten years, no more clandestine priests ventured into Japan. One hundred years after Xavier's arrival, Christianity had been publicly expunged from Japan. Yet, for the Jesuits in Europe, this was not the end of the story. The memory of each and every one of the European and Japanese martyrs in Japan was to be cherished (see Chapter 4). The Japanese martyrs were to be heralded, not just as similar to Europeans, but as exemplars of true Christians; whose lives, and particularly their deaths, set a model to which European Catholics could look for inspiration (Oba et al., 2022).

The saintly people and their cruel masters

In 1951, the historian Sir Charles Boxer published a book entitled *The Christian Century in Japan 1549–1650* (Boxer, 1951/1967). This concept of a "Christian Century" in Japan has been employed by later academics (e.g. Barker, 2009; Ward, 2006; Takao, 2018), although often with the caveat "so-called" or placed inside quotation marks (e.g. Screech, 2012). Indeed, Higashibaba (2001) notes that while Japanese secular historians have sometimes examined the "Christian Century" in terms of the political and economic context of Japan at the time of the Jesuit missionaries, he also acknowledges that

> [a] more influential historiographical perspective in studies of the Christian century is perhaps that which centers on individual or collective biographical histories. Mainly Jesuit church historians have promoted this approach by focusing on the "great figures" of the Jesuit mission to Japan, such as Francis Xavier and Alessandro Valignano.
>
> *(Higashibaba, 2001, p. xiii)*

Yet, in the examination of the Jesuit missionary activity discussed in this chapter, I argue that the Christian Century in Japan was neither Christian nor a century – but a construction of the Western mind.

First, estimates of the number of Christians in Japan in the 16th–17th centuries range from 1 to 2 percent of the population, so Japan was a 98 to 99 percent non-Christian country during this century. Also, many of these "Christians" were only converts at the behest of their lord, converting back to Buddhism when their lord did (Morris, 2018), suggesting a more realistic percentage figure similar to that of Buddhists in the population of the modern United States of America (according to the 2020 census), and historians do not label the current period as "the Buddhist Century in the United States". Second, 1650 is the end of an "arbitrary century" from the arrival of Xavier in Japan in 1549 (Spalding, 1952, p. 399). Ironically, it is also the date of the death of seventy-year-old Chuan Sawano (the apostate Christovao Ferreira). Yet any date from Hideyoshi's first edicts against Christianity in 1587 (barely thirty-eight years after Xavier's arrival) could be identified as the beginning of the end of Jesuit influence. Indeed, a "Christian Century" was not conceived of before Boxer. For example, Murdoch's 1903 three-volume history of Japan discusses the period under the title *The Century of Early Foreign Intercourse*. Hence Boxer's construction of the "Christian Century" creates a Western story of a period of Japanese history that overemphasizes its European Christian influence.

What is more, the European Christians of the early 17th century brought their rival beliefs and philosophies to Japan through which context they perceived the Japanese. As Endo (1969, p. 186), in *Silence*, has his Portuguese Jesuit priest muse:

> How often he had heard at Goa and Macao how the Protestant countries like England and Holland, and the Catholic countries like Spain and Portugal had come to Japan and, jealous of one another's progress, had spoken calumnies about one another to the Japanese.

The Europeans had sought to make sense of the similarities and differences between Japanese culture and that of their own, but in many instances, this revealed more about the purposes and preconceptions of the different European visitors than any fundamental aspects of the Japanese. However, the European experiences of the "Christian Century in Japan" set the foundation for their subsequent interpretations of the Japanese.

The image of the autocratic and cruel Tokugawa administration, putting their own devout people to death "simply" for their Christian beliefs pervaded subsequent Catholic thinking in 17th-century Europe (as will be shown in the following chapter). However, in banning Europeans from Japan (apart from the small Dutch factory on Dejima), Japan avoided the fate of the indigenous people in numerous parts of the Spanish and Portuguese empires involving subjugation and colonization, and the destruction of their local cultures. While Francis Xavier, and his fellow Jesuits, may have dreamt of Japan as a Christian empire of the East, this was only conceivable by ignoring the culture, religion and society of Japan, and the position of Japan within its geopolitical context. The Christian empire of the East was only ever an illusion created by the Western mind.

Notes

1 By this period of "warring states" (sengoku), the emperor now only had ceremonial power, with the dominant warlord (referred to as the shogun, or chief military leader) being the real power in the land.
2 The dominant warlord in the country. See the Appendix for more details.
3 The Western naming convention is used for Japanese names, as the book concerns Western representation. Sorin Otomo was also known as Yoshishige Ōtomo.
4 tratado em que contem muito susinta e abreviadamente algumas contradisões e diferencas de custumes antre a gente de Europa e esta provincia de Japaõ (treatise which contains very succinctly and briefly some contradictions and differences in customs between the people of Europe and this province of Japan).
5 The name Kyushu means nine provinces.
6 The Japanese "kings" were also referred to as "Don" in Spanish or "Dono" in Portuguese, in the Jesuit texts, meaning lord. This European appellation made them appear similar to the European nobility.
7 When a 2019 Japanese television miniseries was made of this embassy, it was entitled "MAGI Tensho Keno Shonen Shisetsu" (Magi: the Tensho Boys Embassy), which was shown worldwide on Amazon Prime Video.

8 Domenico Tintoretto – son of more famous Jacopo (Massarella, 2014).
9 Cooper (2005) gives an account of their later lives.
10 Screech (2012) points out that "William Adams" always referred to himself as William Addames.
11 Ieyasu Tokugawa was given the title of shogun in year 1603.
12 The United Provinces of the Netherlands had no king, but a Stadtholder (steward) who took on the role of head of state.
13 The city of the Takugawa shogun, which later changed its name to Tokyo.

4

THE CLOSED COUNTRY

Plays and propaganda: memories of Japan in the Jesuit stories

Despite their expulsion from Japan, and the end of their letters to Europe communicating their activities in the country, Japan remained a feature of the Jesuit story. As Schwemmer (2022, pp. 54–5) put it: "From the seventeenth to eighteenth centuries, a Jesuit order put on the defensive in Europe would begin to produce triumphal histories of its missionary activities, especially those in Japan, and from here the stories change even more dramatically". Now the Jesuit imagination could be given free rein in representing the Japanese to Europeans. The story of the Christian martyrs in Japan came to the fore in the Jesuit tales – especially through the medium of the performing arts – that circulated within Catholic Europe. The missionaries and their Christian converts were now presented as the saintly heroes of the Jesuit story of Japan.

The idea of the canonization of Francis Xavier was recommended soon after his death, and supported by King John III of Portugal in 1556 (Mormando, 2006). Furthermore, the experience of the Tensho Boys Embassy in Catholic Europe in 1585 had given a boost to the enthusiasm for Xavier's canonization at the time of European fascination with the Japanese Christian "kings" in the East. The devotion to Xavier increased during the latter half of the 16th century, and in 1614 his right arm was placed as a holy relic in the Jesuit mother church in Rome – although his body stayed in Goa (Fernandes, 2000). He was beatified in 1619 and canonized in 1622. In his canonization, numerous miracles were attributed to him, including the gift of tongues, restoring the sight to a blind man and raising the dead (famously shown in the altarpiece painting *The Miracles of St Francis Xavier* by Peter Paul Rubens, now in the Kunsthistorisches Museum, Vienna). Not surprisingly, Protestant critics argued against the existence of these miracles, distinguishing the miracles in the Bible from those of Catholic saints, such as Xavier, which according to the Anglican Bishop of Salisbury

DOI: 10.4324/9781003082088-4

in 1752 were "forgeries of an age posterior to that they lay claim to" (Milner, 1822, p. 322). The claim of Xavier speaking in tongues has been the subject to most criticism. Indeed, Xavier himself wrote about the difficulty of learning Japanese, and modern authors have acknowledged this: for example, Sindemann (2001, p. 123) pointed out that: "Xavier had to make use of a translator during his entire stay in Japan".

Yet in Catholic Europe, it was not just the saintly Xavier who demonstrated the supernatural power of God but also the actions of the martyrs in Japan. The twenty-six martyrs executed on 5 Feb 1597 were beatified by Urban VIII in 1627 (and later canonized in 1862 by Pope Pius IX). Indeed, over 400 martyrs, executed between 1598 and 1639 in Japan, have been canonized by the Catholic Church (the most recent being 188 canonized by Pope Benedict XVI in 2008). The Church has viewed martyrs as witnesses[1] to the truth of the Christian God. Thus, the submission to martyrdom, as evidence of faith, is to be celebrated. As Tertullian wrote, around 197 CE, when the Church was being persecuted in the Roman Empire, "the blood of the martyrs is the seed of the Church".[2] Hence, despite the expulsion of Jesuits from Japan, the stories of the martyrs provided enduring lessons for all time. Thus, the failure of the mission in Japan could be re-presented as a triumph through the stories of the martyrs that echoed those of the early Roman church (Döpfert, 2022). These stories were retold through the "Japan plays" performed in the Jesuit institutions (Takao, 2018), and took "on a life of their own that served the imaginative needs of contemporary Europeans" (Schwemmer, 2022, p. 36).

The Jesuits had appreciated the power of the performing arts from the Society's inception, and plays often featured in their seminaries. Consequently, edifying stories based in Japan became part of the repertoire, featuring saintly characters such as Francis Xavier and his exploits, and inspirational accounts of martyrdom. These plays, combined with the teaching of doctrine, provided a complete world view for the faithful (Schwemmer, 2022). They also offered a vehicle for communicating and evoking spiritual emotionality within the Jesuit teachings (Haskell and Garrod, 2019). Hence, the Japanese converts could be celebrated through these plays: "In them, Europeans went on reimagining the Japan mission according to their own needs" (Schwemmer, 2022, p. 55). Crucially, the Christian "kings" and the Japanese martyrs were presented as idealized Christian heroes in the plays, with a Catholic Christian Japan contrasted with a Europe ravaged by Protestantism. The steadfastness of their faith in the face of death was viewed as bringing about the salvation of the Japanese martyrs (Döpfert, 2022). Different plays were acted out in Jesuit schools throughout Catholic Europe, featuring characters such as Francis, King of Bungo, Protasius, King of Arima, and Bartholomew, Prince of Omura, and even referencing Prester John (Miranda, 2022).

As well as these plays, Jesuit historians wrote about the Japanese experience in their accounts of Church history, such as Cornelius Hazart's *A Church History of the Entire World*,[3] published in four volumes between 1667 and 1671 (which includes a 184-page section on Japan), François Solier's two volume *Ecclesiastical History of the Islands and Kingdom of Japan*[4] (1627–1629) and Jean Crasset's two-volume *A History of the Church in Japan*[5] in 1689 which developed Solier's work. While these are detailed histories, providing much of Western knowledge of the events of the time, they also, not surprisingly, foregrounded the Christian experience interpreted in Jesuit terms; focusing on the actions, fortitude and faith of the Japanese martyrs, to demonstrate the power of faith in the Catholic Christian God in a world full of barbarity and evil. This was graphically shown in Nicholas Trigault's *The Christian Triumphs of the Martyrs of Japan*,[6] 1625, with numerous illustrations of martyrdom in Japan.

The Jesuits were well aware of the power of visual imagery, and the engravings of Hazart's *Church History* and Trigault's *Martyrs of Japan* demonstrated the story that they wished to tell about the Japanese. The section on Japan in Hazart's *Church History* (Hazart, 1667) is interleaved with illustrative prints of the people and events annotated by captions. The images first tell the story of the Christian kings. A picture of the saintly Francis Xavier begins the section. Later is an image of Xavier welcomed by the "King of Bungo" and his retainers (p. 23[7]). Next, "Bartholomew of Omura", the "first Christian amongst the kings of Japan" is shown destroying a Buddhist temple (pp. 34–5), followed by "Francis, King of Bungo" about to set sail (on his retirement) to be "alone with God, beyond all worldly concerns" (pp. 42–3). The Tensho Boys Embassy is illustrated with three (sic) boys about to set sail with their Jesuit companions: "Three young Japanese Princes, envoys of three Japanese kings . . . depart for Rome to recognize the Pope as God's representative on earth" (pp. 62–3). Next, they are seen kneeing before Phillip II, who honourably receives the Japanese "princes". Finally, they kneel before the Pope and the Cardinals in Rome, who also receive them "with great honour" (pp. 64–5). The second part of the illustrated story is that of fortitude by the martyrs. Hazart provided an equal number of graphic illustrations of martyrdom as he did for the story of the Christian kings but, of course, Trigualt's work focused exclusively on images of torture, crucifixion, burning at the stake, drowning in the sea, and being hung upside down over fetid pits. The stoic and at times beatific-looking Japanese Christians – and most of the martyrs were Japanese – endure all heroically. Importantly, the Christian kings and the Japanese martyrs were represented in these engravings as European-like, with no Asian features (Schwemmer, 2022). Despite their difference in clothing, the Japanese were represented as not just "like us" but "as we should be", who (in contrast to those Europeans who had abandoned the Catholic Church for Protestantism) remained a model of true Christian faithfulness. As Verberckmoes (2020, p. 3/20) argued: "This visual and narrative representation stirred affections, and the reworking of these emotions optimized the connection between the European propaganda of Christian martyrs and the agency of the Japanese Christians".

Images of luxury: Japanese products in an Oriental fantasy

By the mid-17th century, the only Europeans with contemporary access to Japan were the Dutch. With the expulsion of the Portuguese (and all other Europeans) from Japan, they now had a monopoly on the European trade with Japan through the VOC factory isolated on the tiny island of Dejima in Nagasaki harbour. The VOC had established their eastern base in Batavia (Jakarta, Indonesia) and, using their military power, had ousted the Portuguese from Ceylon (Sri Lanka) and Malacca and established bases in numerous locations, including Mauritius, South Africa, Tonkin (Vietnam) and Taiwan (called Fort Zeelandia). While gaining trading agreements with China was often difficult for them, they overcame this by dealing with Chinese intermediaries. The VOC had now become the dominant European military power in the East Indies but, unlike the earlier Portuguese aim of conquest and Christianization, its goal was commerce. The Dutch mercantile mentality meant that they were willing to do what was necessary to keep a profitable trading relationship (Clulow, 2014). Furthermore, the Dutch Republic was very different to Catholic Portugal. It was religiously tolerant and bourgeois, with its wealth spreading across society. Indeed, the English writer John Evelyn commented that even the rooms of Dutch farmhouses were covered with works of art (Lindemann, 2008). As a result, desirable goods from all over the East Indies, including Japan, flooded into Amsterdam, which became the rich heart of the largest trading empire of its day, creating the Dutch Golden Age in 17th-century Europe.

During this Golden Age, the wealthy Dutch burgers could afford luxuries, such as silks and porcelain from China, silver from Japan and the silverware made from it, and Imai-ware from Arita, Japan when "china" from China was hard to obtain, tea (to be drunk using the fine chinaware), lacquered tableware and cabinets, and other luxury items, such as spices, fabrics, carpets and craft products from the Near East to India and as far as Japan. Indeed, all the luxuries that Asia could provide found their way to Amsterdam, making the Dutch Republic rich. European interest in Japan no longer involved the Japanese potential for Christian conversion, but a delight in their luxury products by the European wealthy classes, who wanted to show them off by commissioning paintings of themselves surrounded by these items. It is estimated that during this period, five million paintings were produced by Dutch artists (Lindemann, 2008). Dutch paintings typically showed scenes of bourgeois life in the Netherlands, where merchants and their families displayed the products of their wealth. Indeed, these pictures illustrate the mercantile success of the VOC and the richness of the imported Asian products (Corrigan et al., 2015). The pictures also created a fantasy Orient, with Dutch merchants dressing as imaginary Eastern princes, with paintings such as Rembrandt van Rijn's *Man in a Turban* 1632 and *Man in Oriental Costume* 1635, portraying wealthy men showing off their rich silk gowns. These Oriental costumes were also incorporated into Dutch Biblical paintings, such as Rembrandt's *Adoration of the Magi*, c1633, and that of his pupil Salomon Koninck, *Adoration of the Magi*, c1645, where the Magi wear the same sort of rich Oriental silk gowns as those favoured by the Dutch merchant sitters.

Now a stylish Dutch merchant or an English gentleman would pass his leisure wearing an "Indian" turban and silk gown, although neither may have come from India. The European dressing gown emerged from the Japanese kimono although the real item was very costly. In the annual exchange of gifts between the Tokugawa shogun and the Dutch factory in Japan, the gift of kimonos was viewed as highly prized, with the Dutch receiving around twenty per year for the next 150 years, with some Dutch traders commissioning them themselves (Screech, 2002). As their popularity increased, they were often made from Indian fabrics for the European market, and referred to in the Netherlands as a *Japonse rok* (a Japanese skirt or robe) and in England as a *banyan* (a name from India for a loose-fitting garment or robe). Wealthy men wore their banyans to be depicted in paint. For example, around 1673, the Dutch painter Frans van Mieris the Elder painted (what is now known as) *Portrait of a Merchant in a Banyan, Holding a Business Document*: an image of a Dutch merchant, wearing a rich golden kimono, leaning leisurely on a banister holding an account letter. In Michiel van Musscher's 1671 portrait of Barend van Lin (with his brother and future brother-in-law), the main sitter is displayed wearing his luxurious silk gown, learning on a table covered by a Persian carpet. Nearly thirty years later, Musscher's painting of Admiral François Lefort, 1698, has the sitter's luxurious silk gown dominating the image. The passion for "Indian" garments captured the English too. The diarist Samuel Pepys wrote on Monday, 1 July 1661:

> This morning I went up and down into the city, to buy several things, as I have lately done, for my house. Among other things, a fair chest of drawers for my own chamber, and an Indian gown for myself. The first cost me 33s., the other 34s.
>
> *(Pepys, 1906, p. 175)*

In fact, we can see Pepys wearing a banyan in a portrait of him by John Hayls in 1666. His wife was also a beneficiary of Oriental wear. On Saturday, 12 December 1663, Pepys wrote "one Abrahall [*a business contact*] . . . has sent my wife a Japan gowne, which pleases her very well and me also" (Pepys, 1906, p. 438).

The great interest in Japanese and other Asian products, in the Netherlands and England, also offered the prospect of huge profits for successful merchants, compared to the high taxes and lower productivity in European markets (Markley, 2003). During the 17th century, as the English were developing their colonies in North America, the EIC trading in India was unable to challenge the Dutch dominance in the East Indies. Indeed, Markley argued that the Far East represented "exotic realms" beyond the reach of the EIC, and the English envy of the Dutch VOC can be seen in Book 2 of Milton's *Paradise Lost,* 1667, which compares Satan's flight from Hell to a Dutch merchant fleet: "The VOC imaged as 'the flying Fiend' traces a course of both conspicuous consumption identified with Dutch economic power and of frustrated English desires for a share of that trade" (Markley, 2003, p. 502).

The skilled artists and artisans of Japan

The desire for the luxury products of the East often outstripped the supply, particularly of goods from Japan, limited by the Japanese supply and their long journey to Europe. Consequently, European manufacturers sought to replicate Oriental goods.

Whereas a banyan as a fashion item did not have to be made of Chinese silk, or be a genuine Japanese kimono, which only the very wealthy could afford, it was more difficult to copy other items, particularly Chinese porcelain and Japanese lacquerware. It was simply that the European craft workers could not replicate the techniques. Indeed, the Dutch Golden Age would be over before the Meissen factory in Germany could produce good quality European porcelain in the 18th century. And Japanese lacquers were made from resins unavailable in Europe, even assuming that the Europeans could work out how to create and apply them. Hence, there was an awareness in Europe that the artisans of the East had skills unknown to them. Unlike in the previous century when the Portuguese could visit Japanese workshops, in the late 17th century, Japanese craft skills were a mystery. In the case of lacquerware, European furniture makers would seek to preserve genuine Japanese lacquerware panels and incorporate them into new cabinetwork. Then they tried to imitate the process in the manufacture of new panels. They achieved a degree of similarity with the use of varnish in a technique that was termed "japanning" for obvious reasons. During the 17th and 18th centuries, japanning became a popular technique that was gradually refined over time, and applied to wood (and metal) products to supply the demand for Japanese lacquerware. However, the longer that Japan was inaccessible to Europeans, the more the skills of their artisans were admired as their work could be imitated but not replicated. In 1688, John Stalker and George Parker published *A Treatise on Japaning and Varnishing Being a Compleat Discovery of Those Arts,* which included pattern illustrations. However, Parker was very clear on the superiority of Japanese arts:

> Let not the Europeans any longer flatter themselves with the empty notions of having surpassed all the world beside in stately Palaces, costly Temples, and sumptuous Fabricks. . . . The glory of one country, Japan alone, has exceeded in beauty and magnificence all the pride of the Vatican at this time, and the Pantheon theretofore
>
> *(Huissen, 1973, p. 58)*

Accounts of Japan in 17th-century Europe

During the 17th century, there was increasing fascination with exploration in Britain and the Netherlands, particularly concerning the Orient, and North America. In England, Richard Hakluyt (c. 1552–1616) was an enthusiastic collector of travel documents, and his work was continued by Samuel Purchas (c. 1577–1626), an Anglican clergyman, after his death. His 1625 work, *Hakluytus Posthumus or Purchas His Pilgrimes, Contayning a History of the World in Sea Voyages and Lande Travells by Englishmen and Others*, included compilations from Portuguese and Dutch sources as well as publishing material from William Adams and Richard Cocks. It also included a map of Japan that over-exaggerated the size of Kyushu relative to Honshu and Shikoku, possibly because it was most prominent in the Jesuit sources. Purchas's work promoted the idea of English expansion (colonization) and commerce across the world, especially in North America, and defended the EIC in its rivalry with the VOC (Pennington, 1966).

A popular work of the mid-17th century was Peter Heylyn's *Cosmographie* of 1652, a history and chorography of the world. However, much of the work was drawn from other sources, such as Hakluyt and Purchas (Markley, 2003). The problem for authors seeking to write about Japan in the middle of the 17th century was that there was little new information available, except the commercial and accounting information from the VOC in Dejima. However, Markley (2003) argues that works such as Heylyn's *Cosmographie* provided some complexity to the European views of Asia at the time, which did not claim a simplistic view of European superiority. This can be seen in Heylyn's positive account of the Japanese.

> The people are for the most part of good understanding, apt to learn, and of able memories; cunning and subtil in their dealings. Of body vigorous and strong. . . . Patient they are of pain, ambitious of glory, uncapable of suffering wrong. . . . They reproach no man for his poverty.
>
> *(Heylyn, 1677, III, p. 219)*

He noted their olive-colour complexions, and claimed that their customs were opposite ("antipodes") to "ours". However, his account of the geography and history of Japan is a patchwork of other sources with additional errors added.

One way to satisfy the desire for information about Japan was to publish material from before the expulsion of the Europeans. A Frenchman, François Caron had arrived in Hirado in 1619 and worked for the VOC, learning to speak Japanese, and rising to Opperhoofd in 1639, remaining in post until 1641. However, in 1636, he had been asked to produce a report on Japan for the VOC director general, comprising answers to thirty-one questions. This report was now published in Dutch in 1649, and in 1663 in English in the work: *A true description of the mighty kingdoms of Japan & Siam*, translated by Roger Manley. Caron's account is a compendium of Japan, its provinces, the daimyo and details of the government and organization of the society – very much an informational document for the VOC hierarchy. Indeed, much of it presented material to inform the VOC about the benefits of Japanese trade. However, it does include some information about the people and society that he deemed noteworthy, that contrast with European practice, such as crime and punishment. Like Richard Cocks, the English factor, he noted the uniqueness and severity of their justice.

> When a Gentleman, or Souldier, is condemned to die, he is allowed the honour to kill himself, by cutting up his belly with his own hands; whereas the Citizen, Marchant, and meaner persons, suffer by the common Executioner. . . . Lyes are likewise punished with death.
>
> *(Caron, 1663, p. 53)*

He then recounted in detail the various tortures used to get the Christians to apostatize, concluding:

> The greatness of this torment surpasseth all other, being beyond all humaine strength to suffer and be undergone, but by such who are extraordinarilie strengthened from above. This extremitie hath indeed (by reason of its continuance) forced many to renounce their religion.
>
> *(Caron, 1663, p. 69).*

Yet at other places, he noted the hospitality of the Japanese, and their careful and tender child-rearing. However, for curious readers in Europe, as an account of Japan, it left much to be desired by its brevity.

A more substantial account of Japan was published in Dutch in 1669 and in English in 1670. This was the *Atlas Japannensis* by Arnoldus Montanus, a Dutch Protestant cleric; a voluminous account which provided the reader with everything they could wish to know about Japan, the people and their history and geography. Indeed, the book contains the earliest illustration of the VOC factory on the island of Dejima. Montanus had access to the VOC reports of visits to Edo in 1641 and 1661 which formed the basis of the work (van Eeghen, 1972). However, despite being the most comprehensive and best-illustrated account of Japan of its day, Montanus included much material from other (Jesuit) sources, which he rewrote with the addition of his own inaccurate speculations adding to the exoticism of the Japanese (Hesselink, 2002). Unlike the Jesuit accounts of Japan which sought to justify their actions and demonstrate the piety of the Christian Japanese, Montanus provided a sensationalist account, representing the Japanese as exotic to Europeans. The English translator John Ogilby introduced it as: "these strange and novel revelations concerning both the ancient and present estate of the so populous and wealthy Empire of Japan, being a book of wonders" (Montanus, 1670, p. xiii). And, indeed, Montanus used the word "strange" dozens of times[8] throughout the book. He was also anti-Jesuit.

> The Jesuits having laid a Plot to deliver up the whole Empire of Japan to the King of Portugal. . . . But this being discover'd, The Portuguese were presently banish'd and excluded for ever from Japan in the Year 1641, the Jesuits and principal Confederates being all put to death.
>
> *(Montanus, 1670, p. 35)*

Also, his descriptions of the Japanese are a mixture of other sources and misunderstanding. "They are tall with a strong constitution . . . they are a strong people trained to withstand hardship" (p. 67). "They much delight in war" (p. 65) "The customs of the Japanners are opposite to Europeans" (p. 65). The bonzes "under which appearance of sanctity, they commit all the Outrages of

Lust, Avarice and Revenge" (p. 67). However, he also presented a positive view of the Japanese:

> They are generally good natur'd, of a kind and affable Disposition, of quick Apprehension, having ready Memories, and . . . appear rather like Gentlemen in their courteous and civil behaviour. . . . They keep their Houses always clean and neat. . . . They are covetous of good Fame, and fair Reputation.
>
> *(p. 67)*

When suffering, "they bear it with a settled and unchang'd Countenance" (p. 68). Yet he then mentions their cruelty, adding: "Their women are as strangely merciless to their own issues, murdering without any Motherly compassion their tender Infants" (p. 70).

Montanus filled the information gap with his own made-up material, such as fabricating a speech for the apostate Christavao Ferreira to criticize the Jesuits (Hesselink, 2002). He also erroneously claimed that the Japanese word for "self-murder" (presumably hara-kiri or seppuku) meant "happy dispatch" (p. 210). While not giving his sources, it is clear that he drew on the work of Hazart, who he claimed was wrong about the geography of Japan. Hazart, who always listed his sources, came back at Montanus, dismissing him as a fool (Hesselink, 2002, Verberckmoes, 2020). However, Hazart's criticisms of Montanus, and of the Dutch "concealing their religion for the benefit of trade" (van Eeghen, 1972, p. 256), illustrated the debate between the Protestant and Catholic European writers about the representation of the Japanese in late 17th-century Europe: either as heroic Christians suffering under cruel leaders or as responding to the Portuguese Catholics fomenting revolt, causing their own expulsion from Japan. However, despite Montanus's work containing numerous errors, and Engelbert Kaempfer, a later doctor on Dejima – see further – regarding it as not very good (Van Eeghen, 1972), it was translated into other European languages to meet the demand for information about Japan.

Fantasy Japan in 18th-century European fiction

While Montanus had adapted his sources to fit his own speculations about Japan, his work was based on accounts of people who had visited the country. However, as the 18th century began, no Europeans, bar the small group of VOC employees, had visited Japan for over sixty years. Furthermore, war and financial crisis were bringing an end to the Dutch Golden Age (Prak, 2005). When the Dutch William, Prince of Orange, accepted the throne of England in 1689, alongside his wife Mary, it brought peace between the two countries, but it had the ironic effect of promoting British interests at the expense of the Dutch, with the 18th century seeing the rise of British naval power and its increasing interest in the East (especially in India), and North America where its rivalry was primarily with France. In 1715, the Dutch Ambassador to England wrote that the Dutch Republic was "in a bad state and other countries know this all too well" (Prak, 2005, p. 263). Yet in a Japan debarred to Europeans, the Dutch remained the sole source of information about the country.

There was a fascination in Europe, and in England in particular, with the Far East (Conant, 1908), and there was not enough information to satisfy it. It was in this context that the hoaxer George Psalmanazar published his book, *An Historical and Geographical Description of Formosa: An Island Subject to the Emperor of Japan*, in London in 1704. Claiming to be a Formosan (Taiwanese) but probably French, it was a sensationalist made-up account of child sacrifice, cannibalism and polygamy to both scandalize and excite his readers (Shufelt, 2005). However, as well as its description of "Formosa" and its people, Psalmanazar attacked the Catholic Church, in particular the Jesuits in Japan, in his portrayal of them in the book. Eventually, the hoax was uncovered, yet with little public opprobrium towards Psalmanazar, who lived on in London into his eighties. But the work was read by Jonathan Swift, who, among others, saw the potential for the use of a fictional Far East as the location for a satirical reflection on the state of his own country (Shufelt, 2005).

Swift's *Gulliver's Travels*, 1726, has Lemuel Gulliver discovering a number of fantasy countries in the Far East, such as Laputa, Balnibarbi, Glubbdubdrib and Lugnagg, after which he ends up in Japan. Indeed, including the latter in a list of strange and exotic places has left academics such as Cullen (2013) wondering why he included Japan at all in the book, and suggesting that it may have simply been to fix the imaginary places in a known location, and mock the Dutch. As Markley (2004) noted, the story includes the claim of the Dutch willingness to perform the fumi-e (the treading on a Christian image) to show what they would do to keep the Japanese trade. In the brief section of the book concerning Japan, the Japanese are presented more positively than the Dutch, but Japan is presented as just as much of a fantasy land as the other countries Gulliver visits.

Indeed, in a later unfinished satire, entitled *An Account of the Court and Empire of Japan*, 1728, Swift used Japan as a fantasy representation of Great Britain, where the Emperor of Japan, Regoge, is an obvious anagram of King George (and Nena of Queen Anne). This technique of using Japan to write a satirical criticism of Britain or Europe was employed by Van Loon (a pseudonym) in *A Fragment of Japanese History*, 1749, and by Tobias Smollett in the *History and Adventures of an Atom*, 1769. In the latter, events from a thousand years ago in Japan are described by an atom who witnessed them. However, it is actually a satirical criticism of the political system in Britain during the Seven Years' War (1756–1763) and William Pitt (the Elder) the prime minister (who appears in the book under the pseudonym of Taycho). Thus, as knowledge of contemporary Japan was scant, it gradually became a mysterious place, an exotic land in which to locate satirical accounts of contemporary European society (Shimada, 2008).

Kaempfer's Japan: a window into the closed country

In 1690, the German doctor Engelbert Kaempfer (1651–1716) arrived in Japan, as the VOC physician on Dejima, and remained for two years. With few medical duties to undertake, Kaempfer, a keen naturalist, began work on documenting everything he could about Japan, from its history to its flora and fauna. He was fortunate in being able to take part twice in the trip to pay homage to the shogun in Edo (Tokyo), which gave him a greater experience of Japan than just the island of Dejima. Kaempfer's work remained unpublished at his death, after which it was acquired by Sir Hans Sloane, a wealthy British doctor and naturalist and inveterate collector (whose collection, on his death in 1753, formed the basis of the British Museum). Sloane had Kaempfer's manuscripts translated into English by Johann Caspar Scheuchzer, a Swiss doctor who worked as Sloane's librarian. The first English edition was published in 1727. Subsequently, Dutch, French and German translations were made from the English edition (Bodart-Bailey and Massarella, 1995).

Kaempfer's three-volume *History of Japan*, with his own illustrations, comprises a detailed diary of his experiences in Japan, combined with encyclopaedic entries of everything he encounters, from the fish and the temples, to the minerals and the customs. It is clear he has interrogated different Japanese sources; for example, he notes a difference concerning the length of the reign of an ancient emperor when setting down a list of them all. He had read Caron and Montanus, the former who he corrected for claiming that prostitution is only carried out in bawdy houses (which he suggests occurred "out of respect to his lady, who was a Japan woman"), rather than, in Kaempfer's view, in every public inn. He also included detailed accounts of his two trips to Edo. In the first volume, he addressed the Dutch assistance to the Japanese in the Shimabara revolt (when a Dutch ship bombarded Hara Castle for the shogun), and their "submissive readiness to assist the Emperor in the execution of his designs, with regard to the final destruction of Christianity in his dominions". It is clear that he found this submissiveness disquieting, a submissiveness that had accepted so many restrictions in the cause of trade. He wrote: "So great was the covetousness of the Dutch, and so great the alluring power of Japanese gold, that . . . they willingly underwent an almost perpetual imprisonment". His criticism can be easily determined when he continues that the Dutch "patiently and submissively bear the abusive and injurious behaviour of these proud infidels towards us, than which nothing can be offer'd more shocking to a generous and noble mind" (Kaempfer, 1906, II, p. 174). He clearly found the restrictions hard and disliked the numerous Japanese officials seeking to fleece the Dutch at every turn. He even noted that young Dutch sailors have to pay an extortionate price for prostitutes despite them "being none of the best and handsomest" (II, p. 185). He concluded that this Dutch "humble complaisant and obliging conduct" has not made them liked or trusted by the Japanese (II, p. 173).

The journeys to Edo provided Kaempfer with much information about the towns and cities, which are all described in exceptional detail, but he chafed at the restrictions, and the attitude of the Japanese officials, commenting ironically on the "good manners" of the Chief Interpreter "who cried out to the Isje pilgrims, not to pollute themselves, and their holy undertaking, by approaching too near to our unclean persons" (Kaempfer, 1906, III, p. 161) While he is fascinated by the city of Edo, he found the Dutch audience with the shogun demeaning. One passage was considered shocking when the book was read in Europe (Clulow, 2014). Kaempfer described the approach of the Opperhoofd to the shogun in his audience chamber.

> Our Resident [*was conducted*] into the Emperor's presence, leaving us behind. As soon as he came thither, they cry'd out aloud Hollanda Captain, which was the signal for him to draw near, and make his obeisances. Accordingly he crawl'd on his hands and knees, to a place shew'd him, between the presents rang'd in due order on one side, and the place, where the Emperor sat, on the other, and then kneeling, he bow'd his forehead quite down to the ground, and so crawl'd backwards like a crab, without uttering one single word. So mean and short a thing is the audience we have of this mighty Monarch.
>
> *(Kaempfer, 1906, III, pp. 87–8)*

On a second audience, he commented, "We were ask'd a thousand ridiculous and impertinent questions" (III, p. 92). The Dutch visitors were commanded, in Kaempfer's words, to perform "apish tricks" (III, p. 94), such as singing and dancing, jumping, taking off and putting on their cloaks, giving their ages and writing their names on paper and speaking broken Japanese. Indeed, it was these comments, rather than his encyclopaedic account of Japan, that was most noteworthy to his European readers.

Throughout the book, Kaempfer refers to aspects of the Japanese character. In a long discussion about the origin of the Japanese, he rejects their descent from the Chinese, claiming that their character is Tartarian (from Tartary – north of China) rather different to the "effeminate Chinese" (III, p. 312). The book's translator is even more specific in distinguishing the "warlike humour and activity of the Japanese" from the "effeminate slothfulness of the Chinese" (I, p. lv). Kaempfer also noted that the Japanese are "so little apprehensive of death" (III, p. 137), and cites a number of instances of people cutting open their bellies to avoid punishment or shame. He attributed this to a "boldness or heroism" that leads to a "contempt of their life" (III, p. 307). Indeed, he argued that they are "very industrious, and enured to hardships" (III, p. 312), "great lovers of civility and good manners" (III, p. 312), "Keeping themselves, their cloaths and houses, clean and neat" (III, p. 312). He also noted that they are "dextrous and ingenious" in craftwork (III, p. 315) and, like most Western authors, noted their "daily use of bathing" (III, p. 319).

Importantly, it was Kaempfer who established the view that Japan was a closed country. In Appendix 6 of his *History of Japan*, he asked whether it was a good idea for Japan "to keep it shut up, as it now is, and not to suffer its inhabitants to have any Commerce with foreign nations" (III, p. 301). He argued strongly that it went against the laws of nature, the will of God, and kept the inhabitants "prisoners within the bounds of their own Country" (III, p. 302). However, he did note that "their Country was never in a happier condition than it now is, governed by an arbitrary Monarch, shut up, and kept from all Commerce and Communication with foreign nations" (III, p. 336). When Shizuki Tadao, a Nagasaki interpreter, translated part of Kaempfer's work in 1801, he coined the term *sakoku* ("locked country") for Kaempfer's reference to a shut-up or closed country, which became the dominant term for this period in Japanese history. Yet, as Kazui (1982) argued, Japan was in a much more significant commercial relationship with Chinese traders than the Dutch at that time, and also trading with Korea and the Ryukyu Islands. While from a Western perspective, Japan was "closed", it was actually in a trading relationship with all its close neighbours. Furthermore, Kaempfer ignored the argument that the restrictions had been a response to a perceived threat of European aggression, not to deny commerce.

One hundred and fifty more years of seclusion

While Kaempfer's book had been published in 1727, his account of the Japanese referred to his sojourn in Japan thirty-five years earlier, from 1690 to 1692. Yet it remained the definitive text on Japan for the next 150 years. Apart from the mercantile records of the VOC (e.g. Blussé et al., 2021), only a handful of Dejima officials, like Kaempfer, decided to document their experiences in the country. In 1775, the Swedish doctor Carl Peter Thunberg arrived in Dejima and stayed for more than a year. He had trained in medicine and botany in his native Sweden under the famous Enlightenment thinker, Carl Linnaeus, the inventor of modern taxonomy. Following the approach of his tutor, Thunberg set out to classify and categorize the flora of Japan. The result of this work was the *Flora Japonica*, 1784. However, he also published an account of his travels, including his time in Japan (Screech, 2005), in which he described aspects of Japanese history and society, including a record of the shoguns since Kaempfer's time. He claimed that the Portuguese success in trade and evangelism resulted in "avarice and haughtiness [*which*] proved their ruin" (Screech, 2005, p. 184). This explained why Christianity was banned and the Portuguese expelled from Japan. Thunberg also saw the strict rules in Japan, and obedience to them – along with the severe punishment for a crime – as one of the key features that distinguished the Japanese from Europeans (Kijewski, 2014).

> Most crimes are punished with death, a sentence which is inflicted with less regard to the magnitude of the crime than to the audacity of the attempt to transgress the hallowed laws of the empire and to violate justice, which together with religion they consider as the most sacred things in the whole land
>
> *(Screech, 2005, p. 196)*

However, Thunberg also made many Japanese friends and pointed out the Japanese fascination with, and desire to study, Western learning (Kijewski, 2014).

The Opperhoofd Isaac Titsingh served three tours of duty in Japan between 1779 and 1784, and his *Illustrations of Japan* was published posthumously in 1820 in French, and in English in 1822. He followed in the tradition of Frois and Kaempfer in describing, from his observations, the differences between Japan and Europe: the division of the year, weights and measures, the lives of the different shogun up to his day, the festivals and the ceremonies, and also included an illustration of the Dutch factory on Dejima. He noted that most books about Japan discuss "legal suicide", that is, "of being their own executioners by ripping up the belly", and he is no exception. He says that the practice, to avoid the disgrace of having committed a crime, "is so common, that scarcely any notice is taken of such an event". Indeed, he concluded: "This disregard of death, which they prefer to the slightest disgrace, extends to the very lowest classes among the Japanese" (Titsingh, 1822, pp. 147–8).

The VOC was disbanded in 1799, and its operation taken over by the Dutch government, which succumbed to the French dominance in Europe under Napoleon: in 1806, the Kingdom of Holland was established with Napoleon's brother Louis as its king. The upheaval in Europe restricted the ships going to Dejima. Also, the British were becoming more powerful in the East Indies, taking over Dutch territories: the Cape Colony in 1795, Ceylon in 1815 and Malacca in 1825. With the end of the Kingdom of Holland in 1813, and the defeat of Napoleon in 1815, the sailing of Dutch ships to Dejima was restored. Hendrik Doeff had arrived on Dejima in Japan in 1799, becoming the Opperhoofd from 1803 to 1817. His *Recollections of Japan* was published in Dutch in 1833 (with only portions published in English translation). The complete work was finally published in English, translated by Amick M. Doeff, in 2003. Doeff viewed Kaempfer's work as the best account of Japan, and much of his own book told of his difficulties in Dejima at a time of upheaval in Europe. During French-controlled Holland, Dutch ships were prey to the British Royal Navy. In consequence, American and some Danish ships were hired to supply Dejima, evidence that Western ships of many flags in the early 19th century had access to Japan. Both the Russians and the British sought to establish trade with Japan, hoping for commercial benefits but also on the basis of the "natural law" espoused by Kaempfer, which argued that civilized countries should engage in trade. However, Doeff helped to maintain the Dutch monopoly in Japanese trade (with Europe) even when there was no independent Dutch nation. In 1808, the British warship, *Phaeton*, under a young Captain Pellow, seeking to capture a Dutch trading vessel sailed into Nagasaki harbour under a false Dutch flag. Doeff recounts the story in detail, and the failed attempts of the Japanese to prevent the British vessel from leaving, due to a failure to man the guard posts. Doeff records that the governor of Nagasaki was "so sure of the fate that awaited him that he sacrificed himself for his family and cut open his belly" (Doeff, 2003, p. 103).

Doeff served longer in Japan than any other person in the history of the Dejima factory. He learnt Japanese, made Japanese friends (despite the restrictions), and fathered two children who had to remain in Japan when he left. He summed up the Japanese in his book: "Generally speaking these people are courageous and not afraid of any danger in all the world" (Doeff, 2003, p. 16). For eighteen years, Doeff's life combined the long years of humdrum life on Dejima when no ships arrived, with the excitement of his three trips to Edo (Tokyo). This strange life was described in David Mitchell's 2010 bestselling novel *The Thousand Autumns of Jacob de Zoet*, based on Dejima at the start of the 19th century, and inspired by Doeff's experience. Mitchell, with his in-depth knowledge of Japanese culture, wove a complex story of the relationship between the Japanese and the Dutch factors (Larsonneur, 2015) – a relationship that had evolved for nearly two centuries, and which was now on borrowed time.

The "opening" of Japan

The German doctor and botanist Philipp Franz von Siebold arrived on Dejima in 1823 keen to continue the work of Carl Peter Thunberg on classifying the natural world of Japan. He made an extensive collection of Japanese flora and fauna. Crucially, the restrictions on the residents of Dejima were becoming less onerous, and von Siebold was able to offer instruction in Western medicine to the Japanese in their thirst for Western learning. He had a Japanese family, with his daughter later becoming a physician trained in Western medicine. Unfortunately for von Siebold, his extensive collection of Japanese artefacts included maps of Japan were discovered by accident by the authorities, and led to his expulsion from Japan in 1829. His book *Manners and Customs of the Japanese* was published in English in 1841. Like the previous Dejima authors, von Siebold explained the different aspects of Japanese life and described his visit to Edo, although he repeats the error of Montanus by claiming that hara-kiri means "happy dispatch" (von Siebold, 1841, p. 177). However, like Doeff, his account discussed Western ships in Japanese waters – including retelling Doeff's story of the *Phaeton* – and the increasing attempts by Western nations to encourage Japan to open for trade, retelling of the failure of the Russians and the British to achieve that end.

In the 1840s, the American whaling industry was very lucrative, and ships had begun fishing in the rich but dangerous seas near Japan. However, due to the precarious nature of the activity, there were occasions when ships arrived in Japan seeking repairs or refuelling, or sailors were shipwrecked on the Japanese shore. These received mixed treatment as the Japanese simply did not want them there. In some cases, they were given supplies and sent on their way, but on other occasions, sailors were imprisoned – often for months – and accused of spying (Steele and Caiger, 1993). Stories of the inhumane treatment of American sailors reached the attention of the US government. The Americans, like the Russians and the British, saw the lucrative benefits of trade with Japan, and also held the Western view (as expressed by Kaempfer) that Japanese seclusion went against natural law. Western Enlightenment thinkers (like their Christian predecessors) had sought to set down the natural order of human relations, how a civilized society should operate, and how different nations should treat each other. International commerce was considered a feature of a civilized world which required the freedom of the seas – as outlined by the Dutch political theorist Hugo Grotius (1583–1645) in defending the Dutch attempts to break the Portuguese monopoly in the Japanese trade in the early 1600s (Borschberg, 2011). And the idea of natural law had contributed to the Constitution of the

United States (Kirk, 1993). To the United States, Japan, both in its seclusion and in its "uncivilized" treatment of American sailors arriving on its shores, was both violating natural law and acting in a morally unacceptable manner.

US President Millard Fillmore agreed to an expedition to Japan, under the command of Commodore Matthew Perry, who read various books on Japan, including Kaempfer and Von Siebold, in advance of the journey (Perry, 1859). The *Narrative of the Expedition*[9] stated that, for some:

> "Japan had no right thus to cut herself off from the community of nations; and that what she would not yield to national comity should be wrested from her by force". Also, it was argued that "the exclusive system of Japan . . . was caused by peculiar circumstances, long since passed, and was, in fact, in direct opposition to what history proved to be the natural temperament and disposition of the Japanese people."
>
> *(Wallach, 1952, p. 2)*

These "particular circumstances" were listed on the following page: "Portugal had given early and unpardonable offense in encouraging domestic treason" (p. 3). Twelve warships made up the squadron, including "iron-clads" (steam ships) and sail, the most powerful naval force in the Pacific. The Squadron arrived in Japan in July 1852, and, in a classic case of gunboat diplomacy, the Treaty of Kanagawa was signed in March 1854, protecting American ships and providing safe ports for them in Japan. The seclusion of Japan was ended. Subsequently, Japan signed diplomatic agreements with other Western nations. The American envoy Townsend Harris negotiated a trade agreement in 1858, and the European powers followed suit, opening the country to commerce with the West once again. When von Siebold returned to Japan in 1862, he found that it was in a process of rapid change. Five years later, the last Tokugawa shogun, Yoshinobu, abdicated and imperial rule was restored in 1868, under the young Emperor Meiji (Hillsborough, 2014).

The inhabitants of the secret empire

In the late 20th century, the American broadcaster, PBS America,[10] showed a three-part documentary series entitled *Memoirs of a Secret Empire*[11] (1993). This focused on the period of Japanese history from the beginning of the 17th century (and the expulsion of the Europeans) to the middle of the 19th century (and the opening of Japan). This Western image of the "closed kingdom" (from Kaempfer), with the idea that somehow Japan was a "secret" empire for more than 200 years, has permeated the Western mind. Sansom (1950) in his book *The Western World and Japan* referred to "the closing of the country" in his introduction to this period. Yet these descriptions (following from Kaempfer) ignore the fact that Japan was not "secret", and it was only "closed" to keep out the potentially destabilizing foreign powers whilst maintaining thriving trading relationships with its neighbours and, indeed, the Dutch. Ironically, Kaempfer's term was then translated into Japanese as sakoku (closed country) by the translator Shizuki Tadao, in 1801, who entitled his partial translation of Kaempfer's history *Sakoku ron* (discourse on the closed country) (Mervart, 2015). It then began to be employed by Japanese authors too in the later 19th century, adopting this Western interpretation.

The problem with this label of the "closed country" is outlined by Kazui (1982, p. 283):

> Literally interpreted, the ideograms making up the word [*sakoku*] simply mean "the closing of the country". From this we imagine a closed society having absolutely no contact with any other nation. And then, by extension, we find the . . . period itself being defined as "the period of isolation" or "the dark ages" or "the beginning of the Japanese tragedy".

As Kazui pointed out, this was far from the truth. Japan did not stop trading at this time: indeed, as Cullen (2013) pointed out, trade actually increased after the introduction of sakoku. The volume of trade carried out by the Chinese traders in Nagasaki was always greater than that of the Dutch, who themselves brought in valuable materials from Europe and the East Indies, and this continued during sakoku, as did Japanese relations with Korea and the Ryukyu Islands to the south (the latter having become vassals of the Satsuma clan of Kyushu). Yasunori (1988) has called these the "four portals" of Japanese trade, with itself at the centre during sakoku.

Furthermore, the idea that Japan was "isolated" from the outside world during the sakoku period was commonly held in the West (see Chapter 5) in the sense that it was unchanged since the early 17th century and had not advanced in knowledge during these "dark ages". Yet, during this period, a wide range of Chinese and Dutch books were imported into the country (Boot, 2013). Indeed, a whole branch of learning, called Dutch learning (*rangoku*) developed in Japan (Goodman, 2000). The ability to speak and read Dutch by the Japanese interpreters working in Dejima meant that Western books (in Dutch) could be translated and disseminated. And, as noted in this chapter, the members of the VOC in Dejima would often engage in a dialogue with the Japanese involving the transfer of learning that increased throughout the sakoku period. Indeed, the Japanese were gaining an advanced knowledge of Western science and medicine from the imported books and VOC doctors such as Thunberg, and later in the 19th century with Von Siebold as an active teacher of medicine.

Finally, as well as the Japanese trade and knowledge of the outside world that was underestimated in the West during the sakoku period, it was also assumed in the West that Japanese society had somehow stuck in the Middle Ages, remaining socially and culturally unchanged from the time the Portuguese left in the early 17th century until the opening in the 19th century. Yet if we take the period from the mid-17th to the mid-19th century, the period covered in this chapter, there is over 200 years of cultural change taking place in Japan, that was not appreciated in the

West where, in the mid-19th century, people (including Commodore Perry) were consulting Kaemper's *History* (from the 1690s) as a source of information about Japanese society. Indeed, Bolitho (1998) has argued that the 250 years of Japanese history during the Tokugawa shogunate (1603–1868) – from Ieyasu in a continuous line of fifteen Tokugawa rulers through to Yoshinobu – is the least well-known period of Japanese history in the West. Yet, this was a long period of peace in Japan (untroubled by Western colonization) that involved significant social change as the samurai, as a military force, were no longer necessary to defend the domains of their daimyo (who themselves had submitted to the shogun). This time of peace led to a rich growth in the cultural and artistic life of Japan, as shown in the PBS series *Memoirs of a Secret Empire*.

In this chapter, it has been shown that the Jesuits deliberately sought to present an image of the Japanese that perpetuated the idea of the blessed Christian martyrs of Japan in their stories and plays, a construction that had more to do with the Jesuit position in the European Catholic Church than any reflection of the lives of the people actually living in Japan during the sakoku period. While the Dutch remained in Japan, their only real chance to see the country and its people was on the journeys to Edo (Tokyo) to acknowledge the lordship of the shogun, as their position in Japanese society was of a small domain with the Opperhoofd as the daimyo (Clulow, 2014). For many in Europe, this submission to a foreign power was deemed an insult (after reading Kaempfer's account), and for Catholic historians (such as Hazart), it was considered an unforgivable abandonment of fellow Christians in order to maintain trade with their oppressors. Thus, the image of the Japanese became a curious combination of the saintly and the cruel in the Western discourse of the 17th century. Yet for many Protestants, in the 17th century, it was the Portuguese Catholics who had brought about their own banishment from Japan, a view that persisted to Commodore Perry's expedition in 1853 (above). Hence, in the Protestant accounts of Japan such as that of Montanus, the Japanese were viewed as good-natured, affable, and valuing cleanliness. However, they also had harsh punishments for crimes and a sense of duty that might lead them to kill themselves if unable to fulfil it.

As the sakoku period continued and current information about the Japan diminished, authors of European texts filled in the gaps with speculation, seeking to make the Japanese more extraordinary to their curious readers. Yet at the same time, the desire for Eastern products, including those from Japan, contributed to the image of the Orient as a place of luxury, peopled by skilled artisans, the creators of the wonderful products that Europeans found hard to emulate. At times the European image of the exotic Japanese no longer needed a basis in reality but Japan became a place of fantasy, lying somewhere near the fantasy Formosa of Psalmanazar and the fantasy Lilliput of Swift. As well as assuming that Japan remained fixed and unchanging, isolated from the rest of the world for over 200 years, its inhabitants had acquired the trappings of fantasy in the Western mind. With the opening of Japan, this fantasy land now became accessible for Westerners to visit.

Notes

1 Witness was the original meaning of the word "martyr".
2 This phrase from the *Apologeticus*, L13 has been translated in a number of different ways but this is a common paraphrase.
3 Written in Dutch, with the original title: *Kerckelycke Historie van de Gheheele Wereldt.*
4 Written in French, with the original title: *Histoire ecclésiastique des îles et royaume du Japon.*
5 Written in French, with the original title: *Histoire de l'Église du Japon.*
6 Written in French, with the original title: *Les triomphes chrétiens des martyrs du Japon.*
7 These are the page numbers given for the section of the book on Japan. I have translated the captions from the Dutch with the aid of an internet translation service.
8 Three dozen to be exact.
9 The full title of the narrative is: Narrative of the Expedition of an American Squadron to the China Seas and Japan under the Command of Commodore M.C. Perry United States Navy.
10 PBS is an acronym for Public Broadcasting Service.
11 Available to view on YouTube.

5

THE SOUL OF JAPAN

Victorian medievalism and the fascination with Japan

The "opening" of Japan was not seen in the West as the act of gunboat diplomacy – a use of force as a way of demanding trade on advantageous conditions. It was seen as opening the door to bring the modern world to Japan. Yet at the same time, Westerners were fascinated by "medieval" Japan which, particularly to people in Britain, had avoided the evils of the industrial revolution, criticized by the poet William Blake as "dark satanic mills" (Hutchings, 2003). From the medieval romances of writer Walter Scott, the Gothic revival in architecture, the medievalism of the Pre-Raphaelite painters and the Arts and Crafts movement of William Morris, a romantic image of a medieval world, of skilled artisans, artists and chivalric society, imbued the work of the Victorian medievalists (Ibbotson, 2020). Into this cultural context came the Japanese decorative arts.

Added to Victorian romantic medievalism came the Western belief that "Japan emerged from her isolation" (Thomas, 1897 p. vii), like a Rip Van Winkle waking up after centuries of sleep. Indeed, the London *Times* writer Alexander Knox wrote an article on Japan in the *Edinburgh Review* in 1852, claiming that "things remain at the present moment in Japan pretty much as they did in Kaempfer's time" (Yokoyama, 1987, p. 7). Yokoyama (1987, p. 4) also quotes the editor of Cooke's *Universal Library*, published in the following year, 1853, who made the extraordinary claim:

> Having been cut off from almost all intercourse with foreign nations for such a long period, it is not to be expected that, considering . . . the stationary character of eastern civilization, the manners, habits, customs, etc., of the Japanese should have materially changed" [*since Kaempfer's time*].

DOI: 10.4324/9781003082088-5

While William Morris acknowledged that the Japanese had "brilliant qualities as handicraftsmen", he argued that they were limited by their isolation from the "evolution of art" and the "history of mankind" (Vallance, 1897, p. 78). This idea that Japan had not changed in over 150 years, though unrealistic, was not uncommon. Hence, for the medievalists, this offered the opportunity to experience a people that had remained "pure" to their medieval ways in the modern era – the "medieval spirit" of Japan, as writer Clive Holland (1909, p. 251) put it.

The image of the Japanese in the European international exhibitions derived from the displays of their traditional cultural artefacts. In the London International Exhibition of 1862, the Japanese Court exhibited picturesque objects from Japan, such as paper lanterns, fans, bronzes and carved ornaments created by Japanese artisans (Yokoyama, 1987). The medievalist architect and designer, William Burges wrote in the *Gentleman's Magazine* that "if the visitor wishes to see the Middle Ages, he must visit the Japanese Court" (Burges, 1862, p. 10). This was the representation of Japan popular in Europe and, despite the enormous changes taking place in that country, characterized by the Japanese village constructed in Knightsbridge from January 1885 to June 1887 (McLaughlin, 2007), where skilled Japanese artisans demonstrated their skills for the entertainment of visitors, conjuring the image of Japan as a country of "medieval" crafts. A reviewer for the *Furniture Gazette* (1885, p. 56) wrote that the Japanese were working "at their several handicrafts as busily as if they were at home and really gaining their livelihood by their labour". The reviewer went on to explain how the managing director of the exhibition, Dutchman Tannaker Buhicrosan[1] (who had a Japanese wife), had seen in every capital in Europe "admiration and popular demand for every kind of Japanese work, – fans, baskets, lacquer, bronzes, – all were there, unrivalled in beauty and cheapness". The "surpassing superiority of the work . . . was principally due to the painstaking character of the workmen", with "the main characteristic of all Japanese work was its conscientious perfection of detail in every particular". In the 1880s, the Japanese were imagined as working as artisans, in medieval villages, living a simpler life that appealed to the Victorian medievalist imagination (and not viewed in terms of the rapid industrialization taking place back in Japan).

While there is a myth that a visit by W.S. Gilbert to the Japanese village was the inspiration for the famous Gilbert and Sullivan light opera, *The Mikado* (first performed in March 1885 at the Savoy Theatre, London), McLaughlin (2007) showed that Gilbert was working on the libretto in 1884. However, it does illustrate the broad fascination with all things Japanese in Victorian Britain. The comic operetta is based in the Japanese town of Titipu and concerns Nanki-Poo, the son of the Mikado (the Emperor) disguised as a musician to escape marriage to Katisha; and his love for Yum-Yum, the ward of tailor Ko-Ko who she is about to marry. *The Mikado* combines farce about who should be executed for violating a law against flirting, and romantic comedy, ending with Nanki-Poo and Yum-Yum – and Ko-Ko and Katisha – getting married. The "Japanese" characters, with comic names (redolent of an English nursery), were played by Europeans dressed as the images of Japanese ladies and gentlemen as seen on imported chinaware, fans and toys. As Babson (2012, p. 189) pointed out: "there are no Japanese people in *The Mikado*, only objects come to life". Indeed, it follows in the tradition of the Western writers using Japan as a fantasy land in which to set their stories (Nish, 2011; see Chapter 4). However, other academics have argued that the huge popularity of *The Mikado* with audiences actually influenced the Victorian idea of the Japanese.

> The Japanese people themselves were popularly regarded as picturesque and harmless, both "queer and quaint", as the chorus of nobles sing in the opening song of the opera that did so much to stereotype the Japanese in the Western mind, Gilbert and Sullivan's *The Mikado*.
>
> *(Gerster, 2009, p. 319)*

Hence for 19th-century Europeans, after the "opening" of Japan, the image of Japan was firmly established as a "medieval" land of artisans, a fascinating place populated by such quaint people (Lavery, 2019).

Japonisme: an impressionist's dream

The Paris Exposition Universelle of 1867 followed on the success of the International Exhibition in London in 1862. In the park outside the exhibition, a Japanese teahouse was set up and crowds of visitors came to watch three *geisha* sitting inside (Lockyer, 2001). The Exhibition allowed the visitors to wander through the different sections of the exhibition for the different countries to see the objects of their cultures, from architecture and crafts, including the teahouse and its attendant geisha, who like the denizens of the Japanese village later in London, set an image of the Japanese in the European mind. Amongst the objects on display were Japanese wood block prints (*ukiyo-e*[2]), which were to have a major influence on European art. Japanese prints had been seen in Europe before the Exhibition (e.g. in von Seibold's *Nippon*, published in Leiden, in seven volumes between 1832 and 1852). However, the exhibition stimulated a craze for all things Japanese – especially its prints – in the European artistic circles, a craze that was termed *Japonisme* by the French art critic Philippe Burty in 1872 and promoted by the writer brothers Edmond and Jules de Goncourt (Lambourne, 2005).

The French impressionist painter Claude Monet claimed to have discovered Japanese prints while on a trip to Zaandam in the Netherlands in 1871. Subsequently, he collected 231 prints, by over forty artists, including works by the great Japanese masters of ukiyo-e, Hokusai, Hiroshige and Utamaro, among others (Aitken and Delafond, 2013). To some extent, the love of Japanese prints simply reflected the fascination with all things Japanese, and presented images of the Japanese in an apparently medieval society and bucolic landscapes. While Japonisme was embraced by the European art world, those same artists responded to a vogue for pictures of Westerners in Japanese garb (reminiscent of the Dutch merchants in the 17th century: see Chapter 4). Japanese decors, Japanese objects and models dressed in Japanese kimono, all presented an exotic Oriental image that fascinated Westerners, captivated with the representation of the Japanese portrayed in the international exhibitions. An early example is shown in James MacNeil Whistler's *Caprice in Purple: The Golden Screen*, 1864, one of two paintings showing an English woman wearing a kimono, looking at prints by Hiroshige, with a golden Japanese screen behind her (Okamoto-MacPhail, 2005). In 1872, the Belgian Alfred Stevens painted *La Parisienne Japonaise* of a young Parisian woman wearing a kimono and gazing into a mirror. In 1875, Monet succumbed to this fashion, painting his wife Camille in a red kimono, holding a fan, entitled *La Japonaise*. The fashion lasted for the rest of the century, spreading to all Western countries, such as in the United States, with William Merritt Chase's 1890 *Girl in a Japanese Costume*. The vogue for the Japanese decorative arts was further stimulated by each new international exhibition, such as those in 1873 in Vienna, in 1878 in Paris and in 1893 in Chicago. However, the interest in Japanese prints began to change the Western perception of the Japanese from just skilled artisans making exquisite decorative arts to acknowledging their contribution to fine art, and the influence they were having on contemporary Western artists (Coaldrake, 2013).

In 1890, the art dealer S. Bing (Samuel Siegfried Bing) organized the *Exposition de la Gravure Japonaise* at the École des Beaux-Arts in Paris, displaying 750 Japanese ukiyo-e prints, as well as over 400 Japanese picture books. The artists Mary Cassat, Edward Degas and Camille Pissaro all wrote favourably about the exhibition in their correspondence (Kodera, 2016). Indeed, Japanese art had an influence on all three of these artists, as well as the work of Eduoard Manet and Paul Gauguin, and indeed many other French artists of the time, in terms of style, composition, colour, use of space, light and shadow. For example, Henri de Toulouse-Lautrec employed Japanese techniques in his images of Parisian life, without including Japan objects in his work (Raepple, 2008). As well as being one of the first artists to paint Western ladies in kimonos, Whistler was also one of the first to stop, with his work after 1870 showing Japanese stylistic influences without the need for the Japanese décor (Sandberg, 1964). Vincent Van Gogh, another artist who collected Japanese prints, wrote to his brother Theo on 15th July 1888, acknowledging the Japanese influence on contemporary French art, claiming that the impressionists were the "Japanese of France".[3] Indeed, later when Monet was interviewed in 1909 by Roger Marx in the *Gazette des Beaux Arts*, he claimed:

> If you absolutely must find an affiliation for me, select the Japanese of olden times, their rarefied taste has always appealed to me; and I sanction the implications of their esthetic that evokes a presence by means of a shadow and the whole by means of a fragment.
>
> *(Stuckey, 1985, p. 266)*

Furthermore, the French artist Pierre-August Renoir wrote in his notebook:

> The Japanese have a simplicity of life which gives them time to go about and to contemplate. They still look, fascinated, at a blade of grass, or the flight of birds, or the wonderful movements of fish, and they go home, their minds filled with beautiful ideas, which they have no trouble in putting on the objects they decorate.
>
> *(Harrison et al., 2000, p. 858)*

While the notebook entry is undated, Harrison et al. suggest it was written some time between 1880 and 1910. So despite the evidence that the Western view of the Japanese moved from that of a skilled artisan to more of a contemplative aesthetic artist (with the Western interest in the style of Japanese prints), the popular image of the Japanese living contentedly in a medieval society, in a bucolic landscape, as portrayed by both Renoir and the medievalists, persisted even to the end of the 19th century.

Modernization and the romance of Old Japan

For Japan, the second half of the 19th century was a period of rapid modernization. The "opening" of Japan was followed by a major upheaval in the governance of Japan. The fifteenth and last Tokugawa shogun resigned in 1867, and the transition ("restoration") of the emperor to be the ruling monarch followed soon after. Japanese officials began to wear Western clothes and they converted their social hierarchy to a European-style aristocracy, called *kazoku*[4] (Abe et al., 2022). The industrialization of Japan involved numerous foreign advisors to educate the Japanese in new technologies, such as the Scottish engineer Henry Dyer and the American biologist William Elliot Griffis (Gooday and Low, 1998). This led to the Japanese being viewed as students of the West. Indeed, in many cases, the Japanese were actual students, with a group of five young men, the Choshu Five arriving at University College, London, in 1863 to study science. All of them returned to Japan as modernizers, gaining senior roles in the government. For many in the West, there was a positive attitude to Japanese modernization, viewed as seeking to join the community of Western nations (e.g. Morris, 1895; Wittner, 2007). In 1872, the first railway line from Tokyo to Yokohama was built, and the main line from Tokyo to Kyoto was completed in 1889. And in the 1870s, a Western-style army, navy and police, schools, banks, a postal and telegraph system were all created. This led to the view in the West that the Japanese were excellent imitators (Westney, 1987) which was turned by some in the West into the belief that the Japanese were "just" imitators of Western technology (Rosenstone, 1980). While it was acknowledged that the Japanese were having an influence on Western arts (see earlier), Japanese modernization was viewed as synonymous with Westernization, which meant that the West had little to learn from the Japanese.

Yet some Westerners wondered whether the "opening" of Japan was a good thing for the Japanese. Sir Rutherford Alcock, the first British ambassador, noted that "free intercourse and trade threatens them with a participation in all the miseries, mutations, and political struggles from which they have continued so long exempt" (Morris, 1895, p. 129). Also, the Western view of the Japanese during the late 19th century was dominated by the image of the medieval artisan, as portrayed in the international exhibitions, and therefore not suited to the work of a modern factory. As one German commentator put it as late as 1908:

> The Japanese worker is hardly willing to submit himself to the military discipline which according to our standards must rule the modern factory. He takes his holiday whenever he likes, he comes and goes as he pleases, and if he is scolded for such behavior, he leaves the company.
>
> *(Linhart, 1988, p. 271)*

Despite the rapid modernization of Japan (and the acknowledgement of the Japanese as successful imitators), the Western romance of "medieval" Japan (populated by artisans and artists leading simple fulfilling lives) was supported by a number of foreigners living in Japan who had learnt about Japanese history and folklore, and who, fascinated by the Japanese past, which they termed "Old Japan", expressed a loss at its passing – which they could see before their eyes. This echoed the view of the Western medievalists who imagined their own Middle Age as an idyllic, romantic period before their own industrialization. These Japanologists, who had lived, or were living in Japan, wrote romantically about Old Japan for a Western audience that reinforced the idea of the Japanese as having a medieval artistic temperament. In 1871, the British diplomat Algernon Bertram Mitford (later Lord Redesdale), who had returned from more than three years in Japan, published his book *Tales of Old Japan*, stories that he had acquired during his time in Japan. The book began with *The Tale of the Forty-Seven Ronin*, and continued with a collection of fairy stories and supernatural tales set in pre-restoration Japan. As Cortazzi (2002, p. x) argued, Mitford "was never condescending or contemptuous" but his comments were "tinged with a romantic nostalgia", and Mitford "was more inclined to see heroism rather than ruthlessness and cruelty in the behaviour of the Japanese samurai who epitomized for him the spirit of Japanese feudalism". On its publication, Mitford's book became very popular in Britain reinforcing the image of a bygone Japan (Cortazzi, 2002).

Basil Hall Chamberlain arrived in Japan in 1873 and stayed nearly forty years, much of the time working as a professor of Japanese at the Tokyo Imperial University. His friend, the writer Lafcadio Hearn, of Irish and Greek parentage, had worked as a reporter in the United States, and arrived in Japan in 1890. With Chamberlain's help, Hearn became a teacher. He settled in Japan, married a Japanese woman and became a Japanese citizen taking a Japanese name. Both men wrote about Old Japan, with Hearn, like Mitford, writing about Japanese fairy tales and supernatural stories of a time before the restoration (or modernization). Both men reflected on Japan and its past: Hearn in *Japan: An Attempt at Interpretation* (1904) and Chamberlain in *Things Japanese; Being Notes on Various Subjects Connected with Japan* (1902[5]). Chamberlain wrote:

> And what a quaint, picturesque society it was, – that of the time, say, between 1750 and 1850, – the "Old Japan" which all now know and appreciate, because the works of the Artisan School have carried its fame round the world!
>
> *(Chamberlain, 1902, p. 50)*

Yet, in reflecting on the Western "opening" of Japan, Chamberlain continued: "Old Japan was like an oyster – to open it was to kill it" (Chamberlain, 1902, p. 361).

Hearn was even more explicit in his nostalgia for Old Japan and his dislike of Japan's rapid industrialization (Johnson, 1991). He wrote that "the traditions that compelled self-denial and obedience, also cultivated courage, and insisted on cheerfulness" (Hearn, 1904, p. 199), with "the ideals of Old Japan: instinctive unselfishness, a common desire to find the joy of life in making happiness for others, a universal sense of moral beauty" (Hearn, 1904, pp. 504–5). Hearn argued that through their religious beliefs, the Japanese had developed a moral character called *yamato-damashii*[6] (Japanese soul) or *yamato-gokoro* (Japanese mind/heart). He used these concepts to explain why the Jesuit mission had been a threat to the nature of Old Japan and expressed his sympathy in the banning of Christianity. "It [*Catholicism*] was essentially opposed to all the beliefs and traditions upon which Japanese society was founded" (Hearn, 1904, p. 349). He went on to say that the failure of the Jesuit mission "preserved for modern eyes the marvellous world of Japanese art, and the yet more marvellous world of its traditions, beliefs, and customs" (Hearn, 1904, p. 371). Hence, through the works of Western authors, such as Mitford, Chamberlain and Hearn, the most popular books about Japan in English at the turn of the 20th century concerned Japanese fairy tales, ghost stories and the marvellous world of Old Japan that was viewed as nurturing the talent of the Japanese artisans and artists, whose products had become the vogue in Western society. And, for the Western tourists who flocked to Japan after its "opening", it was not the evidence of modernization that they wished to see, but the Japan that they had read about in stories of Old Japan: its strangeness, its quaintness and its exotic delight.

Travellers in fairyland: a playground of the west

With the prohibition on Christianity lifted by the Japanese government in 1873, the American Unitarian Minister Arthur May Knapp was able to lead a mission there in 1888. But like Chamberlain and Hearn he was captivated by Japan – and especially Old Japan. He wrote:

> Of the power and singularity of the fascination which Japan exerts over the Western mind there can be no question . . . no one who has left it after a few years' residence can ever wholly overcome his longing to return to the Island Paradise.

> It is unquestionably the unique nation of the globe, – the land of dream and enchantment, the land which could hardly differ more from our own were it located on another planet, its people not of this world.
>
> *(Knapp, 1900, p. 1)*

It was a "marvellously beautiful land" (p. 195), claimed Knapp, with some parts of Japan offering "visions of romantic beauty beyond the dreams of fairyland" (p. 191). The association of Japan with fairy stories and fairy land had begun almost as soon as Japan had agreed to Western trade. Describing the end of the trade mission of Lord Elgin to Japan in 1858, based on Laurence Oliphaunt's narrative of the mission,[7] James White wrote in *Blackwood's Edinburgh Magazine*: "The fairy tale closes with the last look we get of Nagasaki, and we are brought back to the land of commonplace realities" (White, 1860, p. 276). After the English poet Sir Edwin Arnold returned from visiting Japan in the late 1880s, Basil Hall Chamberlain (1902, p. 3) claimed:

> He lauded it to the skies – and lauded it justly – as the nearest earthly approach to Paradise or to Lotus-land, – so fairy-like, said he, is its scenery, so exquisite its art, so much more lovely still that almost divine sweetness of disposition, that charm of demeanour, that politeness humble without servility and elaborate without affectation, that place Japan high above all other countries in nearly all those things that make life worth living.

Arnold himself wrote: "At very little distance from the surface, which we civilizing westerns have done our best to spoil, will be still discovered the old, changeless, high-tempered, generous, simple, and sweet-mannered Japan" (Arnold, 1891b, p. 323). This image of Japan was also embraced by Lafcadio Hearn who referred to Japan as a "fairyland" (Hearn, 1904, p. 19) as did other Western visitors (see Yokoyama, 1987). As a result, more Western tourists travelled to Japan to see this fairyland inhabited by its charming and artistic denizens.

And they were not disappointed. One of the best-known travel writers of the 19th century was the Englishwoman Isabella Bird, an inveterate solo traveller, who journeyed to Japan in 1878, writing an account of her seven months sojourn in the country, in a book entitled *Unbeaten Tracks in Japan* (1880). Arriving in an unattractive Yokohama, she longed "to get away into real Japan" (p. 21). As she explored further, she found Japan to be like a fairyland. A festival is a "crowded fairy scene" (p. 25) and, on seeing a festival procession, she claimed: "I never saw anything more completely like a fairy scene" (p. 381). A Japanese woman "moves about the house like a floating fairy" (p. 109); Ieyasu's tomb at Nikko is "a fairyland of gold and colour" (p. 116); the gardens of the houses in Niigata "give the effect of fairyland as you look through from the street" (p. 223); a tea-house has "fairy-like rooms" (p. 262). Numerous things in Japan are exquisite to Bird, and in this example, fairy-like too. "I found that we were in the most exquisite garden that I have seen in Japan, a fairy-like creation, small, but seeming large" (p. 248). A festival in a town "turned the whole into fairyland", making the houses look "like fairy scenes" (pp. 296–7). When not fairy-like,

Japan became an earthly paradise to Bird: "The plain of Yonezawa . . . is a perfect garden of Eden" (p. 133). However, she often noted the small stature of the Japanese people which resulted in her descriptions switching from fairy-like to a Victorian image of a toy town. A priest's house "looks like a doll's house" (p. 44); a row of houses is a "doll's street" (p. 105). In a city, she sees "the tiny houses and doll-like women" (p. 204). At a festival, there are "decorated doll-children" (p. 298), In Tokyo, the shops "as elsewhere, are . . . resembling dolls' houses" (p. 184), alongside "tiny houses and doll-like women" (p. 204). The American travel writer Eliza Scidmore (1891, p. 1) agreed: "Japan is a dream of Paradise, beautiful from the first green island off the coast to the last picturesque hill-top. The houses seem toys, their inhabitants dolls, whose manner of life is clean, pretty, artistic, and distinctive".

While Western visitors found so many things in Japan that were charming, quaint and delightful, there were times when they were surprised by customs that jarred with their own, and the major one was public bathing. Yet, rather than viewing this as indecent as it would be considered in the West, it was seen as evidence of Japanese "classical" purity or child-like innocence. White (1860, p. 275) noted: "Women, especially at Nagasaki, perform their ablutions in tubs upon the public street, with the air of being Dianas enjoying the bath in some secluded fountain". Arnold also reported from his experience in Japan:

> The Japanese are not in the least ashamed of the body. . . . This frank exposure goes with the most perfect modesty, and indeed leads to it. Morality rather gains, and sentiment decidedly loses by this candor of Japanese manners as regards nudity; for no one looks at what all the world may see, and it is the veil which makes the sanctum.
>
> *(Arnold, 1891a, pp. 22–3)*

Chamberlain (1902, p. 59) agreed, stating that "cleanliness is more esteemed by the Japanese than our artificial Western prudery. As the editor of the Japan Mail has well said, the nude is seen in Japan, but is not looked at". But some Westerners found they could not overcome their social conditioning. Rudyard Kipling on a visit to a bathhouse recounted:

> I was preparing to wash when a pretty maiden opened the door, and indicated that she also would tub in the deep sunken Japanese bath at my side. When one is dressed only in one's virtue and a pair of spectacles it is difficult to shut the door in the face of a girl. She gathered that I was not happy, and withdrew giggling, while I thanked heaven, blushing profusely the while, that I had been brought up in a society which unfits a man to bathe *à deux*.
>
> *(Kipling, 1899, pp. 167–8)*

Yet this lack of prudery enhanced the view of the Japanese as living in virtuous innocence. Yokoyama (1987, p. 25) quotes an astonished Royal Navy captain describing women bathing in public as the "fair Eves" of Japan. However, this perception of Japanese innocence was not something that all Western men respected for its purity, as illustrated further.

It was also a vision of innocence that the Japanese themselves thought odd. The historian Kenneth B. Pyle agreed that many 19th-century Western visitors regarded Japan as either a playground or a charming, fantasy land of "divine sweetness" populated by the people with the characteristics of "birds and butterflies" (Pyle, 1969, pp. 85–6), a view that frustrated their hosts. In an article in the Japanese magazine *The Nation's Friend* (*Kokumin no tomo*), of 22 June 1889, the writer commented: "these foreigners regard Japan as the world's playground. . . . They pay their admission and enter because there are so many strange, weird things to see". The author went on to encourage reform and progress to "make us a normal, civilized country", a view supported by many Japanese intellectuals wishing to move on from their "romantic" past (Pyle, 1969, p. 85). However, the Westerners continued to see Japan as their playground, and the Japanese as innocent children. Wood (1916, pp. 33–4) wrote, rather tongue-in-cheek, in this vein:

> Japan is too lovely for words. I shall certainly stay here for some little time and take a house – a real Japanese house of the papier-mâché variety – and play in the sunshine. . . . What I have seen already of the Japanese tells me that for all intents and purposes they are children. Easily pleased and amused, they are the happiest people in the world.

Yet for all this delight in Japan and its inhabitants, it was clear that Western travellers to Japan saw the Japanese as a people very different to themselves. Isabella Bird provides a good illustration of this. While viewing them as the denizens of fairyland and doll-like, she showed no hesitation in characterizing them in negative racial terms to her readers. As well as mentioning their small stature, they were clearly not white people: "the skin is very yellow" (Bird, 1880, p. 17), "their yellow faces" (p. 19), "So lean, so yellow, so ugly, yet so pleasant-looking" (p. 29), "His face is very yellow" (p. 48), plus a number of other examples. From Kaempfer's speculation on the origin of the Japanese, through to the Enlightenment distinction of people by their skin colour, Bird reflected Western 19th-century racial distinctions (see Chapter 1) in her descriptions of the Japanese. Clearly, she expressed many positive opinions about the Japanese, but they were not the same type of people as her. As Kowner (2014) and Keevak (2011) have so eruditely shown, the once "white" Japanese had now morphed in the Western mind into "yellow", a difference reflecting the changing ideological construction of them between the 16th and 19th centuries.

Chrysanthemum and butterfly: "the little doll with whom I play"

From 1889 to 1894, Mary Crawford Fraser, wife of the head of the British Legation in Japan, kept a record of her experiences of Japan through her correspondence, which was published in 1899. In it, she discussed the Japanese girl: "a creature of so many attractive contradictions, with her warm heart, her quick brain, and her terribly narrow experience". Yet she also noted that: "The books I have read on Japan have always had a great deal to say about the *musumë* [*musume*],[8] the pretty, plebeian tea-house girl, or the *geisha*, the artist, the dancer, the witty, brilliant hetaira[9] of Japan", who she argued was no more typical of the Japanese girl than a music hall singer is of a European Catholic sister (Fraser, 1904, p. 270). Yet a distorted combination of the geisha and tea-house girl dominated the image of the Japanese woman in the 19th-century Western imagination. The Japanese girl was viewed as having child-like characteristics, illustrated by the infantile names given to the girls in *The Mikado* (Yum-Yum, Pitti-Sing and Peep-Bo), and in the representation of Japanese tea-house girls. Yet at the same time, the Japanese woman was associated with the geisha, and erotic romance. Indeed, Japanese girls as represented in much of the literature about Japan were not like Western women at all – they were fairies, they were dolls, as Isabella Bird, and, more commonly, Western male authors described them (Ni, 2016).

For men such as the French writer and naval officer Pierre Loti, this meant he could ignore the social and moral constraints of his own country and view the Japanese girl as a companion to satisfy his erotic desires for the duration of his visit. His 1887 novel *Madame Chrysanthème* is a semi-fictional account of his visit to Japan in 1885. From the first moment he sets foot on Japanese soil, he seeks a Japanese "wife" by going to a tea-house to organize one. All is arranged for his selection, and he chooses the pretty *Kiku-san* (Madame Chrysanthemum) from the teenage girls on offer, and they are "married". During the ceremony, Loti looks that Kiku-san and muses: "Is it a woman or a doll?" (Loti, 1905, p. 40). The answer comes soon when he describes her as "this little doll, with whom I play at married life" (p. 72). Loti is emotionally detached, describing her when sleeping as looking like "a dead fairy", and resembling a "blue dragonfly" (p. 75). At their parting Loti concludes:

> Well, little mousmé [*musume*], let us part good friends; one last kiss even, if you like. I took you to amuse me; you have not perhaps succeeded very well, but after all you have done what you could . . . in short, you have been pleasant enough in your Japanese way.
>
> *(p. 216)*

While Loti's work was very popular in Europe, Chamberlain (1902) noted that Loti's popularity was much less with the Western residents in Japan, who disapproved of his superficiality and inaccuracy. Arnold (1891b) – whose third wife was Japanese – was highly critical of Loti, calling the work brilliantly offensive, and arguing that Chrysanthemum's character was morally superior to the egotistical Frenchman. Hearn – who also had a Japanese wife – greatly admired Loti's writing, but "apologized for his lack of moral feeling" (Modell, 1933, p. vi). However, the theme of Loti's work, the chauvinistic and sexist Western man and the charming and innocent Japanese girl, was to gain wider popularity in the West with American John

Luther Long's 1898 short story *Madame Butterfly*. In it, Pinkerton, an American naval officer, arrives in Japan and, through a marriage broker, weds a young Japanese girl Co-Co-San (Madame Butterfly). When Pinkerton departs, leaving her pregnant, Co-Co-San insists that their marriage is permanent, and rejects other suitors, seeking help from the American consul who agrees that American marriages are not temporary. However, Pinkerton has married in America and when his ship returns, he does not visit Butterfly. His American wife goes to the American consulate, and on seeing Co-Co-San, patronizes her, calling her a charming plaything. Mrs Pinkerton demands Butterfly's child who she expects to take away. Horrified Co-Co-San attempts suicide, but her maid binds her wound. Next day when Mrs Pinkerton arrives at Co-Co-San's house to claim the baby, it is empty. The story was turned into a theatrical production by David Blasco in 1900, playing successfully in New York and London. And then Giacomo Puccini turned it into an opera, first performed in 1904, which became one of the most successful operas in the Western world.

The effect of the popularity of Madame Butterfly had two outcomes. While it illustrated the callousness of the Western man in his treatment of a Japanese girl (as the story centred on Co-Co-san, with Pinkerton an absent figure), and encouraged sympathy for Madame Butterfly, it also propagated the image of the Japanese girl as a plaything of the Western man in Japan. These views can be illustrated by examples from a "flippant"[10] (fictional) account of a visit to Japan by Eric Erskine Wood. At the start of the visit, an English bachelor arrives in Nagasaki and says:

> The only thing I know about Nagasaki is that it is the scene where is laid the plot of the opera with the most appealing music in the world. Poor little Madame Butterfly, she is but one of many who wait and wait patiently in their best kimono for the returning of Love.
>
> *(Wood, 1916, p. 28)*

When he leaves Japan at the end of his visit, the protagonist stands on the deck of the ship, sad to leave Japan, and writes:

> A big, bluff, red-faced man has already encroached on my misery. "Looking a bit down in the dumps", he said, using the expression that I dislike intensely. "I expect you've left something on shore, eh? Why, bless my soul, we've all left a little girl back yonder", and he pointed a fat finger towards Japan. "Every Englishman leaves a girl in Japan – it's part of the fun", and he roared with laughter, then added, "Come and have a drink, old man; that'll put you right".
>
> *(Wood, 1916, p. 97)*

This image of the Japanese girl as dainty (doll-like) and a charming companion to the Western man was promoted by other authors at the time, such as English writer Clive Holland. Holland wrote books – *My Japanese Wife,* 1902, and *A Japanese Romance*, 1904 – about encountering such a desirable young Japanese woman.

When writing about visiting Japan, he contrasted Japanese girls favourably with their Western counterparts: "They are merry little souls" who remain "singularly happy, cheerful, cleanly and content" in working conditions "that would make the most humble factory girl at home go out on strike" (Holland, 1909, p. 152). It is worth noting that Holland was eulogizing the obedient and submissive Japanese girl at a time when women in his own country were taking part in a struggle for suffrage (Smith, 2014). Indeed, this representation of the charming and obedient Japanese girl – represented by Madame Butterfly – has remained a feature of Western popular culture, typically contrasting the Japanese girl with a Western woman (Morris, 2002).

Bushido and the Japanese spirit

At the turn of the 20th century, three Japanese writers, familiar with Western culture, sought to influence the Western view of Japan by writing about Japan in English for a Western audience: Inazo Nitobe and the brothers Kakuzo and Yoshisaburo Okakura. Inazo Nitobe (1862–1933) studied at Johns Hopkins University in the United States, where he became a Quaker and married an American woman. He obtained his doctorate in economics at Halle University in Germany and wrote works in both English and German before returning to Japan to be a diplomat. Kakuzo Okakura (1863–1913) was an academic, artist and art critic, who visited Europe, the United States and India, before spending the last few years of his life working at the Boston Museum of Fine Arts. Yoshisaburo Okakura (1868–1936) studied English in Tokyo, where he became a successful teacher of English and an academic. As men of intellect, they must have found the child-like representations of the Japanese circulating in Western culture as highly objectionable.

In his 1899 book, *Bushido: The Soul of Japan*, written in English, Nitobe made an association between the samurai of Japan and the knights of medieval Europe, with his book describing a Japanese form of chivalry called *bushido*, typically translated as "the way of the warrior" (Benesch, 2014), the "the code of moral principles which the knights [samurai] were required or instructed to observe" (Nitobe, 1907,[11] p. 4). He argued that Zen Buddhism and Shintoism had contributed to the Japanese approach to the mastery of skills, and their sense of loyalty to their masters. Bushido was also influenced by Confucianism; and patriotism and loyalty combined to bring about a sense of group unity (such as national unity). Hence, the soul of Japan was based on the "wholesome, unsophisticated nature of our warrior ancestors" (p. 18), who lived by rectitude, and condemned lying and cheating. They were guided by giri, a sense of duty (see Chapter 1), and sought to do the right thing for the right reasons, which Nitobe interpreted as courage. This was allied to a sense of honour: "implying a vivid consciousness of personal dignity and worth" (pp. 65–6). Like the Western concept of the "gentleman", the samurai valued truthfulness. Thus, the bushido code of the samurai is exhibited as politeness and good manners. Hence, traditional education was to build character and self-restraint. A samurai would bear suffering without complaint, and "whenever a cause presented itself which was considered dearer than life, with utmost serenity and celerity was life laid down" (p. 74), which explained why seppuku could bring death with honour (as in the classic *Tale of the Forty-Seven Ronin*). Essentially, Nitobe argued, bushido explained the spirit of the Japanese, the soul of the nation, and it had not disappeared with modernization (and Westernization). He claimed that it demystified the rapid industrialization of Japan that was built on the Japanese spirit: "Scratch a Japanese of the most advanced ideas, and he will show a samurai" (p. 173).

Yoshisaburo Okakura in *The Spirit of Japan* 1905, based on a lecture series he gave at the University of London, explained the history of Japan and the various religious influences on its people. He related a number of aspects of the Japanese character to Zen Buddhism:

> [the] self-control that enables us not to betray our inner feeling through a change in our expression, the measured steps with which we are taught to walk into the hideous jaws of death – in short, all those qualities which make a present Japanese of truly Japanese type look strange, if not queer, to your eyes . . . [*the*] love of nature and the desire of purity that we had shown from the earliest days of our history; that serene dislike of loudness of form and colour. That apparent simplicity with a fulness of meaning behind it . . . which we find so pervadingly manifested in our works of art.
>
> *(Y. Okakura, 1905, pp. 80–1)*

Okakura argued that the Confucian ethical code, embraced by the samurai, "form the code of unwritten morality known among us as Bushido" (p. 92), and he then presented a summary of bushido that supported the views of Nitobe. Okakura continued by identifying two symbols of Japan: the serenity and grace of Mount Fuji as "a silent influence on the Japanese character", and the "sunny gaiety" of cherry blossoms, with their "readiness to scatter their heart-shaped petals with a Samurai's indifference to death", which "make them so dear to our simple and determined view of life" (Y. Okakura, 1905, p. 107). This approach to life is constantly reinforcing the "unwritten morality", according to Okakura. To illustrate this, Y. Okakura (1905, p. 43) wrote: "Even such a commonplace thing as the drinking of a cup of tea becomes in our hands something more: it becomes a training in stoic serenity, in the capacity of smiling at life's troubles and disturbances".

In *The Book of Tea* (1906), Kazuko Okakura explained how the ceremony of tea making in Japan was related to the Japanese art of life, and this is central to the "Zen conception of greatness in the smallest incidents of life" (Okakura, 1906, p. 69). He complained that "the average Westerner in his sleek complacency" sees the tea ceremony as quaint and childish, and views Japanese self-sacrifice, in terms of a willing to give up one's life, "as the result of fatalism" (Okakura, 1906, pp. 7–8). As a consequence, Westerners misunderstand the Japanese as an odd contradiction of the quaint and the barbaric. Yet, Okakura argued, the true spirit of the Japanese can be determined in their "teaism", the cultural influences on the way that they make tea. Fortunately, Nitobe had spelt out what this meant for his readers: "That calmness of mind, that serenity of temper, that composure and quietness of demeanor, which are the first essentials of *cha-no-yu* [*the tea ceremony*] are without doubt the first conditions of right thinking and right feeling" (Nitobe, 1907, p. 51). Rather than simply making a cup of tea, Nitobe argued that the cha-no-yu had attained the status of fine art, of poetry.

These authors were arguing that the Japanese were not quaint and charming and culturally "undeveloped", in comparison to the West. Rather, they had a different aesthetic: the Japanese mind (the yamato gokoro), or spirit (yamato-damashii), was different to its Western counterpart, and guided by different aesthetic principles, which they had explained. Crucially, this meant that to understand Japanese culture – both the Japanese themselves and their cultural products – Westerners had to adopt a different aesthetic to their own. Crucially, they were putting forward intellectual arguments to counter the racist discourse about the inferiority of other "races" circulating in the West (e.g. Pickering, 2001). It was not that the Japanese were inferior, they were simply different: which meant that in certain spheres, their ways were superior to Western ways. The impressionists had seen this in their love of Japanese art, which had changed their way of painting. Thus, to understand Japanese cultural products, Westerners did have to appreciate Japanese aesthetics. Many in the West accepted this view, and for those Westerners, fascinated by aspects of Japanese culture, from art, gardening and flower arranging to self-control and martial arts such as in judo or ju-jitsu, the only way to learn how to do these things properly was to learn from the Japanese masters. Thus, when Isabella Christie wanted a Japanese garden at her estate at Cowden (Scotland), after returning from a visit to Japan in 1908, it was to the Japanese garden expert Taki Handa that she turned.

The works of Nitobe and the Okakura brothers had a very persuasive effect on their Western readership. In the West, a new image of the Japanese emerged of a people with a mature and sophisticated ethical and aesthetic tradition – a Japanese soul. However, this image of the Japanese as custodians of ancient wisdom also made their psyche appear very different to that of the West. By associating bushido to Western chivalry, Nitobe had linked the concept to Western romantic medievalist ideas of a more authentic life. However, whereas chivalry, associated with the European Middle Ages, was now a distant memory in the West, bushido was still present in Japan (according to Nitobe), and could provide an explanation for the Japanese success in rapidly modernizing. For many people in the West, Japan had retained admirable, and enviable, values that had disappeared in the West. Hence, there were aspects of Western life that would gain by the incorporation of the Japanese values – its moderation and selflessness. *Bushido: The Soul of Japan* was reprinted numerous times due to its high sales in the West. In the introduction to the revised edition of 1905, Nitobe said how flattered he was that the US President Theodore Roosevelt had read his book and given copies to his friends. Roosevelt was also a keen student of the Japanese martial art, judo, which had gained much popularity in the United States and he wrote about its benefits to his children (Tierney, 2007). Also, amongst those in the West embracing

Nitobe's idea of bushido was the founder of the scouts, Robert Baden-Powell, who wanted to create a scouting movement that contained the ideals of the samurai within it, as "an anglicized version of bushido" (Hashimoto, 2007, p. 396).

However, it has been argued that Nitobe and the Okakuras were constructing a new representation of the Japanese (for the reasons discussed earlier) rather than providing an academic account of the history of Japanese culture and society. Indeed, the detailed analysis by Benesch (2014) of bushido and Nitobe's writing demonstrates that Nitobe's concept of bushido is full of contradiction and inconsistency. Benesch also showed that this representation of bushido (promoted by the Japanese writers at the beginning of the 20th century) was not an account of Japanese history but was invented for their own purposes. "By focusing on the timeless 'way of the warrior' rather than the more limiting historical samurai, this invented tradition can be mobilized for almost any contingency" (Benesch, 2014, p. 247). At the time of the success of its publication, Basil Hall Chamberlain (1912) described the contingency he believed that bushido was being mobilized for. He argued that the idea of bushido served the Japanese nationalists and the Japanese government at this time, in representing themselves to people of other cultures. Chamberlain argued that history did not show that the Japanese had demonstrated any special loyalty to their leaders – who have been assassinated, and deposed, at various times throughout Japanese history. He also pointed out that Kaempfer – a detailed observer of Japan – had made no mention of bushido, and there had been no reference to the concept in Japanese dictionaries before 1900. In fact, Chamberlain argued, the concept of bushido was an aspect of a new "religion" emerging in Japan, focused on loyalty and patriotism, a religion that had created an emperor cult – with obedience to the divine emperor above all else – which promoted the idea of the superiority of the Japanese and Japanese values over other nations.

While many in the West – such as President Roosevelt and Baden-Powell – found bushido as a chivalric ideal very appealing, in the context of their newly industrialized and modernized society, the rising power of the Japanese, who had defeated China in the war of 1894–5 over their influence in Korea, was a source of anxiety in the West. Nitobe's statement that it only took a scratch to reveal the hidden samurai under the surface of the modern Japanese, added to Western anxieties, also expressed by Baden-Powell, about the military pretensions of the Japanese (Hashimoto, 2007). People in the West had been persuaded that the Japanese had a different "soul" but, rather than viewing them as equal but different, the Japanese were now viewed as a threat to the global hegemony of the Western powers. This would be expressed in the West in the discourse about the "yellow peril", which will be examined in the next chapter.

From artists in fairyland to the samurai within

For the second half of the 19th century, following from the opening of Japan, the popular image of the Japanese, in the West, was of members of a medieval society, of artisans working and living simple lives in a village setting in an idyllic landscape;

ironically, a similar image of Japanese life to that described by Captain Álvares to Frances Xavier back in the 16th century (see Chapter 2). This representation of the Japanese played into the romantic medievalism permeating Victorian society in Europe, which combined a sense of a loss of innocence and a more authentic life than that brought about by their own industrialization, with an industrial dominance that had forced Japan to open in the first place. The renewal of trading relations with Japan appeared to present the possibility of experiencing the Middle Ages come to life in Japan, conceived of in the Western mind. The delights of the Japanese village in London in 1886 supported this image of the artisanal "medieval" Japanese. International exhibitions in Europe and North America featured all the expected trappings of this imagined Japan: the kimono, the fans, the ceramics and the woodblock prints. Pictured in these works were the Japanese themselves, going about their everyday activities, such as walking along the *Tokaido* (the main route from Tokyo to Kyoto), or crossing a bridge in a snow storm carrying a staff and wearing a straw hat, as the seasons changed about them. The *sakura* (cherry blossoms) of springtime became the kiku (chrysanthemums) of autumn. Serene Mount Fuji dominated the landscape as the seasons changed about it. Women in kimono populate the prints which Claude Monet surrounded himself with in his house in Giverny in France, carrying on their daily lives in a world seeming unchanging bar the passage of the seasons.

Western writers who lived in Japan, very aware of the rapid changes to the society and lamenting the increasing pace of modernization, fed their Western readers with stories of Old Japan, full of ghosts and spirits conjuring up a world that resonated with the pictures that Western artists enthusiastically sought to emulate. Like the Dutch merchants of the 17th century, Westerners could collect Japanese objects and play at being Orientals by dressing in a kimono; only this time the fans, the figurines and other imported Japanese knick-knacks were cheap enough for anyone to buy. On a night out, an opera lover could embrace fantasy Japan in the town of Titipu by watching the *Mikado* and, as the 20th century dawned, feel sympathy for poor, little, abandoned Co-Co-san as she attempted to kill herself in Puccini's tragic *Madama Butterfly*.

Western travellers flocked to Japan and, like Isabella Bird, they benefitted from the modern technology, such as the new railways of Japan, yet they eschewed these modern developments to seek out "real" Japan ("I long to get away into real Japan", claimed Bird, 1880, p. 7, early in her visit). Western travellers sought out the Japanese "paradise" and the Japanese "fairyland" of their imagination. Indeed, as wealthy visitors, the poorer Japanese were willing to supply their entertainment. As Pierre Loti found to his delight, he just had to negotiate a fee with Kiku-san's parents and he had bought himself a little kimono clad doll for his erotic entertainment while in Japan. For the more reserved Rudyard Kipling, he just had to keep out the "innocent" Japanese maidens from his bath house, to save his blushes.

Yet this Western fantasy representation of Japan could not fail to come up against the rapid modernization taking place in the country. For many in the West, Japanese industrialization was viewed as flattering, as "less developed" people sought to emulate West society, characterized as a student seeking to imitate a master. Indeed, a

Western sense of superiority meant that a patronizing approach to the Japanese persisted during much of its development (Henning, 2000). The Japanese saw this very clearly, from their chagrin at the Western attitude to Japan as a playground for their fantasy games, through to the end of the 19th century, when Japanese intellectuals challenged Westerners about their belief in their superiority. The shock in the West of the success of Japanese "rapid" industrialization meant that they were persuaded by the new image of the Japanese constructed by Nitobe and other Japanese writers in English, in that the Japanese "soul" – very different to that of Westerners – was guided by the tenets of bushido. However, rather than seeing it in terms of a common chivalric heritage, bushido was interpreted as the source of a military threat to the West.

Notes

1 A Japanese-style name adopted by Frederik Blekman.
2 Ukiyo-e literally means "pictures of the floating world" but described a style of painting and woodblock print from the 17th to 19th century in Japan depicting aspects of life in Japan. The term "floating world" was a reference to the entertainment district of Edo (Tokyo).
3 http://webexhibits.org/vangogh/letter/18/511.htm
4 While literally meaning "family", it meant that Japanese aristocrats now used titles such as Count or Baron.
5 I have referred to the fourth edition, but the book was first published in 1890 and continued to the sixth edition in 1936.
6 Yamato is the old region of Japan that was adopted as a name for the country. See Appendix.
7 Narrative of the Earl of Elgin's mission to China and Japan in the years 1857, '58, '59. With illustrations from original drawings and photographs. By Laurence Oliphant, Private Secretary to Lord Elgin.
8 While literally meaning daughter, it was a term employed for a domestic or servant girl.
9 Fraser is relating the geisha to a type of courtesan of ancient Greece (the hetaira), acknowledging that both are the educated elite of courtesans, making a clear distinction between the geisha as a highly skilled entertainer from the uneducated tea-house girl.
10 The copy of this book presented by Professor and Mrs Kofoid to the University of California Library (available online) contains a dedication by the author with the statement: "This was written with my tongue in cheek, it was not intended to be serious literature merely the flippant juxtaposition of words". Certainly, Kumojima (2022) refers to it as a novel, and it is devoid of any detail of Japan, which suggests that the illustrative examples chosen here represent common images about Japan circulating in Britain at the time.
11 This is the 12th edition.

6

BANZAI

The west and the rising military power of Japan

In the late 19th century, an industrialized and modernized Japan entered the global stage as a rising military power. In 1876, Japan signed a treaty with Korea, shifting the outside influence in the country from China to Japan. The Ryukyu Islands were formally annexed in 1879, becoming the Okinawa Prefecture. The rivalry with China in Korea led to war in 1894, which the Japanese won, with China giving up all claims to Korea in the Shimonoseki Treaty of 1895, establishing Japanese dominance in the region. Japan also gained control of Taiwan. The Russian Empire took this opportunity to extend its influence into Manchuria (North-East China, north of Korea), and with the help of other European powers, forced Japan to give up the Liaotung Peninsula to Russia – much to its displeasure – which gave Russia jurisdiction over Port Arthur (Lüshun). At the same time, Britain (which already administered Hong Kong), France, Russia and Germany all took (leased[1]) territory from the Chinese government, giving them control of a number of Chinese ports. In 1901, an alliance of eight nations – six European powers, the United States and Japan – defeated Chinese attempts to expel the foreign powers (in the Boxer Rebellion), leaving China further weakened militarily. The 19th-century imperial "great game"[2] was being played out in China, with Japan now a "player" (Sibey, 2012).

The Western powers had not expected the Japanese to imitate them as a military power through their modernization, and began to express their concerns. In the aftermath of the Japanese victory over China in 1895, the German Kaiser Wilhelm II was alleged to have used the term "die gelbe Gefahr" (the yellow danger) to refer to the threat from the East to the Western powers, which was rendered into "the yellow peril" in English, a term that became common in the Western discourse about Japan (Shi, 2019; Keevak, 2011). While some Western nations, particularly Great

DOI: 10.4324/9781003082088-6

Britain, forged alliances with Japan in their mutual interest, a clash between Japan (from the south) and Russia (from the north) in Manchuria was inevitable. On 12 July 1900, the *London Times* newspaper published a letter from the former British diplomat in Japan Lord Redesdale (A.B. Mitford, the author of *Tales of Old Japan*. See Chapter 4), arguing against Japanese dominance in Manchuria. He accepted that Japan had "donned a veneer of Western Civilization", but the warrior spirit (yamato-damashii) remained in the Japanese. He claimed: "The national character of Japan is restless, ambitious, and aggressive in the highest degree". He counselled that Russian control, not Japanese, would be better for "civilization in the North of China" (Cortazzi, 2013, p. 703; Gubinskaya, 2020).

In 1903, the British Minister in China Sir Earnest Satow (who had spent many years as British Minister in Japan) wrote in his diary that Japan would not be recognized as a major power on the world stage until "it had crossed swords with an European power" (Kowner, 2001, p. 19). This came in the following year, with the Japanese surprise attack on Russian shipping in Port Arthur (without a declaration of war), followed by their victory in the resultant Russo-Japanese War of 1904–5, which caused shock in Europe at the time. Indeed, Kowner (2001, p. 31) argued that the prevailing stereotypes of the Japanese "played an important role in the Russo-Japanese War. [*Tsar*] Nicholas perceived the Japanese as feminine, weak, and racially inferior, a view that led him to underestimate the Japanese national character and military capability". Now Japan had shown itself to be superior militarily and strategically in a conflict with a Western power. Furthermore, the Japanese scrupulously followed the international conventions on the treatment of Russian prisoners, and in the treatment of casualties, which led to favourable reports of the Japanese military in the American and British press. The British Red Cross representative Ethel McCaul noted: "I had witnessed a treatment of their enemies which would reflect the greatest credit on any nation. The Russians were being treated as guests of the country, not mere prisoners of war" (Kowner, 2001, p. 31).

At the end of the war, US President Theodore Roosevelt brokered the Treaty of Portsmouth (in Kittery, Maine) in 1905. The United States was now the major Western "player" in the Pacific region. It had purchased Alaska in 1867, taken over the Philippines on winning the Spanish-American War in 1898, and annexed Hawaii in the same year. It had established a Pacific empire that now faced the Empire of Japan in the Pacific region. In 1905, the US Secretary of War Taft and Japanese Prime Minister Katsura discussed mutual concerns in the Western Pacific, and agreed that Japan would give up any interest in the Philippines to the Americans and the Americans would leave Korea to the Japanese – which was viewed as a betrayal by the Koreans, as it repudiated their 1882 treaty with the United States (Trani, 2014). While the Russians had to give up their interests in Manchuria and Korea, leaving Japan dominant in the region, the Japanese were denied war reparations from Russia which, in Japan, led to rioting in Tokyo, at the assumed weakness of the Japanese negotiators in the face of Western pressure (Kowner, 2006). In 1908,

Roosevelt established the Pearl Harbor Naval Shipyard in Hawaii, creating a military chain across the Pacific to the Philippines.

The effect of the Japanese victory over Russia was felt around the world. In South Africa, the lawyer Mohandas K. Gandhi wrote in his *Indian Opinion* newspaper, "so far and wide have the roots of Japanese victory spread that we cannot now visualize all the fruit it will put forth. The people of the East seem to be waking up from their lethargy" (Steinberg et al., 2005, p. 610). This sense of the Japanese "waking" had also been proffered by Japanese intellectual Kakuzo Okakura in his 1904 book *The Awakening of Japan*, written in English (while in Boston, United States) for a Western audience. He complained of the hypocrisy of the West.

> Until recently the West has never taken Japan seriously. It is amusing to find nowadays that such success as we have achieved in our efforts to take a place among the family of nations appears in the eyes of many as a menace to Christendom. . . . What sweeping condemnation, what absurd praise has not the world lavished on New Japan? We are both the cherished child of modern progress and a dread resurrection of heathendom – the Yellow Peril itself.
>
> *(K. Okakura, 1905, pp. 3–4)*

Okakura argued that Japan was not simply a follower of Western ideas, but he promoted its culture and civilization as distinct and important, rather than subordinate to the West. He claimed that there was no "yellow peril" but the problems in Asia were related to the involvement of the Western imperialists: a "white disaster" (K. Okakura, 1905). While the American Japanologist Sidney Gulick proposed a similar argument in *White Peril in the Far East* (1905) concerning the Russian-Japanese War, for many in the West, this academic analysis hardly troubled their thoughts. For example, as Nish (2011, p. 16) pointed out, at the time of the 1910 Japan-British Exhibition in London, one commentator noted that "The home-keeping Englishman has even yet nothing but a very hazy notion of the yellow man". However, as Nish (2011, p. 22) argued, they were now discovering that "Japan was no longer a Mikado-land, an idea which had been deep-rooted since 1885".

The perception of the Japanese in the aftermath of the First World War

Japan had sided with the Allies in the First World War, and declared war on Germany in 1914, allowing it to take over German islands in the North Pacific (including the Marshall Islands). At the end of the war, its delegates arrived at the Paris Peace Conference of 1919 seeking permanent control over their gains. However, the Western allies' view of Japan was mixed. Japan and Britain had signed a naval treaty in 1902 and Japan had honoured that treaty in assisting Britain to maintain control of its Pacific possessions. Crewdson (1915), in his book *Japan Our Ally*, praised the Japanese help in defending the dominions of Canada, Australia and

New Zealand. As a result, the British agreed to support the Japanese claims to the north Pacific islands (Meehan, 2014). But the crucial relationship for Japan was now with the United States in the Pacific. And the opening of Japan in 1853 had also resulted in Japanese emigrants joining their Asian neighbours in crossing the Pacific to seek work in America.

By the end of the First World War, in California, there was increasing concern about immigration from Japan (and China), with restrictions already put on land ownership and segregation in the schools. The Alien Land Law had been passed in 1913 (and later strengthened in 1920 and 1923) barring "foreign" land ownership (i.e. by immigrants denied citizenship on the basis of their "race") in an attempt to discourage further Japanese immigration. The American press (in particular that owned by William Randolph Hearst) sought to portray Japanese immigration as a "yellow peril", which threatened the American Pacific region (MacMillan, 2001). However, to the Japanese, the Paris Peace conference, and the founding of the League of Nations, was an opportunity to establish "racial equality" and change the Western view of Japan as a second-rate power. Importantly, this was not a demand for universal racial equality but for Japan to have equal status to the European powers and the United States, as "honorary whites" (Shimazu, 1989, p. 94). However, this was not something that the West were willing to agree to. Their British allies kept a back seat in the discussions to placate Australian Prime Minister Hughes, whose "White Australia" policy sought to keep out Asian immigrants (Bridge, 2011). The US President Woodrow Wilson was chair of the Commission deciding whether to include the Japanese proposed racial equality clause in the covenant of the new League of Nations. While originally sympathetic to Japanese demands, he was also acutely aware of the politics in his own country. In the Committee, he argued that the clause was unnecessary as it was clear that "everyone in the room knew that the League was based on the equality of nations" (MacMillan, 2001, p. 329). When the Japanese insisted on a vote, which carried, Wilson rejected this, on the basis that there were objections (i.e. the vote was not unanimous), and the clause was not included in the covenant. The outcome sent a strong message to the Japanese, who

> had shown themselves ready to participate in the international community, and yet they were still treated as inferiors. . . . [*This*] was to be an important factor . . . in turning Japan away from co-operation with the West and towards more aggressively nationalistic policies.
>
> *(MacMillan, 2001, pp. 329–30)*

Despite their failure on the equality clause, in the South Seas Mandate, the Japanese retained permanent control over the north Pacific Islands. This brought it into a dispute with the United States, who claimed that it had not assented to the Yap islands (in the Caroline Islands), being given to Japan, as in the Mandate. Yap was a hub of the cable system connecting the United States to the Philippines, and it was in American national interest to control the cables. In 1922, Japan agreed that not just on Yap but also on the mandated north Pacific Islands, American interests and property rights would be respected, which led to a reduction of tensions in the Pacific and the improvement of relations between the countries (Rattan, 1972). However, in California, the concerns about Japanese immigrants did not go away. Despite the Japanese government working with the Federal administration to limit Japanese immigration, a new Immigration Act passed through the US Congress in 1924 which excluded immigrants from Asia. A quota system, seeking to maintain a specific racial pattern of the country, now banned rather than restricted any new Japanese immigration into the United States. In signing the act into law, President Calvin Coolidge stated "America must be kept American" (Yuill, 2021, p. 12).

The response in Japan was one of outrage. It was argued that Japan should both militarize and turn away from the West, and focus its interests, and its expansion, in Asia (Hirobe, 2001). Beyond the damaging effect on US-Japanese relations, the law institutionalized race, rather than nationality, as the basis for US immigration. Specifically, it banned Japanese immigration to the United States "because they were deemed racially ineligible for citizenship" (Ngai, 1999, p. 72–3). Enshrined in the law was now the definition of the "white" race, the unassimilability of races, and the anti-miscegenation laws that maintained it. Crucially, it was argued "that Japanese cannot be Caucasian because they are not white" (Ngai, 1999, p. 84). Thus, 350 years after Europeans had first landed in Japan and decided that the Japanese were white, the United States enacted a law stating that they were definitely not.

Western perceptions of the Japanese in China

While the Great Depression dominated Western minds in the early 1930s, at times events in China, and the action of the Japanese Kwantung Army,[3] did reach the headlines. In 1931, the *New York Times*[4] reported an explosion near the Japanese-owned South Manchurian Railway line, with a Chinese claim that it had been contrived by the Japanese (known as the Mukden or Manchurian Incident), which led to the full-scale military take-over of Manchuria by the Kwantung Army. In 1932, the puppet state of Manchukuo was proclaimed. The Japanese took more and more control of the area, developing it economically to counteract their own depressed economy. Some Western newspapers sought to explain the incident as a dispute over the control of railways and China's claim that Manchuria was part of China.[5] The League of Nations set up a Commission of Inquiry led by the British politician, the Earl of Lytton, who travelled to the area to investigate the incident and its aftermath. The Lytton Report did not present a cause of what happened, but acknowledged the situation on the ground in terms of Japanese control in Manchuria. It put forward ten recommendations, mostly supportive of China's case (Kuhn, 1933). Subsequently, a widespread view emerged in the West that the Mukden Incident had indeed been staged by the Japanese as an excuse for their aggressive take-over of Manchuria (Chang, 2003). The US government stopped havering, and the US Secretary of State Henry

Stimson issued a statement, now known as the Stimson Doctrine, stating that territorial gains made outside of treaty agreements (i.e. through aggressive military action) will not be recognized (O'Mahoney, 2018). The League of Nations adopted the Stimson Doctrine on 11 March 1932, and on 25 March, Japan announced its withdrawal from the League.

The former Ambassador to Japan and Undersecretary of State William R. Castle claimed that the crisis in Manchuria was "war madness" on behalf of the Japanese military and "not on behalf of the Japanese people, who are among the finest in the world"[6] (Gripentrog, 2010, p. 248). Indeed, the *New York Times* reporter in Japan, Hugh Byas, was a key proponent of the distinction between what was happening in Manchuria and the moderate views of the Japanese back home (Gripentrog, 2010). However, the image of Japanese aggression dominated Western views of the Japanese with their attack on Nanking (Nanjing) in 1937. The *New York Times* (18 December 1937) splashed the headline "All captives slain. Civilians also killed as the Japanese spread terror in Nanking". The reporter F. Tillman Durdin, an eyewitness, wrote:

> Through wholesale atrocities and vandalism at Nanking the Japanese Army threw away a rare opportunity to gain the respect and confidence of the Chinese inhabitants and of foreign opinion there. . . . It was felt Japanese rule might be severe, at least until war conditions were over. Two days of Japanese occupation changed the whole outlook. Wholesale looting, the violation of women, the murder of civilians, the eviction of Chinese from their homes, mass execution of war prisoners . . . turned Nanking in a city of terror. . . . Just before boarding the ship for Shanghai the writer watched the execution of 200 men. . . . The men were lined against a wall and shot. Then a number of Japanese, armed with pistols, trod nonchalantly around the crumpled bodies, pumping bullets into any that were still kicking. . . . A large group of military spectators apparently greatly enjoyed the spectacle.

The horrors of the Nanking massacre resonated through the following decades. Buruma (2002, p. 5) noted:

> The Nanking Massacre was an atrocity on a huge scale. . . . In sheer inventiveness, the cruelty of the Japanese troops was on a par with the worst twentieth century barbarities, of which, as we know, there have been many.

Some later authors, such as Chang (1997) in *The Rape of Nanking*, argued that the massacre had been forgotten, and Japanese revisionists had sought to deny it. However, Buruma (2002) rejected both of these claims, arguing that the Nanking Massacre remained in the Western mind as an image of Japanese militarism that would have effects on the later American engagement with the Japanese at the end of the Pacific War (see the reference to the Tokyo Trials further); an enduring image of the Japanese "warrior" that now was overlaid with cruelty and callousness.

While the actions of the Kwantung Army in Manchuria were criticized in the West, with its sympathies for the Chinese, actions such as the Stimson Doctrine had no influence on the Japanese in the military takeover and colonization of Manchuria. However, as the Japanese expanded north, it encountered Soviet Russia and its Mongolian allies. This time the situation was very different to 1904. While there had been a series of border clashes since 1935, matters came to a head in the Nomonhan Incident of 1939, or more properly described, the Battles of Khalkhin Gol, which involved over 100,000 combatants. The "mighty" Kwantung army faced the Russian and Mongolian troops, but this time the Soviet commander, Georgy Zhukov, had a well-planned strategy, and his successful use of artillery, fighter planes and especially tanks – techniques he would later use effectively against the Germans – defeated the Japanese Army. Unlike the Nanking Massacre, the Nomonhan Incident did not have Western newspaper reporters on the spot, and it has remained obscure to the Western public.[7] However, it has been argued (Goldman, 2012) that it had a significant impact on the Second World War. The Soviet Union, having secured its eastern border, could now turn to Europe. It signed the Molotov-Ribbentrop Pact with Nazi Germany, and followed the Germans in invading Poland, carving up the country between them, the day after the victory at Nomonhan. For the Japanese, blocked in their expansion in the West, their focus now turned east – and to the Pacific – as the Second World War began in Europe.

The representation of the Japanese during the Pacific War

With the defeat of France by Nazi Germany in 1940, the Japanese occupied French Indochina (Vietnam), which restricted the supply routes to the Chinese resistance to the Japanese invasion. In the same year, the United States, concerned about the Japanese expansion into Asia, put an embargo on oil supplies to Japan. While there were expectations of war, what followed produced shockwaves in the West. The Japanese attack on Pearl Harbor on 7 December 1941 will remain forever in the American psyche – "a date which will live in infamy" as US President Franklin D. Roosevelt put it – an attack that took place while the Japanese special envoy was still seeking to negotiate an agreement in Washington, and without a declaration of war (Rosenberg, 2003). Nearly 200 Japanese airplanes destroyed 200 US ships, 300 airplanes of the Pacific Fleet but crucially no aircraft carriers (which were elsewhere), and killed more than 2,400 people. "Well, it's finally come", commented the editor of the Osage Press, Iowa,

> that war with Japan we middle-aged ones have for forty years been hearing must some day happen; and it has come with a deceitful treachery that bears out what we in boyhood used to read about the tricky Japs in the pulp-magazine thrillers.
> *(Petersen, 1942, p. 38)*

Within the next twenty-four hours, Japan successfully attacked the American Philippines, British Hong Kong and the Dutch East Indies (Indonesia), the latter a major source of oil.

The shock of these first attacks was not simply that they took place before a declaration of war, but that they signalled a series of Japanese victories over Western nations. The Japanese were sweeping through the Asian colonies of the West; including the fall of British Singapore in February 1942, which was viewed as a humiliation for the British Empire (Farrell, 2017). By May, British troops had retreated from Burma under the Japanese assault. In March 1942, President Franklin D. Roosevelt ordered General Douglas MacArthur, the commander of the US forces in the Far East to leave the Philippines[8] before its fall to the Japanese in May, one of their worse defeats in US history. In the West, the question was proposed: How was it possible to be defeated by a Japanese military viewed in the West as "scrawny, near-sighted, poorly trained and equipped"? (Johnson, 1991, p. 19). Ferris (1993) argued that some military analysts in the West did have a reasonable estimate of Japanese military strength, but the dominant view of the Japanese was influenced by racism and related ideas of the Japanese character, as inferior to the Western soldier. Indeed, increasingly derogatory racial representations of the Japanese were to dominate the Western view of them during the war (Dower, 1986).

The forced march of Filipino and American prisoners after the Battle of Bataan (Philippines) in 1942 to a Japanese prison camp was called the Bataan Death March due to the cruel treatment by the Japanese guards. The use of prisoners in the building of the Burma-Thailand Railway, known as the Death Railway, resulted in tens of thousands of deaths of Allied prisoners of war (POWs) (Houghton, 2014; Havers, 2003). Towle (1975) argued that the stark difference between the Japanese treatment of Russian prisoners in 1904–5 and their treatment of prisoners in the 1930s and 1940s was related to societal changes in Japan, the rejection of Western values and the harshness of the Japanese military code during this period. However, the cruel treatment of Allied prisoners of war by the Japanese was viewed in the West as proof that the Japanese were ruthless and uncaring. Havers (2003) analysed a variety of experiences of Allied soldiers held as Japanese POWs, and points out that the common Western view was that "Allied POWs were beaten, starved and worked to death by their Japanese captors, for whom the very idea of surrender was abhorrent and alien". To which he adds: "To a large extent this apparent simplification is a more than adequate description" (Havers, 2003, p. 2).

In February 1942, President Roosevelt – with public support – signed an order to have all Japanese-Americans living in the West coast region, mostly in California – over 100,000 persons – relocated to internment camps away from the coast. Explanations for the internment were based on the view that the Japanese-Americans were not to be trusted, and might act treacherously, at the risk of American security (Nagata, 1990). Lieutenant General John L. De Witt, commander of the Western Defence, opined that it was not possible to be Japanese and American: "the Japanese race is the enemy race" and "racial strains are undiluted" by American acculturation (Wu, 2002, p. 53). In a climate where California, and the American government, had supported a "yellow peril" ideology with respect to Japanese immigration, there was little criticism of the policy of Japanese internment at the time, despite the fact that German and Italian Americans were not interned despite the Axis powers fighting the Allies in Europe (Renteln, 1995).

Westerners sought to find the factors that had led to the shocking (to them) success of the Japanese military. The British university teacher, John Morris, had lived in Japan between October 1938 and December 1941, and on his return to England, he wrote *Traveller from Tokyo*, published in 1943[9] (Morris, 1945). He identified three features in explanation. The first was Emperor worship. In a chapter entitled "The Japanese Mentality", he wrote:

> The outward signs by which the Emperor's divinity is proclaimed are many and various. . . . Every school and university in Japan has a photograph of the Emperor, and in a fire or any other calamity this portrait must at all costs be saved. There are cases on record when a school principal has lost his life in attempting to save the Imperial photograph; or, having failed in his attempt, has committed suicide.
>
> *(pp. 49–50)*

The second was nationalism, rooted in the Japanese education system: "elementary education in Japan has become extremely nationalistic" (p. 51), with children taught "to worship the armed forces, and told that the greatest honour is to die in battle" (p. 127). "Many [*violent reactionaries*] have received a western education and are nationalistic almost to the point of insanity; they understand the necessity for a close study of the West, but only as a means of destroying it" (p. 51). Finally, the third feature was the harsh discipline in the Japanese army. "The Japanese idea of discipline is based on fear; the soldier is taught not to think but only to obey" (p. 135). Morris stated that on joining the Japanese army, "the first thing that he [*the recruit*] is taught is that he must look upon dying as a duty" (p. 133). Morris went on to explain that this was why Japanese soldiers returning to civilian life or taken as prisoners feel a sense of shame, but he argued: "The sentiment has often been described as fanaticism; but it equally deserves the name of bravery". (He also pointed out that some of his students did not wish to join the army and had committed suicide rather than doing so.) Morris concluded that the Japanese had tricked the West into underestimating their true military strength; yet he was convinced that the Western allies could defeat the Japanese army, but: "It will go on fighting until the bitter end" (p. 140).

Western wartime propaganda presented the Japanese soldiers as fanatics, dedicated to the Emperor, and fighting with a savage ruthlessness in obedience to a military "death cult", linked to a construction of bushido, associated with unquestioning loyalty and nationalistic fervour that resulted in soldiers' willingness to give up their lives rather than surrender (Trefalt, 2004). Trefalt argued that attributing the characteristic of fanaticism to the Japanese soldiers implied that their behaviour was "robot-like" and hence dehumanized them. This representation of the Japanese was aligned with "the pseudo-scientific academic discourses that gave the

Japanese national character the attributes of childishness, mental illness, inferiority complexes, neuroses, abnormality and so on" (Trefalt, 2004, p. 34). The image of the fanatical and treacherous "Jap" now became a feature of Western popular culture, such as in the animation *Japoteurs*, 1942, with Superman uncovering a Japanese plot to steal a new bomber, or in 1943, *Action Comics* (no. 58), which has a cover image of Superman printing posters with a slapping hand next to a typical caricature of a bespectacled and buck-toothed Japanese soldier's face, with the caption: "Superman says you can slap a Jap with war bonds and stamps!" (Gutierrez, 2019). Popular songs had titles such as "We're Gonna Have to Slap the Dirty Little Jap", "You're a Sap, Mister Jap" and "Mow the Japs Down" (Koppes and Black, 1987, p. 251).

The hard-fought battles of the Coral Sea (May 1942), Midway (June 1942) and Guadalcanal (August 1942 to February 1943) turned the tide for the American forces in the Pacific. During the Guadalcanal campaign, the flamboyant Vice-Admiral Halsey was appointed the naval commander in the South Pacific, which had an immediate effect of raising morale (Dillard, 1997). Halsey described his mission at a Press Conference in a phrase that became the battle cry of the American troops, and was painted on a large sign at the boat landing at Tulagi (Solomon Islands), stating: Admiral Halsey says: "Kill Japs, kill Japs, and keep on killing Japs!" Halsey's most frequent description of the Japanese was "yellow bastards" (Dower, 1986). Journalist John Hersey who reported on the Guadalcanal campaign wrote in his book *Into the Valley*, 1944, that, unlike the marines, the Japanese seemed comfortable in the jungle, using all sorts of tricks to disguise their presence. This added to the view that the Japanese were animal-like, and devoid of humanity. As the Americans fought them across the Pacific, the term "monkey" became a popular way of referring to them (Dower, 1986; Trefalt, 2004). Dower (1986, p. 85) gives an example of

> a witticism that the New Yorker carried to its upper-class readership in cartoon form late in 1942 and Reader's Digest reproduced for its own huge audience soon after. It portrayed white riflemen lying in firing position in a dense jungle, where the trees were full of monkeys along with several Japanese snipers. "Careful now", one white soldier is saying to another, "– only those in uniform".

In the Hollywood movie *Guadalcanal Diary* (1943) the Japanese are

> described as apes and monkeys who hide in trees and use unfair tactics to lure unsuspecting Americans to their death. When Nolan [*the tough veteran sergeant*] is asked how he feels about killing people, he replies: "Well, it's kill or be killed – besides they ain't people".
>
> *(Koppes and Black, 1987, p. 260)*

Hence, the animal-hunting metaphor was frequently used in the description of fighting the Japanese. A common send-off was "Good luck and good hunting", alongside descriptions such as "flushing out" the enemy, which was extended to the image of the enemy as "vermin [*that*] must be exterminated" (Dower, 1986, p. 90).

Eventually, American firepower began to dominate the battles, with Japanese positions destroyed by weapons of massive destructive power.

> "It gave me a beautiful feeling", [*an American soldier*] wrote, "to see such a display of might and to know this is only a fraction of the power America possesses". He also confessed to "a feeling of satisfaction to know that little yellow men are in there taking the brunt of this – a part payment for some of the suffering and agony they have caused".
>
> *(Schrijvers, 2010, p. 248)*

In October 1944, a triumphant General MacArthur waded ashore on Leyte Island in the Philippines and uttered his famous phrase "I have returned". Yet it was also in the Battle of Leyte that the first *kamikaze* fighters appeared: Japanese pilots willing to kill themselves by deliberately flying their planes into Allied ships in the hope of causing maximum damage. In the Battle of Okinawa (April to June 1945), there were 1,900 kamikaze attacks leading to 36 ships sunk and 102 damaged, causing nearly half of all the destruction to US seaborne forces (Timenes, 1970). The appearance of the kamikaze pilots confirmed the worst fears about the fanatical Japanese in Western thinking. Even worse, in Okinawa, the Japanese co-opted school children to fight, and civilians were willing to commit suicide rather than surrender. Despite the victory, the high toll of American casualties and the very large number of Japanese dead led to concerns that the planned invasion of Japan would be opposed by every Japanese man, woman and child in the country (Fussell, 1981; Johnson, 1991). This fear that the fanaticism of the Japanese would make the invasion extremely costly in terms of American lives led to the decision to drop the atomic bomb on Japan (Miscamble, 2011).

One day after a successful demonstration of the atomic bomb, in July 1945, the US President Truman met with British Prime Minister Churchill and the Soviet leader Stalin at Potsdam. They issued a declaration to the Japanese government demanding unconditional surrender, but with an offer to choose their own form of government. If refused, the declaration promised "prompt and utter destruction" (Walker, 2004, p. 71). The Japanese refused. On 6 August 1945, an atomic bomb was dropped on Hiroshima and, three days later, on Nagasaki. Japan surrendered. After the war, Truman claimed that his decision to drop the atomic bomb on Japan not only ended the war swiftly but saved half a million American lives (Bernstein, 1999). Bernstein (1986) has argued that this is a post-war myth, with 40,000 deaths a more realistic figure of the estimates prior to the bombings. However, at the time, the dropping of the bombs was welcomed in the United States, especially by those soldiers who had fought in Okinawa (Fussell, 1981; Sledge, 1981).

The Chrysanthemum rather than the Sword

The American Occupation of Japan began on 2 September 1945, and lasted until 28 April 1952. Its main purpose was to demilitarize Japan – including disbanding the armed forces of six million people – and create new institutional structures which would deny any possibility of future Japanese military aggression (Ward and Sakamoto, 1987). This was crucial, as the "warrior" aspect of Japanese culture (and seen as part of the Japanese character) had emerged so strongly in the first half of the 20th century. Ruth Benedict with her book *The Chrysanthemum and the Sword* – see Chapter 1 – gave anthropological significance to the idea of a contradiction within the Japanese character: between the mild-mannered, polite, artistically minded aspect, which engaged in flower arranging, gardening, and arts and crafts – *the Chrysanthemum* – and the fanatical, emotionless aspect, devoid of mercy for the "damaged" (wounded), with a dedication to the Emperor, and duty, following the "way of the warrior" (bushido) rooted in their culture (and character) that meant they were willing to give up their lives to avoid shame (the greatest of all human failings) – *the Sword*. It was this "warrior" aspect of the Japanese character and culture that now had to be suppressed. From the work of Benedict, it was argued that the occupation should create a new Japanese democratic political context within which the ultra-nationalistic warrior aspect of the Japanese character could never arise again, and the mild-mannered, polite Japanese would be the norm (Dower, 1999). Thus, the Emperor was not tried for war crimes but stripped of his "divinity" and kept as a figurehead (echoing his position from before the restoration), former Japanese leaders were tried in the Tokyo Trials,[10] and executed or imprisoned. The American administrators wrote a new Japanese constitution, including the now well-known section on women's rights written by Beate Sirota Gordon, and set up democratic institutions to bring this about (Gordon, 2014). Also, it was in the United States' interest to suppress any communist sentiments where possible, as the Cold War with the Soviet Union had begun. Perpetual non-aggression was enshrined in the new constitution, denying the Japanese the use of armed forces, as they were not trusted to wage war again (Buruma, 2002).

One of the most enduring images of the occupation that appeared in the Western media was that of American soldiers in their jeeps handing out chocolate and chewing gum to smiling Japanese children amongst the devastation of Tokyo (Dower, 1999, p. 72). The American soldiers, with their image of the fanatical "Jap", were surprised at these smiling children and polite Japanese citizens, and a new image of the Japanese arose in the West, that of a people "embracing defeat" (Dower, 1999); subservient to the conquerors and friendly and helpful.[11] American soldiers turned into tourists, seeking souvenirs to take back home, trying Japanese food (such as *sukiyaki*, beef stew), and fraternizing with the Japanese (despite restrictions on doing so). In the desperate poverty of a destroyed country, the Japanese on the receiving end of American generosity – often young women – found it gave them some respite from the harshness of their lives. This fraternization only increased with the relaxing of restrictions. However, with the outbreak of the Korean War in 1950, Japan became the centre of rest and recreation (R&R) for American soldiers. The Korean War was a further opportunity for the American administration to suppress the Japanese communists and increase its influence in Japan (Dower, 1999). The Occupation formally ended in April 1952.

In the 1950s, the US government wanted to represent Japan in a way that echoed the situation after the arrival of Commodore Perry, with a poor Japan learning from the West that helps it create a modern (Western-style) society. Indeed, it was the United States which was financing Japanese reconstruction and, with the increasing fears of communism during the Cold War, there was a need for Japan to be located amongst the friendly, democratic, capitalist nations. As Mettler (2018) argued, it was important for the American government to make Japan safe for the American public. In the 1954 film, *The Bridges of Toko-Ri* – based on a James Michener novel – set in the Korean War, the main character Lieutenant Harry Brubaker (William Holden) comes out of retirement to lead a bombing raid in Korea, but, relaxing in Japan with his wife (Grace Kelly) and family, they inadvertently share an *onsen* (hot spring) with a Japanese family where awkwardness turns to friendship. Also, Mickey Rooney – playing the light relief – portrays a helicopter pilot whose Japanese girlfriend leaves him for another American. Thus, a positive image of Japan, and American-Japanese relations, was contrasted with the war in Korea.

One of the most powerful images of the Japanese, which helped suppress the Western wartime representation of the fanatical Japanese, was a love story of a Western man and a Japanese woman. James Michener's novel *Sayonara* (1953–4) became a best-seller in the United States, and influenced the popular image of the Japanese, especially when it was made into a film, starring Marlon Brando and Miiko Taka, in 1957. The protagonist, twenty-eight-year-old Major Lloyd Gruver, is a flying ace of the Korean War, and has a glittering military career before him. His girlfriend, the beautiful, Vassar-educated Eileen, is the child of a general, just like him. Yet, when he feels the pressure of marriage from Eileen's mother, he questions his love for her, and thinks of his own parents who he knows did not marry for love. Now based in Japan, he exhibits the casual denigration of Japan and the Japanese, typical at the time. He cannot understand why so many American soldiers have Japanese girlfriends, telling a colleague: "They're all so dumpy and round-faced. How can our men – good average guys – how can they marry these yellow girls?" (Michener, 1970, p. 11). Yet he agrees to be the best man of Airman Joe Kelly from his unit, who is desperate to marry his Japanese girlfriend Katsumi, despite the regulations against it. When shown a picture of Katsumi, Gruver dismisses her as "one of the millions of girls who could never be pretty, who did all the heavy work and who dressed as if the only clothes in Japan were made from old flour sacks" (Michener, 1970, p. 16). However, he begins to question his view of Japanese women and acknowledges that his friend Mike's Japanese girlfriend is beautiful. She works at the Takarazuka[12] all-girl theatre troupe, and he sees them perform *Swing Butterfly*, a pantomime version of *Madame Butterfly*, where he feels uncomfortable at the mocking of Americans by the lead male-role performer, a woman of his own age called Hana-ogi, playing Lieutenant Pinkerton as "arrogant, ignorant and ill-mannered" (Michener, 1970, p. 84). Yet when Gruver sees her again, he falls madly in love with her and, with Joe and Mike's help, he is able to meet her. Despite knowing nothing of each other's language, they begin a relationship and share a house. Gruver's view of Japanese women changes radically:

> I concluded that no man could comprehend women until he had known the women of Japan with their unbelievable combination of unremitting work, endless suffering and boundless warmth – just as I could never have known even the outlines of love had I not lived in a little house where I sometimes drew back the covers of my bed upon the floor to see there the slim golden body of the perpetual woman. I now understood why ten thousand American soldiers had braved the fury of their commanders and their country to marry such women.
>
> *Michener (1970, p. 128)*

Crucially, for Gruver, his lover is no longer "yellow" but her skin has become "golden", and now, for him, a Japanese woman represents the perfect woman. Despite his passionate desire to marry her and return with her to the United States, he has to accept that anti-Japanese sentiments would destroy their careers and happiness. Hana-ogi knows that their marriage is impossible, telling him "Because I know you, now I better Japanese. You better American" (Michener, 1970, p. 194). Finally, accepting that they must part, Gruver sadly says *sayonara* (goodbye) to his lover and all the things he loves in Japan. And then he leaves, with Eileen driving them to the airport. Michener (who married a Japanese woman), like the Western men who had married Japanese women fifty years earlier, such as Hearn and Holland (see Chapter 5), presented the Japanese woman as an archetypical woman – in contrast to their anxieties about the more emancipated Western woman. Michener, however, admitted his anxiety about American women, with their ambitions and potential to humiliate men, which he contrasted with the "secret" of the Japanese woman "who just simply loved" their man (Michener, 1970, p. 55). Michener indicated that it is this secret that made the Japanese embrace her "feminine mystique"[13] and be the perpetual woman (to American men such as Gruver). However, when the married couples returned to the United States, the American husbands found their Japanese wives did not always share their image of domestic bliss, and were not the obedient, submissive women that they had imagined (Storrs, 2000).

In the 1950s, this romantic representation of the Japanese woman, combined with a revitalized American interest in traditional aspects of Japanese culture, suppressed the image of the (male) wartime Japanese fanatic and (to some extent) returned the Western image of the Japanese to a feminized, ancient – mysterious Eastern – Orientalist representation, from whom Westerners might learn to enhance in their everyday lives (Shibusawa, 2006). Thus, during the depths of the Cold War, Japan could be viewed as a close Western ally, with the fears of its militarism and nationalism consigned to an aberrant period of its past (Mettler, 2018). Books on Japan in the West promoted traditional crafts, such as the cultivation of Japanese *bonsai* trees and flower arranging (*ikebana*). In 1956, Ellen Gordon Allen set up Ikebana International, an organization devoted to promoting the Japanese art of flower arranging internationally. The Japanese way of everyday life – viewed in terms of the spirit of Japan – once more fascinated the West.

In 1955, the Beat poet Gary Snyder spent a year learning about Zen Buddhism in Japan, funded by the First Zen Institute of America. In turn, he was to influence his fellow Beat, the writer Jack Kerouac, who in 1958 mixed Zen with his critique of American consumer society, in his book *Dharma Bums*.

> Dharma Bums refusing to subscribe to the general demand that they consume production and therefore have to work for the privilege of consuming, all that crap they didn't really want anyway such as refrigerators, TV sets, cars, at least new fancy cars, certain hair oils and deodorants and general junk you finally always see a week later in the garbage anyway, all of them imprisoned in a system of work, produce, consume, work, produce, consume,
>
> *(Kerouac, 1972, p. 72)*

He proposed an image of Zen unlike anything that was actually happening in Japan, with its drive for economic power. Alan Watts, in *The Way of Zen*, 1957, had sought to bring the wisdom of the Zen masters to the West, noting:

> Since the Second World War this interest [*in Zen Buddhism*] has increased so much that it seems to be becoming a considerable force in the intellectual and artistic world of the West. It is connected, no doubt, with the prevalent enthusiasm for Japanese culture which is one of the constructive results of the late war.
>
> *(Watts, 1957, p. 6)*

In the following year, Watts ("a leading U.S. exponent of Zen", according to *Time* magazine[14]), felt the need to distinguish "the underlying protestant lawlessness of beat Zen" (professed by Kerouac) with the square Zen "of established tradition in Japan with its clearly defined hierarchy, its rigid discipline and its specific tests of *satori*"[15] (Watts, 1973, pp. 103–4). Watts, while presenting the differences, also sought to see the positive in both ways of viewing Zen, arguing that "the atmosphere of Zen is free from all one's unpleasant childhood associations" with Christianity (Watts, 1973, 109). Watts had set the groundwork for the ongoing interest in Japanese Zen that would also be a focus in the American counterculture of the 1960s (see Chapter 7).

The Japanese "way" began to influence other aspects of American society. The editor of *House Beautiful* magazine in the United States, Elizabeth Gordon, had been critical of the Western international styles of architecture and design, by modernists such as Le Courbusier, but she found it difficult to find a clear Western definition of beauty. She found her answer in Japan, with the concept of *shibui*, translated as simple elegance, which she learnt about from designers and architects on trips to Japan. In the August 1960 edition of the magazine, the cover proclaimed "Discover *shibui* the word for the highest level in beauty" (Penick, 2017, p. 203). She contrasted the beautiful design of objects in daily use in the Japanese house with the cheap Japanese products available in the United States (see Chapter 7), and sparked a fashion for American shibui in design, that she had learnt from the Japanese aesthetic of simplicity and imperfection. As well as shibui being a design aesthetic in middlebrow American homes, "In its postwar American context, the 'shibui' aesthetic primarily helped reinforce the 'chrysanthemum' image of Japan" (Mettler, 2018, p. 11).

The rehabilitation of Japan in the Western mind was finally complete with the 1964 Olympics in Tokyo, with Western television viewers seeing a modern city, totally rebuilt less than twenty years after its complete destruction. Visitors could travel on the "bullet train" (the *shinkansen*) or take the monorail from the international airport to central Tokyo (Abel, 2012). As well as displaying their new technological achievements, the Japanese demonstrated their hospitality to foreign visitors which the *New York Times* reported "is helping project the friendly image for which Japan has been yearning in the years since World War II" (Abel, 2012, p. 216). The Olympic Games were very successful, both in terms of their organization and in representing Japan to the world as a peaceful and internationalist nation at the forefront of the modern world. Its wartime military aggression was absent from the message of peace, with the horrors of the nuclear strikes on Hiroshima and Nagasaki brought to the fore, with the final bearer of the Olympic torch being born on the day the Hiroshima bomb struck. The Olympic Games were accompanied by an exhibition of traditional Japanese arts and crafts. Japan was presented as a forward-looking modern peaceful country built on its traditions, with its wartime aggression now positioned as an aberration to be mostly ignored (Droubie, 2011).

However, the role of the Japanese in the Pacific War was relived in numerous films, books and comics in the popular culture of the West in the years following the end of the war, along with the numerous academic accounts by historians. The famous films, *From Here to Eternity*, the winner of the Best Picture at the Oscars of 1953, portraying the attack on Pearl Harbor, and the 1957 film *The Bridge on the River Kwai*, also a Best Picture Oscar winner, showing the lives of POWs building the Death Railway, showed the treacherous and heartless wartime Japanese military in technicolour detail. Combatants in the Pacific War wrote their accounts of the bloody hard-fought victories over the Japanese, such as US marines Robert Leckie's *Helmet for My Pillow* (1957) and later E.B. Sledge's *With the Old Breed: At Peleliu and Okinawa* (1981). Indeed, the Pacific War continued to be a rich source of material for the numerous war comics that were produced in the United States and Britain, for a Western audience. In 1961, the publisher DC Thompson introduced a new comic into Britain, called *Commando*, where the Second World War continued to be fought, with the "Japs" a constant threat. Issue number 48, from December 1962, featured a full-colour image on the front of two samurai-sword-wielding, camouflaged Japanese soldiers bursting out of the jungle with a cry of *Banzai! Banzai! Banzai!* with the words emblazoned in red across the cover, with the following text underneath: "when their savage war-cry rang through the jungle, it was every man for himself".[16]

The Sword and the Chrysanthemum

The Western image of the Japanese in the first half of the 20th century was dominated by the Japanese military. At the start of the century, in a West dominated by representations of the Japanese as the child-like denizens of fairy land, making arts and crafts in medieval villages, the Japanese victory over Russia in 1905 came as something of a shock. Yet for fifty years, Japan had been assisted by the West in its development into a modern industrialized power. The Japanese, as "students" of the West, had sought to join the community of Western imperial nations, such as by signing the Anglo-Japanese Alliance, in 1902, with Great Britain (which was still the largest economic power in the world, before being overtaken by the United States in the following decade). It was developing its own empire on the Asian mainland, and had defeated a European power (Russia) suggesting, as Satow noted earlier, that now it had achieved all of the qualifications to be "recognized as a major power on the world stage" (i.e. join the community of Western imperial nations). It had also demonstrated its honourable treatment of defeated Europeans (Russian prisoners) in the war of 1904–5.

Yet rather than acknowledging Japanese Westernization, and Japan as a modern Westernized nation – a new member of the imperial "club" – two alternative representations of the Japanese dominated the popular Western image of them. On the one hand was a representation that attempted to disregard their industrialization, as a regrettable loss of Old Japan: a view that tourists adopted, like Isabella Bird, looking for the "real" Japan (see Chapter 5), meaning an idealized "medieval" society, a Mikado-land, where they could act out their fantasies of Old Japan while patronizing the inhabitants. On the other hand was the awareness of Japan's rapid industrialization but now this was accompanied by an anxiety about the "yellow peril", a racist discourse in the West that was employed to exclude the Japanese from the community of "major powers". It was no surprise therefore that Kakuzo Okakura (1905, p. 95) wrote:

> To most Eastern nations the advent of the West has been by no means an unmixed blessing. Thinking to welcome the benefits of increased commerce, they have become the victims of foreign imperialism; believing in the philanthropic aims of Christian missionaries, they have bowed before the messengers of military aggression. For them the earth is no longer filled with that peace which pillowed their contentment. If the guilty conscience of some European nations has conjured up the specter of a Yellow Peril, may not the suffering soul of Asia wail over the realities of the White Disaster.

Japanese intellectuals, such as the Okakura brothers, sought to change the Western perception of the Japanese by writing in English, with Nitobe's tract on bushido the most popular. While it did conjure up the image of the Zen-following, chivalrous samurai, whose values were appealing to many in the West (such as President Theodore Roosevelt and Robert Baden-Powell), it did not result in the perception in the West of a common chivalric heritage. Both in Japan, and in the West, the invention of bushido, as Benesch (2014) has shown, was used for different purposes, but essentially to represent the Japanese and Westerners as fundamentally different. In Japan, nationalists employed the concept of bushido as representative of the nation with their military and imperialist goals. In the West, bushido was combined with the "yellow peril" rhetoric to represent the Japanese in the construction of a fanatical other, to be kept in check rather than treated as an equal member of the community of civilization nations. The actions of the League of Nations after the First World War simply entrenched these positions.

The horrific massacre of Chinese civilians by the Japanese military in Nanking in 1937, the shocking attack on Pearl Harbor, the appalling treatment of Allied POWs and the self-destruction of the kamikaze pilots were all aspects of Japanese behaviour that required explanation in the West. For Benedict (1947, p. 101), the answer lay in an "alien" Japanese culture (see Chapter 1). Despite acknowledging the modern construction of bushido, she does not interrogate other aspects of pre-war Japanese society in the same way. For example, in employing the concept of *on* (a "limitless devotion"), she says:

> Every kamikaze pilot of a suicide plane was, they said, repaying his Imperial *on*; all the troops who, they claimed, died to a man defending some island of the Pacific were said to be discharging their limitless *on* to the Emperor.

Yet, this view of *on* was argued to be a modern construction, promoted by the Japanese military in the 1930s after the Manchurian Incident (Ryang, 2002). Critically, Benedict generalizes from the extreme nationalistic ideology of the Japanese military (the dominant power in pre-war and wartime Japan) to Japanese culture more generally (Ryang, 2002). Yet we know from Morris (1945) that there were students who preferred to die rather than join the army, and from Ohnuki-Tierney (2007) that kamikaze pilots were forced to "volunteer", rather than choosing a suicide-mission for their Emperor. The pre-war "moderate views" (according to the *New York Times*) may have been silenced in wartime but the holders of these views were Japanese too.

We can compare the interpretation of the actions of the military in the Japanese state (between 1932 and 1945) with the Nazi party in the German state (1933–1945). Yet the explanation of the atrocities of the latter have typically been attributed to the Nazi ideology in a particular time and context of German history (e.g. Weinstein, 1980), rather than a generalization to all the Germans, or German culture, with the concept of the "good German" commonly being contrasted with the Nazi in post-war literature about wartime Germans (e.g. Dochartaigh and Schönfeld, 2013). Hence, Benedict's attempts to attribute Japanese military wartime behaviour to cultural causes may result from her initial claim that the Japanese were "the most alien" enemy – a claim that would not have been made about Europeans (i.e. Germans). In seeking to explain the Japanese in terms of character and culture, Benedict ignored aspects of the historical context to Japanese wartime militarism and nationalism, particularly its imperial ambitions and colonial activities in Asia that preceded it (Ryang, 2002). However, as a codicil, it is worth noting that Harry Emerson Wildes, who worked for the Occupation, agreed that the goal of the Occupation was to make sure that Japanese ultranationalism could never return, but said that Benedict's work was ignored. "The occupationnaires preferred and trusted unskilled and undiscriminating folk who saw all things American as glistening white, all things Japanese as jet black or blood red" (Wildes, 1954, p. 2).

Consequently, it can be argued that the surprise that the post-war Japanese were amenable, mild-mannered and polite people (rather than the wartime fanatics) resulted from the conflicting Western representations of the Japanese, rather than the character of the Japanese themselves. Furthermore, a new democratic-friendly image of the Japanese was crucial to the American government in its attempts to fight communism globally, and in Japan, with the United States funding much of the reconstruction of Japanese industry post-war to create a capitalist economy. Hence, throughout the 1950s, the representation of a Japan based on Zen philosophy, but one that influenced household product design (shibui) rather than one that challenged capitalism (Elizabeth Gordon rather than Jack Kerouac), suited the American government's political goals. The surprise that Japan had emerged phoenix-like to produce the modern, technological, international Tokyo, which hosted the 1964 Olympic Games, may reflect the lack of focus of the Western media on Japan post-war, and the enduring memories of the Second World War, acted out by Western children, and in Western popular culture (such as in comics of the 1960s) portraying the Japanese as fanatical soldiers, forever crying "banzai!"

Notes

1 These leases were obtained in the context of a military threat.
2 A term to describe the political and diplomatic power struggle between the European imperial powers at this time.
3 The Japanese army formed to support its interests in China, especially Manchuria.
4 Report by Hugh Byas in the *New York Times*, 19 September 1931.
5 Such as the British Manchester Guardian, 16 November 1931.
6 *New York Times*, 1 February 1932.
7 Although, in 1997, the Western readers of the translation of Haruki Murakami's novel *The Wind-up Bird Chronicle*, 1994, may have been intrigued to read about it.
8 Arriving in Australia, MacArthur uttered the famous "I shall return".
9 Page numbers are given from the 1945 edition, listed in References.
10 International Military Tribunal for the Far East (1946–48). Amongst those hanged was General Matsui, who had been in charge of the Japanese troops in Nanjing in 1937.

11 This is not to deny the presence of criminal gangs in post-war Japan, but smiling children receiving candy at the hands of the GIs was a more common image in the Western media.
12 Jennifer Robertson's 1998 book *Takarazuka* gives the history of the group.
13 A term invented by Betty Friedan in her 1963 book critical of the assumption that women gained fulfilment through the traditional caring role of women in American society, which heralded the second wave feminist movement in the United States.
14 *Time* magazine, "Religion: Zen: Beat & Square", 21st July 1958.
15 The Japanese word *satori* can be translated as enlightenment, awareness or understanding.
16 A key difference between the image of the Japanese in this comic and the Japanese in wartime propaganda is that they no longer wear glasses or have buckteeth: https://commandocomics.fandom.com/wiki/Banzai!_Banzai!_Banzai!

7

MADE IN JAPAN

The makers of "cheap imitations"[1]

The reconstruction of the Japanese economy after the Second World War began under the financial and political umbrella of the United States. In the American media, Japan was patronized in a similar way to its 19th-century modernization, as needing to learn the ways of the West, in terms of democracy, and capitalism, an American ideal of the free-trade marketplace (Mettler, 2010, Yoffie, 1983). However, after the Occupation, the US secretary of state, John Forster Dulles, argued that Japan ought to look for markets in Southeast Asia, telling the Japanese Prime Minister Yoshida in 1954 "that Japan should not expect to find a big U.S. market because the Japanese do not make the things that we want" (Havens, 1987, p. 8). However, the United States was one of the markets in which Japan could succeed. When the newly formed Japan Air Lines planned its regular flights to San Francisco in 1953, it employed the Austrian-American psychologist Ernest Dichter to advise on its advertising. He identified two problems: the wartime image of a fanatical kamikaze pilot, and concerns about safety at a time when Japan had a reputation for making unreliable cheap products (Nakano, 2018). Reassurance was given that the planes and pilots were American, yet this did not provide a reason to choose JAL over any other carrier. The answer came in the promotion of the care and service of the kimono-clad Japanese stewardesses, representing once more what Dichter called the "luxury, mystery and romance of the Orient" (Nakano, 2018, p. 173). The aeroplane cabin was designed to evoke a classic Japanese interior of tatami mats, shoji screens and chrysanthemum motifs. American passengers could relax in the luxury of a new Japan that echoed an earlier "safer" image of Japan half a century ago (Nakano, 2018).

By 1955, Japanese industry had regained its pre-war output levels, with over 20 percent of its exports going to America, with textiles as the dominant product

DOI: 10.4324/9781003082088-7

(Yoffie, 1983). Japan became known for its cheap products which undercut the American producers. For example, American textile manufacturers could not compete with the Japanese "one-dollar blouse" (Mettler, 2010). With American companies suffering, there were calls for a restriction on Japanese textile imports, and for local boycotts of Japanese clothing. To avoid this, the Japanese government had little choice but to offer voluntary restrictions. After difficult negotiations, an agreement was signed and there was a drop in Japanese textile exports to the United States in 1957. However, these recovered in the following years and, despite the efforts of the Japanese government, unauthorized shipments, and differences in definitions about what was restricted, led to greater than quota exports. As Yoffie (1983, p. 61) put it: "Thus, in an ironic way, Japan got most of what it had failed to achieve in bargaining by unintentional cheating".

The Western view was that the label Made in Japan indicated cheap imitations of better-quality American or European products (Mettler, 2010), and was reinforced by the Japanese mass production of low-price goods. In the mid-1950s, Japanese imports were cheap and regarded as poor quality, for example, the "tinny" Sony transistor radio (invented in 1955) which had poorer audio quality than contemporary American products (Lynn, 1998). However, a small, cheap personal radio appealed to the youth market at the time when teenagers were emerging as a major commercial sector in the United States. It also meant that Sony, with its investment in transistor technology, could improve the audio quality of its products, and later capture the hi-fi audio market on quality from the Western producers, as well as maintaining its reputation for convenient and popular products (Lynn, 1998). Similarly, the Honda 50cc Super Cub motorcycle (invented in 1959) was derided in the West as a cheap under-powered toy compared to the popular large motorcycles that dominated the market in the 1950s: for example, the British Triumph and the American Harley Davidson brands. Motorcycles were associated in popular culture with nonconformist leather-clad young men – motorcycle gangs such as the Hells Angels in the United States and the "ton-up boys"[2] in Britain. The iconic image of a motorcycle rider in the West was actor Marlon Brando driving his Triumph T6 Thunderbird in the movie *The Wild One*, 1953, or fellow actor James Dean, who owned a Triumph TR5 Trophy. However, as Christensen and Raynor (2003, p. 252) pointed out, Honda appealed to "people without leather jackets", who wanted a cheap, easy-to-maintain, lightweight and convenient run-around, that was also a lot of fun riding off-road (Christensen, 1997). Once they had entered the Western motorcycle market, Honda were later able to develop larger vehicles that surpassed the Western manufacturers in quality and reliability (Flavin, 2017). Yet it was not just consumer goods that the Japanese were producing. Japan was also building its heavy industries in the 1950s, with its new steel plants being more efficient and better located for export than the older ones in the West. For example, Britain with its older plant undertook 50 percent of global shipbuilding in 1950, yet by the early 1960s, it had been overtaken by the Japanese, who went on to dominate the market (McMillan, 1996).

On 1 October 1964, nine days before the start of the Olympics in Tokyo, with the Western media already in Japan, the Japanese National Railways launched a new high-speed train, the *shinkansen*, soon dubbed the "bullet train" in English, between Tokyo and Osaka (Hood, 2006). The image of a bullet train racing past Mount Fuji was to become the image of modern Japan, appearing on posters and guide books for tourists, as

> an icon of modernity or, more precisely, a meeting of two icons representing modernity and tradition, the new Japan and the old. . . . The pure lines of Mount Fuji rise upwards and the pure lines of the bullet train intersect its base, composing themselves into a perfect aesthetic image.
>
> *(Littlewood, 1996, p. 62)*

The Tokyo Olympics showing the new modern rebuilt capital city, the smooth-running infrastructure and the sleek aeroplane-like bullet trains, presented a radical change in image of Japan from that of its post-war poverty. In Europe, at the time, countries such as Britain were still phasing out their main-line steam trains and only introduced high-speed trains capable of the 200 km/hr of the first *shinkansen* during the 1970s and 1980s (Chen and Hall, 2011). While Western surprise at the speed of Japanese modernized recalled that at the turn of the 20th century, now the sense of military peril from Japan was absent. The Japanese people had suffered nuclear devastation at Hiroshima and Nagasaki, and had a constitution (written during the American Occupation) that forever committed it to peace. In the context of the Cold War, the Japanese were now viewed as demonstrating the success of democratic capitalism, at the same time as evoking a past that once again became a source of fascination in the West. In 1960, the Japan expert Donald Keene wrote in the *New York Times* Sunday magazine about "the prevalence of hibachi stoves, cochin lanterns, and shoji screens in American living rooms" (Mettler, 2018, p. 1). Mettler continued: "New Japanese restaurants were opening throughout the country. Indeed, in the twenty years following World War II, Japan loomed large in the personal tastes and leisure pursuits of the Times' main readership of upper-middle-class white Americans" (Mettler, 2018, p. 1).

Japanese influence, Western lifestyle

During the 1950s, there had been a fascination with aspects of Japanese culture and Japanese design, as noted in Chapter 6, but mass-produced Japanese products – with the exception of some textiles – had not yet dominated Western markets. However, this all changed during the 1960s. For example, post-war, the Japanese government had encouraged toy production, with Japanese toy manufacturers growing rapidly in the 1950s. By the early 1960s, Japan was the largest exporter of toys (Cross and Smits, 2005). Cheap Japanese plastic toys had obtained a global market, bought for and by children. Also, Japanese toy manufacturers were able to exploit the popular interest in science, and science fiction in 1950s' and 1960s' America and Europe by creating tin robots – a product easily shaped to create angular humanoid characters – that could move by wind-up, battery or friction mechanisms (Phoenix, 2006). In particular, children's toys could be made of popular characters from movies, television programmes, cartoons and comic books.

A problem was that the image of the Japanese developed in the 1950s, as in shibui design for the middle and upper classes, did not resonate with the mass market (see Chapter 6). For example, the Japanese film *Seven Samurai*, 1956, now one of the most famous Japanese films, was initially unsuccessful in the United States, as "it failed to conform to American critics' expectations of Japanese films: that they should reflect an artistic Japan and offer something different and better than the usual Hollywood product, that they should be more shibui than spectacular" (Mettler, 2018, p. 67). Yet, the Japanese were not just looking for high-brow critical appreciation of their products, but mass sales in the West. To achieve this, they had to alter their own cultural products to meet the expectations of Western culture. This was particularly the case with children's entertainment. The sales of toys linked to films needed the films to be popular. The successful Japanese movie *Gojira*, 1954, about a fire-breathing monster, combining live-action and special effects, was severely edited, with scenes taken out and new ones added to produce the American version, called *Godzilla: King of the Monsters*, released for American audiences in 1956 (Kerner, 2007). This began the process of Western children discovering characters from Japanese popular culture, and then buying the merchandise – toys – associated with them. In 1963, NBC[3] bought the English language rights to the popular Japanese animated cartoon series *Tetsuwan Atomu* (Mighty Atom) by Osamu Tezuka. Renamed *Astro Boy* in the United States, it began syndication in 1963. However, changes were made due to cultural differences, with many restrictions demanded by the NBC censors (by changes in translation or cuts). For example, Schodt (2007, p. 85) cites the example of a character dying and Astro Boy saying "he's dead". This was not acceptable in an American children's show so, to avoid death in the English edition, it was translated as "He's unconscious, get him to hospital!" Astro Boy continued to be shown on American television, with repeats, until the 1970s, setting the foundation for Japanese animation (now referred to by its Japanese name of anime) forming a significant part of children's entertainment in the West. West (2008) has referred to this process as the Japanification of (Western) children's popular culture. However, due to cultural differences and cultural misinterpretation when unedited Japanese media was later introduced into the West, it risked being regarded as unsuitable for children, and indicative of the "weirdness" of the Japanese (e.g. Hinton, 2014a). Hence, the Japanification of Western children's entertainment only occurred due to the Americanization of the source material.

This cultural issue did not arise with Japanese consumer products, in the 1960s, which did not reference Japanese culture – or in many cases Japan at all – in their advertising. The manufacturer's name was Japanese, but the focus of the advertising was on enhancing the American lifestyle. An advert headlined "Wash n' Watch" shows a woman in a laundrette able to watch her portable Sony television while washing her clothes; another headlined "Bach n' Roll" shows a "square" older man and a "hip" young man both listening to their Sony portable transistor radios; a picture of a sunny day with a young American couple riding their Honda Cub past a yacht, wearing their normal fashionable clothes (without risk of getting dirty), tells the viewer, "You meet the nicest people on a Honda"; smartly dressed people always "Go Prepared!" with the handy Canon portable Auto Zoom Super 8 camera, the perfect accompaniment for the traveller; a Mitsubishi advert suggests a dog for a friend but the Mitsubishi Colt for a journey – "a car you will be proud to own".[4] Ownership of Japanese products represented the modern, technological aspiring Western lifestyle.

As the 1960s wore on, Japanese products for sale in the West combined precision manufacturing on a mass scale, along with innovative features, such as portable televisions and radios or autozoom on cameras. This led them to dominate the consumer technology markets on quality as well as quantity. For example, during this time, the German Leica cameras (with their historical reputation for quality) could no longer compete with the Japanese SLR (single lens reflex) cameras of Nikon and Canon (Windrum et al., 2019), and by the end of the decade, Japan was the leading manufacturer of television sets (Littlewood, 1996). Japan overtook the United Kingdom in terms of gross domestic product (GDP)[5] in 1967, and France the following year, as its "economic miracle" of rapid growth continued apace (Francks, 2015).

In 1964, sociologist Ezra Vogel introduced the salaryman (*sarariman*) to a Western academic audience, as a key element of the new Japanese middle class, who later became well-known in the wider Western society. The salaryman was usually well-educated, worked in a white-collar job for a Japanese corporation, had a nuclear family, with a wife at home looking after the household (Vogel, 1971). The salaryman's social life took place primarily with his work group, involving, for example, drinking with colleagues after work. His long hours away from home resulted in quite separate lives of the salaryman and his wife. Indeed, "if a man carries on an affair with a girl in the office, it need not disrupt his relationship with his wife" (Vogel, 1971, p. 108). While the Japanese salaryman would later be viewed in the West as one of the stereotypical reasons for Japanese economic success (Matsumoto, 2002), in the 1960s, this representation of the Japanese man – in a traditional role of "male dominance" – was clearly very appealing to male chauvinist Western men, in the context of second-wave feminism in their own society, just as their forebears had eulogized Japanese gender relations during first-wave feminism in the West (see Chapter 5). Japan as an imagined male chauvinist paradise was illustrated in the 1967 popular movie *You Only Live Twice*. When the fictional British secret agent, James Bond, has a mission to Japan, it is a place of not only modern technology, with a spaceport hidden in a caldera, but also tradition, illustrated when he visits a sumo wrestling bout. At one point, Bond and his Japanese colleague Tiger Tanaka go to a bath-house where they are bathed by four young bikini-clad Japanese women. Tanaka says to Bond: "in Japan, men always come first. Women come second". Yet, in Ian Fleming's original text, the description has a very different connotation. In the book, James Bond is told by Tanaka: "Our American residents . . . enjoy the subservience, *which I must say is only superficial*, of our women" (Fleming, 1978, p. 59, my emphasis). The writers of the movie had altered Fleming's meaning to present Japanese women as subservient, echoing similar Western representations from the past (see Chapters 5 and 6).

In 1967, the same year that the film of *You Only Live Twice* was released, Karlins et al. (1969) showed that two-thirds of the Princeton University students they asked, characterized Americans as materialistic, and not necessarily in a good way. In contrast to the technological, consumerist world of James Bond, the 1960s "hippie" subculture in the West – like the 1950s "beats" (see Chapter 6) – sought to challenge their own materialistic culture and embrace new ways of living. The Japanese Zen teachings of D.T. Suzuki, and developed by Alan Watts (see Chapter 6), set the basis for a "California Zen",[6] employing aspects of Zen Buddhism in concert with contemporary American psychological questions about the self, and self-development – a form of Zen made in America (Prohl, 2014). In California, the interest in Zen was nurtured in the Esalen Institute in Big Sur and the San Francisco Zen Centre, as a part of a movement for a more spiritual life and personal transformation, which developed within Western societies (e.g. Goldman, 2012). But this still had its roots in the Zen teachers, such as D.T. Suzuki, who offered a traditional Japanese way of spiritual fulfilment. Ignoring the materialism of modern Japan, this Zen approach to life saw the Japanese spirit, as enacted through Zen, as a basis for living in harmony with the world. A clear description of the traditional Japanese spirit, as an approach to life, was given by the famous Japanese writer Yasunari Kawabata in his 1968 Nobel Prize for Literature speech (Kawabata, 1968). Kawabata through his novels had eulogized "Old Japan" and criticized the "blight of Americanization" (DeVere Brown, 1988, p. 378). He argued that the Zen disciple in a long period of silent meditation

> departs from the self and enters the realm of nothingness. This is not the nothingness or the emptiness of the West. It is rather the reverse, a universe of the spirit in which everything communicates freely with everything, transcending bounds, limitless. . . . Enlightenment comes not from teaching but through the eye awakened inwardly.

To Kawabata, this "spirit of Zen" (the Japanese spirit) could be observed in Japanese painting, gardens (including the bonsai dwarf gardens), in the display of a single flower in a vase, in poetry and the tea ceremony. The Japanese influence in the 1960s Western society was not simply in terms of its consumer products but also in questions of lifestyle.

The American Japan scholar Donald Keene (1969) sought to explain Japanese aesthetics to his academic peers, without rejecting modern society. He began with the term "shibui", which he assumed was familiar to English-speaking readers, arguing that the Japanese aesthetic sense is demonstrated in the mundane aspects of Japanese life, such as the arrangement of flowers and food. He identified four key aspects of Japanese aesthetics that particularly distinguish it from that of the West: suggestion, irregularity, simplicity and perishability. These are reflected in Japanese arts, such as poetry, garden design and the tea ceremony, creating an ambiguity of meaning (as in *haiku* poetry) and transient beauty (as in the fragile cherry blossoms). For Keene, "much of what is considered most typical in Japanese aesthetics stems from Zen. Or, it might be more accurate to say, it coincides with Zen" (Keene, 1969, p. 297). The idea that there was a Zen way of approaching everything in life pervaded Western thinking, which led to a raft of popular books linking Zen to almost every aspect of Western society. In 1974, Robert Pirsig's best-selling novel *Zen and the Art of Motorcycle Maintenance* was published. While a book of analytic philosophical reflections during a motorcycle journey from Minnesota to California, discussing the meaning of the self, Pirsig, in the introduction, acknowledged that it was not really about orthodox Zen at all. But "Zen" had now become a familiar term in Western popular culture, especially for book titles.[7]

Return of the samurai in the Western media

After the war, and up to the 1970s, the martial image of the Japanese had been deliberately suppressed in the West, as noted in Chapter 6, with the Japanese typically represented as feminine or wise in ancient wisdom. The American Occupation had sought to make the Japanese "safe" for the West. However, in the early 1970s, two news items from Japan captured Western media interest, and recalled the martial samurai "spirit" of the Japanese. The first was the death of the "internationally renowned literary superstar" (Flanagan, 2014, p. 7), Yukio Mishima, aged forty-five, by committing seppuku, which was widely reported across the Western press. With English translations available of his books, Mishima had been nominated for the Nobel Prize in Literature[8] five times between 1963 and 1968, and had become a celebrity in both Japan and the West, appearing in *Life* magazine in 1966 and on the cover of *The New York Times Magazine* in August 1970, as "Japan's Renaissance Man", three months before his death. On the morning of 25 November 1970, Mishima and four members of the Shield Society (his private military-style organization), all wearing uniforms, visited the headquarters of the Japanese Self-Defence Force in Tokyo, and took hostage a surprised general in his office. They demanded the soldiers assemble outside so Mishima could speak to them from the balcony. In his speech, he claimed that:

> Japan's glorious samurai traditions, its manliness and heroism, had been suppressed as something of which to be ashamed. Instead, the so-called Peace Constitution had turned Japan into an effeminate, anodyne, culturally barren society. Only by overthrowing the Peace Constitution could a new Japan, at one with itself and in tune with its noble history and traditions, be reborn.
>
> *(Flanagan, 2014, pp. 8–9)*

In modern 1970s Japan, the listening soldiers were not interested and jeered him. Mishima returned inside and committed a well-prepared seppuku.[9] The explanation for his death was debated: it could have been a political statement or derived from personal reasons. Yet this flamboyant death of Mishima – a public seppuku – rather than being viewed as a traditional honourable act, was considered very incongruous in modern Japan (Flanagan, 2014, Inose and Sato, 2012). But in the West, it was a reminder of the "samurai within" the Japanese man, as Benedict (1947) had implied.

The second event, which also captivated the world's press, was the discovery in 1974 of Second Lieutenant Hiroo Onoda, hiding in a mountain hideout on Lubang Island in the Philippines, unaware that the Pacific War had ended twenty-nine years earlier. His companion had been killed by the Philippine police two years earlier, and his existence was known but it required a young "explorer", Norio Suzuki, to make contact, and only when his former wartime commanding officer was flown in to order him to surrender that Onoda gave himself up. On 13 March 1974, the *New York Times* reporter Richard Halloran (Halloran, 1974) wrote that on arriving back in Japan, he was given a hero's welcome. "Lieutenant Onoda's ordeal has tremendous appeal to the Japanese, a deeply emotional people. The tragedy of his 30 years of deprivation in the jungle seemed to stir the deepest and most melancholic feelings in people here". Rather than dismissing his behaviour as foolishness – he had ignored leaflets informing him of the end of the war as disinformation – the lean fifty-two-year-old, with a military bearing, was viewed as an exemplar of dutiful behaviour. Halloran explained further:

> The lieutenant has come out of the jungle during a time of self-examination by the Japanese, especially the postwar generation. While they enjoy the material benefits their hard work has brought them, they have begun to despise the label "economic animal". They have started to believe that Japan must stand for something more, though few here seem to know just what.

He also noted that the Japanese press applauded the "Onoda spirit" of doing one's best.

In 1975, the Japanese samurai was once again in the public eye, when a new book captured the imagination of the Western world, through a retelling of the story of the first Englishman in Japan, William Adams, who became the samurai Miura Anjin, the Miura pilot (see Chapter 3). Writer James Clavell had served in the British artillery during the Pacific War and survived for three years as a Japanese POW. After the war, he turned to write for the film industry and moved to the United States in the 1950s, where he became highly successful, before focusing on novel writing. His best-selling book, *Shogun*, told the story of the pilot "John Blackthorn" (based on Adams) arriving in Japan in a Dutch ship in 1600, meeting the shogun "Lord Toranaga" (based on Ieyasu Tokagawa), and falling in love with "Mariko" a Christian married woman who acts as his translator. It was hugely successful, with sales of seven million copies over five years (Johnson, 1991), and "Shogun mania engulfed the American public" (Hurst, 1981, p. 158). In the *New York Times* Book Review, Webster Schott wrote:

> Clavell creates a world: people, customs, settings, needs and desires all become so enveloping that you forget who and where you are. "Shogun" is history infused with fantasy. It strives for epic dimension, and occasionally approaches that elevated state. It's irresistible, maybe unforgettable and, finally, exhausting.[10]

While some academics criticized its historical accuracy, up to half the students arriving onto an academic course about Japan in the United States had read the book, which inspired Smith (1980) to edit the short academic book *Learning from Shogun* as a guide to the fact and fiction. Subsequently, *Shogun* was made into a five-part television mini-series starring Richard Chamberlain as Blackthorn, Toshiro Mifune as Toranaga and Yoko Shimada as Mariko, shown in the United States in 1980. An interesting twist was that the words of the Japanese speakers were not translated into English subtitles, so that the viewer shared Blackthorn's initial lack of understanding and his gradual learning of Japanese phrases. As a result, *Newsweek*, 29th September 1980, reported:

> An outbreak of Samurai Night Fever gripped the nation. . . . For all its mystifying plot twists and inscrutable dialogues, NBC's adaptation of James Clavell's "Shogun" rang up ratings . . . [*of*] . . . nearly 75 million people watching each episode of the five-night mini-series. The epic about medieval Japan also set off a wave of Shogun chic. Bars sold out their supplies of sake, boutiques reported runs on kimonos. . . . Pop-cultural trendies began sprinkling their conversation with words like *arigato* (thank you) and *wakarimasu* (I understand).

Along with the miniseries, the publisher printed three and a half million more copies of the book, to meet the demand. The combination of the book and the television series brought back all of the Western ideas of sengoku (civil war) Japan. Blackthorn adopts Japanese ways and enjoys the cleanliness of regular bathing. He discovers that all the Japanese, from a great lord to a humble retainer, are willing to sacrifice their lives for a dereliction of their duty, no matter how slight their misdemeanour. The violence underlying the samurai sense of honour is revealed in the treatment of enemies and the swift capital punishment given for any disloyalty to their lord. Mariko tells Blackthorne not to wish for things he cannot have (i.e. marriage to her) and emphasizes that Japanese customs are different to his, and he must accept them. As Johnson (1991) argued, Mariko is like Hana-ogi in Michener's *Sayonara* (see Chapter 6), beautiful but strong-willed. Aware of the need for Blackthorne to follow Japanese customs, she acts as his mentor, teaching him Japanese ways. She tells him that "life and death are the same thing". He tries to understand this strange culture; slowly coming to appreciate it, and realizing that they can never be together.

While it was set in 1600 and added to the Western fascination with Japan, it also reminded Westerners of the "fanatical Japanese male", which Johnson (1991, p. 114) argued was "clearly intended to remind the reader of future events" (i.e. the Second Word War). The television series was applauded in the United States, with actors Chamberlain and Shimada winning Golden Globes and both being nominated for Emmy awards. However, on 13 September 1981, Paul Bernstein, reporting in the *New York Times Magazine* (Bernstein, 1981), said that when it was shown in Japan, it was panned by the critics, and denounced for its inaccuracies. He wondered if its success in the United States was because "it provides stereotypes which Americans can recognize, feel comfortable with and accept as authentic".[11] He also noted that Clavell's explanation for its success was that it was a "crackerjack story".

Competing with the corporate samurai

During the 1970s, the Japanese "economic animal" (see earlier) was going from strength to strength. In 1972, the Japanese overtook the other "economic miracle" (West) Germany in terms of GDP. The once-dominant British motorcycle industry was now in decline, and far exceeded in sales by the Japanese manufacturers: Honda, Kawasaki, Suzuki and Yamaha (Koerner, 2012). By the mid-1970s, American imports of colour televisions were dominated by Japan (Yoffie, 1983). The Japanese automotive industry increased its share of the American market threefold during the 1970s. However, just as the Western motorcycle manufacturers had not appreciated the threat of the Japanese producers, now in the 1970s, the major American manufacturers (General Motors, Ford and Chrysler) did not yet regard the increasing imports of Japanese small cars as competition with their larger vehicles, the major source of their revenue (Yoffie, 1983). Yet the writing was on the wall in 1975, when a Japanese car worker could produce the same value of car production in nine days that it took a Western car worker forty-seven days to produce[12] (Vogel, 1979), Now the balance of the US-Japan import-export trade began to shift radically in favour of the Japanese, with an increasing US deficit (Johnson, 1991).

In 1979, in his book *Japan as Number One: Lessons for America*, Vogel's explanation of Japanese success, compared to the United States, during the previous thirty years began as follows.

> Most Japanese understate their successes because they are innately modest, and more purposive Japanese, wanting to rally domestic forces or to reduce foreign pressures, have chosen to dramatize Japan's potential disasters. On the American side, our confidence in the superiority of Western civilization and our desire to see ourselves as number one make it difficult to acknowledge that we have practical things to learn from Orientals. I am convinced that it is a matter of urgent national interest for Americans to confront Japanese successes more directly and consider the issues they raise.
>
> *(Vogel, 1979, p. ix)*

Vogel listed all of the economic and social successes of post-war Japanese society, including achieving, from 1977, the longest expected lifespan of any nation. However, he claimed that it was easier for Americans to accept that the Japanese were using underhand tactics, such as underselling and violating antitrust regulations, than acknowledge "Japanese superior competitiveness" (Vogel, 1979, p. 225). He identified governmental organization, economic policy and the lack of company modernization as the real reasons, and argued that the United States should learn from Japan.

Others disagreed with Vogel's positive view of Japan, with Woronoff (1990) entitling his book *Japan as (Anything But) Number One* in rebuttal. During the 1980s, Western businesses were adapting Japanese management techniques, yet the trade imbalances were increasing (van Wolferen, 1986). Just as Japanese textile exports had led to demands for protectionism to defend the American industry in the 1950s, now the American car industry was suffering as Japanese exports increased. There was talk of a "Japan problem" in the West (van Wolferen, 1986). It was not simply that the West needed to learn from Japan but, as van Wolferen (1986) argued, Japan was not operating a capitalist free-market economy, and had put up barriers to foreign competitors seeking to enter the Japanese market. Furthermore:

> Japanese competitiveness and the inhospitality of its own market to foreign products are helping to bring about further de-industrialization in the United States and Europe. After the virtual loss of the motorcycle industry and consumer electronics industry in the United States, the Japanese are gaining leverage over such crucial industries as semiconductors, machinery and telecommunications equipment.
>
> *(van Wolferen, 1986, p. 295)*

He continued: "the essence of the problem is not that Japan exports much more than it imports, but that its exports systematically undermine Western industries". He referred to this as "adversarial trade"; and very different to the "competitive trade" of Germany and the United States, where a country freely imports and exports the same category of product (van Wolferen, 1986).

It was during the 1980s that the term "corporate samurai" became popular as a description of the Japanese salaryman. In *Forbes* magazine, Kathleen Weigner entitled her article about a successful Japanese businessman, "corporate samurai".[13] The Japanese salaryman was viewed as something very different to a white-collar worker in the West: "the suited 'corporate samurai' in the office from early morning to late at night, with the same firm until retirement" (Tipton, 2007, p. 44). Japan was now "the corporate samurai giant to be emulated and feared" (Law, 2000, p. 136). It was not just the practices of Japanese companies that was viewed as the problem for the West but the samurai culture of these dedicated salarymen. In the West, Japan began to be perceived as an economic threat driven by these "corporate samurai" in echoes of past conflicts. "Ask the average American the reason for our trade deficit", wrote Eason (1984, p. 53), "and you are likely to get a one word answer: Japan". A number of commentators began to speak out against the Japanese and their trade practices, in what became known as "Japan bashing" (Morris, 2010), although Woronoff (1990) claimed that there were more "Japanapologists", such as Vogel (1979) eulogizing the Japanese system, than Japan bashers criticizing it.

In the Western media, images of the Japanese now resonated with the wartime descriptions of the ruthless, treacherous, bushido-following man, but now dedicated to the company rather than the Emperor (Johnson, 1991). Reminders of the war came from the blockbuster movie *Tora! Tora! Tora!*, 1980, a historical account of the attack on Pearl Harbor, and *Merry Christmas, Mr Lawrence*, 1983, a story of the experience of Sir Laurens van der Post in a Japanese POW camp in 1942.[14] The comedy *Gung Ho!*, 1986, showed the problems of American workers adapting to a new Japanese car plant in their town. A dark, dangerous Japan was portrayed in the box office hit *Black Rain*, 1989, with Michael Douglas and Andy Garcia as New York cops seeking a Japanese murder-suspect in the Osaka criminal (*yakusa*[15]) underground. Within these films was a reminder to the audience that the Japanese were very different to Westerners. When Fujitsu made a billion-dollar bid for a large stake in a British computer company, *Financial World* magazine headlined it as *The Samurai Have Landed* (Meyer and Siwolop, 1990), combining the word samurai with the title of a film set in the Second World War.

However, negotiations between the United States and Japan, and European countries and Japan, sought to solve the "Japan problem". At times the Western countries would institute protectionist legislation and at times Japan would agree to change its restrictions on foreign trade. However, certain factors led to a resolution. The performance of Western economies improved. Japanese factories in Western countries were providing Western jobs. The yen was allowed to rise in value, making Japanese exports to the West more expensive. Also, Japanese growth was slowing and, in the early 1990s, it shrank to almost nothing with the bursting of Japan's "bubble economy". Asset values had risen unsustainably due to Japanese monetary policy and, from 1990, stocks and assets had begun to fall, and collapsed at the end of 1991, leading to a decade of economic stagnation, known as the lost decade (Berggren, 1995; Itoh, 2000). In 1995, the management academic Mark Dodgson wrote: "With scarcely concealed schadenfreude, observers point to the painful upheavals taking place in industry as a country used to a rapidly expanding economy has had to cope with three years of zero growth" (Dodgson, 1995, p. 112). Five years later, Woronoff (2001, p. 1) commented:

> The views of Japan at present are quite different [*compared to the end of the 1980s*]. They include a degree of *Schadenfreude*, especially among those who had earlier been beaten by the Japanese. So, it appears, Japanese businessmen, bureaucrats and politicians are not nearly as wily as thought.

As the Japanese economy stagnated, the anxieties about the corporate samurai disappeared, with stories emerging from Japan that "waves of corporate restructuring have caused a spate of suicides among middle-aged corporate samurai" (Elkington, 1997, p. 26). The salaryman became an object of scrutiny in the modern 21st century, having lost his age-related seniority and job-for-life as new business practices took hold. In Japan, the challenges to the salaryman were played out in popular culture with stories of job loss, reconnecting with the family, and taking on new roles (Dasgupta, 2012, 2014). This "crisis" of the salaryman was also played out in manga – Japanese comics – (Matanle et al., 2008), a word that had become very familiar in the West. At the end of the 20th century and into the 21st century, the Western image of the Japanese shifted from the corporate samurai, particularly in the minds of its young people, to the exciting creators of manga, anime, video games, fashion and many forms of innovative popular entertainment.

Entertainment for children?

Japanese manufacturers had dominated the children's toy market in the United States since the 1960s, which were often characters from film or comic franchises. In the mid-1980s, the Japanese company Nintendo released into the American market a home video game console called the Nintendo Entertainment System (NES). A cartridge was inserted into the console, and the game was played on the home television. Famously, a cartoon character called Mario, a stocky Italian plumber wearing a boiler suit and cap, had to negotiate obstacles of increasing level of difficulty to rescue Princess Peach who has been kidnapped by the evil villain, Bowser. Sheff (1993) reported that in 1990 Mario was more popular with American children than Mickey Mouse. In 1991, the rival Japanese company Sega introduced their signature character Sonic, a blue hedgehog, and his world, for their console, the Sega Genesis (also known as the Mega Drive).[16] The advantage of these iconic characters was that they also featured in comics, in children's television cartoons, and could be produced as a variety of toys and plushies. Sheff (1993) described the rise to dominance of Nintendo in the children's entertainment market in his book *Game Over*. He also gave it the subtitle: "How Nintendo zapped an American industry, captured your dollars, and enslaved your children", which expressed the concerns of American adults about Japanese companies. While children (including Sheff's own) clearly loved these characters, it was not long before parents, medical practitioners and psychologists were concerned that children were being adversely affected by these Japanese video games. On 21 May 1990, *The Washington Post* (Okie, 1990) reported cases of "Nintendinitis" (muscle strain from pressing the buttons on the controller), and there was increasing research into "video game addiction" (e.g. Phillips et al., 1995).

The appeal of video games didn't affect just children but also adults, and young adults in particular. The shoot-'em-up arcade games, such as the 1980s favourite *Space Invaders*, could now be played on a home games system, as could the beat-'em-up games such as *Street Fighter* (released in the United States in 1991). In 1993, the release of the *Mortal Kombat* video game created controversy in the

United States and the United Kingdom. Sega released it with an MA-13 rating (that is, for mature audiences of the age of thirteen and over) and Nintendo released it with the gore removed; with the Sega version proving the most popular by far (Pyle and Cunningham, 2014). For the remainder of the 20th century, the controversy resulted in most Western countries introducing various age-rating systems for video games (and banning some), with psychologists examining the effects of video game playing (e.g. Ballard and Wiest, 1996; Kirsh, 1998). However, certain academics, who had previously challenged the assumed relationship between television violence (as dramatic performance) and real-life violence, now questioned the implied negative effects of video games on children's lives, suggesting that they may have a positive influence on cognitive functioning (e.g. Gunter, 1998).

The Japanese in the British media

In 1982, a new show was launched on British television on Sunday evenings: *Clive James on Television*, fronted by the popular Australian writer and wit. Clips from foreign television shows were selected for their perceived quirkiness for the amusement of the British audience. One foreign show became particularly well-known, due to its frequent appearance on the show, the Japanese gameshow *Endurance*, where young student-aged adults undertook unusual "endurance" tasks, such as: who could keep holding a large block of ice for the longest time while being sprayed with cold water, or remain covered in insects for the longest time. This was at a time when Japanese people rarely appeared on British television (except in war films or as "corporate samurai" businessmen in news reports). And here they were being portrayed as particularly odd (kooky) in frequent clips, in a show that remained on British prime-time television for over twenty years (Hinton, 2014a).[17] Yet this was not the only representation of Japanese "weirdness" in the British media. In an analysis of British media reports about the Japanese, entitled: "Fear and loathing in the British press", cultural scholars Hammond and Stirner (1997) listed numerous British newspaper articles characterizing Japanese "weirdness". Even Japanese schoolgirls' interests in the Beatrix Potter character Peter Rabbit, and in Lucy Maud Montgomery's book *Anne of Green Gables*, were reported in the British press in terms of fanaticism and "cult obsession" (Hammond and Stirner, 1997, p. 89). Hammond and Stirner explained these representations in terms of British anxiety about Japanese economic success – and its own economic difficulties – at the same time as the celebration of the fiftieth anniversary of the victory over Japan in the Second World War. Newspapers drew on the popular British television programme *Tenko* (1981–5), a drama about the harsh conditions of Western women prisoners in a wartime Japanese internment camp after the fall of Singapore; claiming that working life in a Japanese factory in Britain was "like *Tenko*". As Hammond and Stirner (1997, p. 111) argued, citing *Tenko* was a way of claiming that the Japanese were imposing unacceptable conditions on British workers and, at the same time, "to remind ourselves who won the war".

The 1990s also saw a rise in the import into Western countries of Japanese comics (manga) and animated films (anime). By the mid-1990s, Japanese manga books were being published in English translation and anime movies were becoming available in cinemas, on television and on videotape (McCarthy, 1996). The anime of Studio Ghibli, and its animator-director Hayao Miyazaki, became very popular in the West. Appealing to adults and children alike, Miyazaki's anime combined beautifully drawn images with contemporary themes, such as ecological devastation, weaved into fantasy stories of young characters finding their way in a complex and sometimes seemingly irrational adult world (Hinton, 2016). However, anime took on a wide range of topics in the fantasy genre. The two-hour anime *Akira* was released in 1989 in the United States, and in 1991 in the United Kingdom. About a biker gang in a dystopian fantasy Tokyo, it has subsequently been rated as one of the best anime of all time by Western critics, with Hoad (2013) stating: "Led by Akira, anime expanded the idea of what animation could be: violent, abrasive, radically stylised, thoughtful and above all, adult".

However, despite the growing success of anime in Britain, with Miyazaki's 1987 *Laputa: Castles in the Sky* shown on the BBC[18] in the early 1990s at a time for children to watch, the mainstream British print media highlighted specific manga and anime (targeted at an adult market) as a disturbing aspect of Japanese "weirdness". This was combined with a misperception that comics and animation were entertainment solely for children, and hence any adult material was viewed in the mainstream British media as unacceptable even for adults (Hinton, 2014a). For example, the 1987 adult anime *The Legend of the Overfiend*,[19] containing violent and sexual cartoon imagery, was released on video in 1993 in its uncut form in the Unites States by Anime 18 (for adult viewers). However, in the United Kingdom, before its release by Manga Video in the same year, it was edited, and then cut by the British censors. Despite the censorship, which had taken out the "shocking" scenes, it still became

> the bête noire of the early British anime market, [*and*] gained an infamous reputation, mostly from reviewers and moral commentators who, even if they have troubled to do more than read the sensationalist press releases, have no understanding of its source manga, background or context.
>
> *(McCarthy, 1996, p. 66)*

The adult anime *LA Blue Girl*, 1992 – set in a fantasy world where strange tentacled monsters sexually assaulted the female protagonists – was released in the United States by Anime 18 in 1995, but a planned release in the United Kingdom by Manga Video was given an outright ban by the British censors. The vast majority of anime for mature audiences covered a wide range of topics, such as the "beautifully crafted" *Wings of Honneamise*, 1987, about an early space fight in an alternate world, to *Grave of the Fireflies*, 1988, about two children starving to death after the wartime firebombing of Japan (McCarthy, 1996). Yet, in Britain, anime was represented in the popular press as all about "sex and tentacles",[20] resulting in a negative representation of all anime, and, after its initial appearance, anime for adults disappeared from the main television channels (Hinton, 2014a).

Images of *otaku*

Yet for Western youth, Japanese products were becoming the focus of their popular entertainment. Video game consoles were booming, with the games becoming more sophisticated each year, and imports of manga and anime were increasing. The *Pokemon* game was released in 1998 in the West. *Pokemon* would become, alongside *Super Mario*, one of the most successful Nintendo products on various platforms. In 1996, Schodt published his book *Dreamland Japan: Writings on Modern Manga* (Schodt, 1996), which explained the Japanese term *otaku* to a wider Western readership. A term for a dedicated fan of Japanese popular culture, especially manga and anime, otaku also had connotations of a rather socially isolated nerd (Hinton, 2018), yet was adopted by American fans of manga and anime as "a badge of pride" (Schodt, 1996, p. 43). He also noted that the popularity of manga in the West was potentially becoming, like the tea ceremony, a positive feature of Japanese culture that its government might promote in the West. However, Schodt also identified a subgenre of manga called *rorikon*, or "lolita complex", featuring young cartoon characters in sexual contexts which might be misinterpreted in the West. And it was.

The name Lolita is forever associated, in the West, with the paedophilic desires of the middle-aged Humbert Humbert for a twelve-year-old girl, called Lolita, in Nabokov's famous eponymous book, first published in 1955. Yet in Japan, Lolita, like *Alice in Wonderland* and *Anne of Green Gables*, was related to the youth culture of *kawaii* (cute, or cuteness). In the 1990s, Japanese youth, aware that their adulthood would be one of duty, hard work, and dedication to the company (as a salaryman) or to the family (as a wife), sought escape into a fantasy world of a romanticized, idyllic Victorian-style childhood. For schoolgirls, cute things from soft toys (such as *Hello Kitty*) to cute fashion reflected this interest, with Lolita-style fashion reflecting the clothing style of a British Victorian doll (Hinton, 2013). Popular boy bands in the Japanese music charts had become more feminized in their style, rejecting macho imagery in favour of kawaii (cuteness) (Schodt, 1983). Manga and anime allowed these young Japanese to explore different concepts of adult gender identity within their stories (Hurford, 2009; Saito, 2014; Hinton, 2014b).

The manga style of drawing, involving large eyes and small mouths, made the cartoon characters appear young to Westerners unfamiliar with the genre, even when they were clearly adults. Indeed, in the United States, the anime distributor Anime 18 issued a notice with their adult anime videos, such as *LA Blue Girl*, making this point and emphasizing that the characters were over eighteen years. Also, the otaku interest in the cute characters in rorikon was argued as reflecting a rejection of the traditional Japanese adult gender roles, rather than a paedophilic interest (Azuma, 2009, Hinton, 2014b). Indeed, a cute "young girl" character in rorikon often had superpowers (such as being able to fly or use magic), was a robot or an android, or a 300-year-old demon princess, clearly distinguishing these cartoon characters from any association with actual girls (Hinton, 2014b). Furthermore, ignoring the vast majority of Japanese men, who had no interest in manga or anime, the British press tended to present the otaku as representative of the Japanese male, and highlighted his "weird" interests in manga and anime (Hinton, 2015).

This British media image of the "perversity" of the manga and anime loving Japanese man persisted into the 21st century (Hinton, 2015). As the stagnation of the Japanese economy became better known in the West, media reports told of its "economic crisis" (BBC, 2001), describing its population decline as a demographic "time bomb" (BBC, 2007), and reporting its "lost decades" (BBC, 2009). Twenty years after the bursting of the "bubble economy", Japan was being described as an economic "basket case" (Mitchell, 2013). In Britain, the explanation of some of these problems was attributed to the "weirdness" of the Japanese man. *The Guardian* newspaper asked: "Why have young people in Japan stopped having sex?" (Haworth, 2013). In a BBC report that focused on two Japanese men, labelled as otaku, who played a Nintendo simulated dating game on a hand-held games console, the question was repeated (BBC, 2013), with an accompanying article claiming: "The Japanese men who prefer virtual girlfriends to sex" (Rani, 2013) – despite one of the men acknowledging that he was married. In presenting the otaku (erroneously) as typical of Japanese men and associating the Japanese with "giving up sex", the reports on Japan's ageing population ignored the evidence of ageing populations across all developed countries, which had been ameliorated in the West by significant immigration, a solution that the Japanese had rejected (Strausz, 2019).

The cool Japanese

At the beginning of the 21st century, the number of anime and manga titles was increasing in the West, with imports and translations available to meet the increasing demand of the youth market, both in Western countries and worldwide, despite demand declining in Japan (Kinsella, 2000). In Britain, television personality Jonathan Ross presented the show *Japanorama* (2002–7), an affectionate look at Japanese popular culture, from anime and fashion, to otaku and robots, that represented Japanese "kookiness" as innovative, technological and modern. The show supplied information to fans in Britain, especially young adults. While innovative Japanese fashion designers, such as Issey Miyake, Yohji Yamamoto and Rei Kawakubo, had had to battle the criticisms of traditional Western designers before establishing themselves at the forefront of modern fashion styles (Kondo, 2010), now Japanese street fashion, associated with Harajuku in Tokyo, was viewed as a dynamic and innovative aspect of Japanese youth culture, that young people in the West wanted to see, and wear, with Lolita-style (in all its variations from Gothic to Sweet) gaining a following amongst young women fans in the West (Hinton, 2013; Aoki and Zabel, 2001). In 2003, the Miyazaki anime *Spirited Away*, 2001, won the Oscar for Best Animated Feature Film. Japanese popular culture could no longer be characterized in the West as "weird", with Japanese anime now appreciated as innovative and beautiful story-telling. Miyazaki's follow-up anime *Howl's Moving Castle*, 2004, combined his unique anime style with an adaptation of the story by the well-known British children's author Diana Wynne Jones. Fan conventions in the West, which attracted huge crowds of science fiction, fantasy and gaming fans, embraced Japanese popular culture. Alongside fans donning *Star Trek* and *Star Wars* outfits, in an activity called *cosplay* (costume play), now numerous fans dressed up as their favourite characters from manga and anime (Woo et al., 2020; Nelson, 2018; Crawford and Hancock, 2019). The image of the Japanese in the Western media was changing, with Japanese games, manga, anime and fashion (including cosplay) now considered a part of mainstream Western youth culture.

Other factors, including changing international trade and the expansion of the internet, all led to a more positive view of the Japanese and their culture in the West. First, the rapid rise of the Chinese economy in the 21st century resulted in Western concerns about a trade threat shifting from Japan to China. Indeed, in 2010, China took over from Japan as the second-largest economy (Barboza, 2010). Also, this emphasized the relationship of Japan with the United States in the Western Pacific (Envall, 2017). In 2008, the US ambassador to Japan J. Thomas Schieffer said: "The United States has no better friend in the world than Japan. The United States has no more important alliance in the world than the U.S.-Japan alliance".[21] The reduction in anxiety about Japan as an economic threat was also accompanied by a lessening in the concerns about its popular culture. Gaming was no longer the province of youth (and a cause of parental concern) but, with the release of the Microsoft Xbox, Sony Playstation and Nintendo Wii consoles, gaming became a part of Western family entertainment (Chambers, 2012). Manga and anime had become a global phenomenon (Bryce et al., 2010) and the British media concerns about Japanese cartoons paled into insignificance in the context of the explicit pornography now available on the internet (e.g. Short et al., 2012). Furthermore, the mainstream media, particularly newspapers, had lost their dominant position in the Western media landscape, and their relevance, in the context of the internet, as a source of information about Japanese popular culture for Western fans. An increasing range of manga and anime was available online and large fan communities had developed; purchasing licensed translations where available, and creating fansubs (fan-produced translations) of titles only available in Japan (and in Japanese). The unwritten rule was that the fansubbed versions were withdrawn when a title was licensed for foreign markets (Lee, 2011). Japanese popular culture was being fully embraced by Western youth, who had integrated these Japanese products into their own lives.

By the second decade of the 21st century, Schodt's prediction that anime was becoming like the tea ceremony (see earlier) was coming true. In 2012, the products of Japanese popular culture were achieving global sales of over 17 billion dollars (Nagata, 2012), and the Japanese government's Ministry of Economy, Trade and Industry (METI) had initiated the "Cool Japan" project, promoting Japanese popular culture worldwide (Hinton, 2018). At the same time, anime was being appreciated as art, and featuring in exhibitions in art galleries and museums in the West (e.g. in the British Museum). The Studio Ghibli Museum had been set up in Mitaka, west of Tokyo, Japan, and featured on any Western tourist itinerary to Japan, as a part of a popular "anime tourism" (Denison, 2010). Now when a British media celebrity took part in a televised travelogue about Japan, as well as following the traditional tourist itinerary (for example, observing a tea ceremony, or visiting temples, gardens and geisha), they would include a pop culture stop-off: such as a trip to Harajuku or Akihabara in Tokyo, or visit a robot hotel or a Japanese popular music (J-pop) concert, which were reported with affectionate delight, yet at the same time emphasizing the exotic difference of the Japanese (Jones, 2019). The success of Japanese popular culture had created a new image of the Japanese in the West with, at the end of the decade, Japan being the number one choice for a foreign visit by young people in the United States.[22]

Anxiety and allure: Japanese products, Western lives

After the American Occupation of Japan, the Japanese had been viewed as embracing their defeat, and they now had a new constitution that debarred them from making war. Thus, a new image of the Japanese was constructed in the West, contrary to the wartime fanatic, but now imbued with aestheticism, that middle- and upper-class Americans could embrace in terms of shibui, or the counter-cultural beats could integrate Zen Buddhism in their distaste of materialism (see Chapter 6). Yet, at the same time, the Japanese had to find a way to rebuild their economy, which required hard work and dedication; a need for endurance in the face of difficulties. This was achieved through mass production and innovation, creating products which were initially viewed in the West as cheap and imitative. While Japanese hard work might be applauded in the West, the tinny radio and the small slow motorcycle were not considered good products by Western manufacturers. Yet, gradually these Japanese products began to out-sell their Western counterparts. A portable television, a neat little run-around motorcycle and a handy camera all appealed to the Western consumer in the 1960s. The Japanese who made these products were clearly doing something right, and modern Japan – that seemingly emerged with the 1964 Olympics – was both fascinating (with its fast bullet trains) and different, and Japanese success required explanation. The Japanese salarymen, with their identical blue-linen-suits, who hardly spent any time with their families and seemingly worked all hours, appeared to be the driving force of the Japanese economy, and provided a simple cultural representation of Japanese success in the Western mind. For the male viewers of the James Bond film *You Only Live Twice*, 1967, the Japanese man seemed to have created a chauvinist's paradise. Yet there was also something disturbingly different in the dedication of the Japanese worker to his employment compared to his Western counterpart.

While counter-cultural images of the Japanese could still draw on Zen Buddhism and Kawabata's criticisms of Americanization, which mirrored the hippies' rejection of materialism, the dominant view of Japan was increasingly of its economic success and the very appealing consumer goods that the Western family wished to buy. But Western manufacturers of televisions, cameras, motorcycles and numerous other goods found it increasingly hard to compete with these new Japanese "corporate samurai", a representation of the salaryman that resonated with the image of the samurai in the Western mind, but now devoted to his company rather than his lord. Echoes of wartime Japanese fanaticism entered the rhetoric of the trading relations between Japan and the West. While Vogel (1979) argued for adapting to, and adopting, Japanese business ways, the behaviour of Japanese salaryman appeared to reflect the "warrior" culture and character, as argued by Benedict (1947). Western media coverage of Yukio Mishima's suicide and Lieutenant Onoda's dedication to the war effort nineteen years after it finished suggested the latter in the Western representation of the Japanese. The image of the samurai – and the subservient Japanese woman – were further reinforced with the success of Clavell's *Shogun*, capturing Western delight in its intercultural love story in a bygone Japan. However, in the 1980s, the trade deficit between Japan and Western countries was represented as "the Japan problem". Yet despite the "Japan bashing", the "problem" was solved in the early 1990s by economic factors: the Japanese "bubble economy" burst, and Western economies grew. And the image of the samurai salaryman dissolved with the Japanese economic malaise. Now, the salaryman – once the corporate samurai – was suffering a crisis of identity along with the collapsed economy, with Western schadenfreude reinforcing ideas of the defeat of the samurai by the West. Yet this character explanation of the Japanese economic success and subsequent stagnation was now represented as a crisis of Japanese masculinity (both in the West and in Japan; see Kumagai, 2013), which tended to ignore the social and economic context, and that adaptation in working practices with economic change affects all societies.

A second strand, in the Western representation of the Japanese during the later 20th century, was associated with them as the producers of popular culture, in terms of games, manga and anime. While hugely popular in the West, and among Western youth, anxieties about the effects of playing games or reading manga were associated with the "weirdness" of the Japanese, and used in the British media to explain their concerns about the effects of manga and anime on British youth. This continued an idea of Japanese "weirdness" that had permeated the British media in its earlier attempts to explain Japanese economic success and their own lack thereof. Yet this image now served another purpose – of explaining Japanese economic and social problems. With the change in the Japanese economy from its rapid growth in the 1980s to the stagnation in the 1990s and beyond, coupled with Japan's ageing population, the image of the Japanese man as "weird" – and now an otaku – "explained" Japan's problems – as they were more interested in manga and anime than having sex! Yet, just as the "corporate samurai" representation ignored the social and cultural context of Japan – where most workers were not salarymen, the otaku representation ignored the simple fact that the vast majority of Japanese men were no more otaku than the majority of men in the United States or Europe.

Further, it is worth noting that the image of the Japanese man as otaku changed with the increasing interest in Japanese popular culture in the West. With manga and anime embraced as art forms, Hayao Miyazaki winning an Oscar, and manga being displayed in art galleries and museums in the West, the "weirdness" of otaku interests had to change – as those interests were also embraced by many in the West – and now shifted to admiration. Japanese popular culture was no longer viewed as a sign of Japanese "weirdness" but of an admirable cultural difference – Japanese "coolness" – so that tourists added Japanese popular culture (such as the Studio Ghibli Museum or a trip to Akihabara) to their itinerary of a trip to Japan. Indeed, the lure of Japan made it the top destination for American youth. Rather than these representations of the Japanese – corporate samurai or "weird" otaku – reflecting aspects of Japanese character, they reflected Western attributions of a Japanese character in order to explain the current state of intercultural relations between the two. While these attributions may be labelled as "stereotypes" in Western academic psychology – as they clearly are not true of all Japanese – this ignores the cultural context of their construction, and the intercultural relations that underlay their use.

Notes

1 "Japanese Sail Into West Coast Markets", *Business Week*, June 6, 1953, p. 144. (Mettler, 2010).
2 Motorcycle riders who had ridden at 100 miles per hour.
3 National Broadcasting Company (of America).
4 All these vintage advertisements are available by searching Google images online.
5 https://countryeconomy.com/gdp?year=1967
6 As practised in the Esalen Institute, established in 1962 at Big Sur in California.
7 From *Zen and the Art of Making a Living* (Boldt, 1993) *to Zen and the Art of Fly Fishing* (Syring, 2018).
8 www.nobelprize.org/nomination/archive/show_people.php?id=12680
9 Masakatsu Morita, a Shield Society member, and possibly Mishima's gay lover, also committed seppuku.
10 www.nytimes.com/1981/09/13/magazine/making-of-a-literary-shogun.html
11 www.nytimes.com/1981/09/13/magazine/making-of-a-literary-shogun.html
12 Vogel gives the examples of English car workers here.
13 *Forbes*, 13 October 1980; Features, p. 168.
14 Both involved significant Japanese involvement, including the latter's director Nagisa Oshima.
15 Yakusa is the Japanese criminal organization, often viewed as the Japanese version of the mafia.
16 Sony joined the American video games console market with the introduction of the PlayStation in 1994.
17 Yet *Endurance* (*za gamen*) was not particularly well-known in its own country, and was not unusual in the context of current British game shows such as *It's a Knockout* (1966–2001) and later reality shows, and certainly not representative of Japanese adults.
18 British Broadcasting Corporation.
19 Chojin Densetsu Urotsukidoji.
20 Associated with girls being sexually assaulted by tentacle monsters (as in *LA Blue Girl*).
21 https://japan2.usembassy.gov/e/p/2008/tp-20080925-71.html
22 From a survey of thirteen- to thirty-nine-year-olds – https://www.ypulse.com/article/2022/05/24/the-top-20-places-gen-z-millennials-want-to-travel/

8

MAKING SENSE OF THE CULTURAL OTHER

Explaining the unexpected in the cultural other

Having surveyed the history of the Western-Japanese relationship from the Western perspective, the key finding of this book is that there have been a wide variety of views of the Japanese by Westerners during almost 500 years. Indeed, there is no consistent view as to what the Japanese are like. For every agreed view at one point in time, there is an alternative view at another. At one time, the Japanese were viewed as white and civilized and, much later, they were racialized as yellow and barbaric. When Japan was closed to Europeans, they were considered mysterious artisans, creators of wonderful decorative arts, living in a secret land that bordered on the realms of fantasy. Then, again, when Japan "opened" to the West, they were viewed as child-like and innocent inhabitants of an idyllic medieval land, and in the first half of the 20th century as fanatical warriors. At one time they were considered as "just" imitators of the West yet, later, as economic miracle-workers and innovators that people in the West should copy. However, each of these representations was related to the state of the relationship between Japan and the West, and contained explanations for that relationship in Western terms. In many instances, we can argue that these accounts of the Japanese were based on misunderstandings – or even wishful thinking – but they cannot be regarded as fallacies, as there is an underlying cultural rationale to each of these judgements, which reflected the prevailing ideology and cultural belief systems of their Western creators. What we can conclude is that in many cases these representations of the Japanese were not based on ignorance, but were often constructed by having to explain the (culturally) unexpected (as discussed further).

In many instances, we cannot simply reject these Western representations as simplistic ideas as an outcome of a lack of knowledge about the Japanese. Francis Xavier

DOI: 10.4324/9781003082088-8

may have been delightfully surprised when he met the Japanese (in contrast to the other non-Christian peoples he had encountered). However, under the guidance of Francis Xavier and Alessando Valignano – both intelligent and university-education men – the Jesuits made the point of integrating into Japanese culture. For example, Luis Frois spent years in Japan: he learnt Japanese and adapted to a Japanese lifestyle, such as eating Japanese food, using chopsticks, and dressing as a (Buddhist) priest. This was a model Valignano encouraged for all the Jesuits "in respect for Japan's culture and love for its people" (Hoey, 2010, p. 22). Indeed, it was said of the Jesuit Organtino Soldo Gnecchi that

> "his whole life was attuned totally to the Japanese way". Organtino himself, after having spent twenty years in Japan, wrote, "I am more Japanese than an Italian, for the Lord of his grace has transformed me into one of that nation".
>
> *(Hoey, 2010, p. 27)*

Organtino wrote of the Japanese: "Since I have begun to understand their language I have formed the judgment that in general no people are as discerning as they [*are*]" (Hoey, 2010, p. 36). Also, Valignano made his support for a Japanese clergy very clear, indicating that, for these Jesuits, the Japanese were people of a status and standing like themselves. Yet, the Jesuits were influenced by their European world view and held such strong religious convictions, and faith in the value of their mission, that the Japanese clampdown on their activities came as a great shock (Cieslik, 1954c, see Chapter 3).

Yet for the English, arriving later in Japan, the Japanese suppression of the Jesuits mirrored their own expulsion of Catholic priests from their own country, and was not surprising at all. The Englishman William Adams was another Westerner who had learnt the language and took on Japanese ways. While he gained the position of samurai, there were still many aspects of Japanese life that he found strange (and unexpected): such as their willingness to commit ritual disembowelment (seppuku). Indeed, this emphasis on seppuku in Japan permeates many of the Western accounts of the Japanese, from the Jesuit Luis Frois, in the 16th century, who wrote: "To us it is a very grave sin for a man to kill himself; whereas the Japanese, when in battle they are unable to go on, deem it to be an act of great valour to disembowel themselves" (Willis, 2012, p. 422), to the Dejima Opperhoofd Isaac Titsingh, in the 19th century, writing about Japanese "legal suicide" and the Japanese "disregard of death" (see Chapter 4). The European shock of Japanese seppuku was because it was socially acceptable behaviour in Japan, unlike in their own society. The Christian position on suicide was based on the view that human life was given by God, and therefore it was not up to the person to decide when it could be terminated (as this is the province of God) but people should respect the sanctity of life. Murder is against God's commandment, and suicide is self-murder and rejects God's gift of life, usurping God's authority over it. As St Augustine argued, no one has the right to condemn themselves to death (Barry, 1995). The Protestant Church made the same claim. In the 18th century, sermons against self-murder were preached in England by the Bishop of Rochester, Zachary Pearce and the latitudinarian Dr Francis Ayscough, for example; the later noting that the punishment for self-murder in England was the forfeiture of the person's estate, so suicide was often taken as evidence of madness (which heirs sought to establish as this did not result in the loss of the estate) (Andrew, 2013). Thus, for much of the relationship between the West and Japan, the Western view of suicide made the Japanese position an indication of their strangeness, in their seeming acceptance of death with equanimity.

A second topic that keeps appearing in the Western accounts of the Japanese is their frequency of bathing and their general cleanliness. While these are regarded as positive characteristics of the Japanese, it was the Japanese acceptance of public bathing that many Westerners found shocking. From a Christian perspective, nudity was associated with the prelapsarian innocence of Adam and Eve, which was lost when they disobeyed God and ate the apple of the tree of knowledge. They acquired a sense of shame and covered themselves. Now nudity became "the shame of nakedness" (Revelation, 3:18). They were cast out of Eden, and they could not return to the pure state of innocence. In the Christian tradition, nudity became associated with sin and sexuality, with the locus of shame on the sexual organs which must remain covered. Nakedness became "indecent", as explained by St Augustine, and exposure of the body risked provoking the evils of lustful desires. As Velleman (2001) argued, this can be interpreted as forming the Christian (Western) sense of privacy. Thus, when the Portuguese arrived in Japan, public nudity was a shock, and something worth noting as it was unexpected in terms of Western cultural expectations (as Captain Álvares did in his report to Francis Xavier – see Chapter 2). When the Victorians arrived in Japan, 300 years later, this Christian view of nudity still permeated their perceptions: Japanese public nudity still shocked them, but this time the accounts were framed in terms of Japanese innocence. The Victorian image of the "child-like" Japanese suggested that they had maintained their prelapsarian innocence, which was why Japanese women bathing in public were referred to as Eves (see Chapter 5). Also, in tracing Western civilization back to classical Rome, the Victorian imperialists could refer to naked Japanese women as classical "Dianas", associating them with the pre-Christian classical world which had public baths. Also the Western embarrassment of being naked in company, deriving from the Christian tradition of privacy, was felt by Rudyard Kipling, although he presented it humorously, when a young Japanese woman invaded his bathing privacy (see Chapter 5).

The long period when Westerners were excluded from Japan had two effects on the Western mind. First, it allowed speculation about the Japanese, particularly as Japanese luxury goods still arrived in Europe via Amsterdam, resulting in the Japanese being represented as exceptional artisans in the decorative arts. Westerners tried but could not emulate their skill in arts and crafts, such as lacquerware, chinaware and prints. Second, it led to the belief that, as Japan was cut off from international commerce, its society was in some way frozen in time, described as it was by Kaempfer in his *History* as a "closed country" (see Chapter 4). At this time, the representation of the Japanese became a contested space in Europe. For the Jesuits, it involved eulogizing the Japanese Christians, and presenting the Japanese martyrs as exemplars of Christian devotion for the Europeans to see. For the Catholic historians of Japan, such as Hazart, the Protestant Dutch had denied their Christian faith in supporting a despotic regime in its suppression of the Japanese Christians – all in the cause of maintaining the profits of Japanese trade. To the Protestant historians, such as Montanus, it was the Portuguese who brought about the expulsion of the Europeans from Japan, as a "fifth column" to prepare the way for an Iberian invasion of Japan (under a Spanish king). During this time, English and Dutch ships fought the Spanish and Portuguese, with the Dutch taking over much of the Portuguese East Indies. The English, though sometimes allied with Dutch, also fought four wars against them in the 17th and 18th centuries. Thus, the English view of the Dutch at times matched the Catholic view that they would do anything for a commercial profit. This anti-Dutch sentiment was expressed by writer Jonathan Swift, who had his fictional character Lemuel Gulliver travel to a fictional Japan. This image of the Dutch was further emphasized when Kaempfer's *History* was published in 1727 in England. Despite Kaemfer's admirable account of the flora and fauna of Japan, with numerous details of Japanese society, the most memorable aspect of his account was of the Dutch Opperhoofd crawling on hands and knees before the shogun, a shocking image of a European prostrating himself before an Oriental despot. Not only did Kaempfer express his distaste at the "apish tricks" the shogun requested of them, but it confirmed the image of the avaricious mercantile Dutch – now rivals in the East Indies – in the English mind.

Western belief in the "natural law" of commerce between nations, combined with a desire for trading profits, led Western powers to seek to "open" Japan to trade in the early 19th century. Despite the increasing military power of these nations, Britain and Russia failed to do so. In support of their whalers who wanted safe ports in Japan, and a belief in natural law, the United States decided to send a squadron of gunboats to Japan to "open" the country to trade. For the Japanese, there was little choice but to rapidly modernize and industrialize, if they were to avoid the colonization by Western powers that was prevalent across the globe. Western travellers were delightfully surprised to find "medieval" Japan populated by charming and enchanting people, with whom they (especially Western men) could play out their fantasies, away from the condemnation that would greet this behaviour in their own lands. Western authors decried the loss of "Old Japan", eulogizing its medieval ways, and the charm and innocence of its inhabitants. The English travel writer, Isabella Bird, visited Japan seeking to meet the "real" Japanese and learn about their culture. In her book *Unbeaten Tracks in Japan*, she specifically sought to give her impressions of the Japanese "in the interests of truth", saying that "accuracy has been my main aim" (Bird, 1880, p. ix). She also consulted academic Basil Hall Chamberlain, about whom she wrote: "although an accomplished scholar, [*he*] does not think anything beneath him which is in any way illustrative of Japanese life and customs" (p. 245). After months of travel across

Japan, Bird was shocked by the Western influence on the Japanese in the ports open to Western trade, but waxed positively about the rest:

> The Japanese of the treaty ports are contaminated and vulgarised by intercourse with foreigners; those of the interior, so far from being "savages", are kindly, gentle, and courteous, so much so, that a lady with no other attendant than a native servant can travel, as I have done, for 1200 miles through little-visited regions, and not meet with a single instance of incivility or extortion.
>
> *(Bird, 1880, p. 8; see Chapter 5)*

Chamberlain became a professor of Japanese at Tokyo Imperial University, and helped Lafcadio Hearn when he arrived in Japan (see Chapter 5). Later Chamberlain suggested that, for anyone wanting to know about the Japanese people, Hearn's books "are perfect mines for the enquirer to dig in" (Chamberlain, 1902, p. 261). His only criticism of Hearn was his frequent praising of the Japanese at the expense of the Europeans. He wrote in an account that brought out his ideological belief in Western superiority (Minear, 1980):

> Lafcadio Hearn understands contemporary Japan better, and makes *us* understand it better, than any other writer, because he loves it better. . . . Our only quarrel is with some of Lafcadio Hearn's judgments: in righting the Japanese, he seems to us continually to wrong his own race. The objectionable character in his stories is too apt to be a European.
>
> *(p. 65)*

Yet Chamberlain was also critical of Westerners, and defended the Japanese when they were described as simply imitative.

> Foreigners have often stood in amaze at Japan's ability to swallow so many new ideas and institutions whole. They have dubbed her superficial, and questioned the permanence of her conversion to European methods. This is because they fail to realise two things, – the innate strength of the Japanese character, and the continuous process of schooling which has enabled this particular Oriental race to face the new light without being blinded.
>
> *(Chamberlain, 1902, p. 153)*

He also shared the Western admiration of Japanese arts and crafts, considered superior to those in the West, which was viewed as evidence of a distinct Japanese aesthetic spirit. Chamberlain synthesized the accounts of various Western commentators to provide a description of the Japanese character that reflected the general Western view of the Japanese at the time:

> To sum up: the average judgment formed by those who have lived some time among the Japanese, seems to resolve itself into three principal items on the credit

side, which are cleanliness, kindliness, and a refined artistic taste, and three items on the debit side, namely, vanity, unbusinesslike habits, and an incapacity for appreciating abstract ideas.

(Chamberlain, 1902, p. 261)

It is important to note here that Chamberlain spent nearly forty years in the country, speaking the language fluently; and Hearn too lived in Japan, marrying a Japanese woman (with whom he had four children), taking a Japanese name and becoming a Japanese citizen. Both Chamberlain and Hearn made the Japanese and Japanese culture the subject of their writing, and their views were nuanced and involved many positive opinions about the Japanese. Hence, while their interpretations of the Japanese reflected their Western cultural background, these authors cannot be criticized for a lack of knowledge, or a simplistic understanding of their subject. Even Bird who only spent a few months in Japan has been regarded positively for her account of the country and its people. For example, Williams and Clark (2017, p. 1) have argued:

Isabella Bird's *Unbeaten Tracks in Japan* (1880, written 1878) is one of the rare Victorian travelogues about Asia that has not only won continued readership and critical prestige in the West, but has also been frequently valued by readers in the country it describes as an insightful perspective by an outsider.

Yet the Victorian image of the "medieval" Japanese was shockingly shattered as the 20th century began; as an industrialized, modern Japan, with its own colonial aspirations, defeated Russia in the war of 1904–5, with Western reporters acknowledging its impeccable treatment of Russian prisoners. Yet the recognition of Japan as a global power, at a time of a pervasive racial ideology of the West, was not acknowledged by Western nations, who saw Japan as a threat to their own global hegemony (a "yellow peril"). This rejection of the Japanese from the "club" of Western nations was confirmed nearly twenty years later, when the Japanese racial equality clause was rejected by the League of Nations (and, in the United States, Japanese immigration was banned on racial grounds). While Japanese authors such as Nitobe and the Okakura brothers had sought to explain the Japanese and their culture (the Japanese spirit or soul) to a Western audience, their representations of the chivalrous and artistic Japanese lost out to a more dominant image, where bushido was interpreted as the Japanese martial spirit, brought about by rising nationalism and militarism in Japan (and Western concerns about Japanese expansion). In the 1930s, the appalling actions of the Kwantung army in Manchuria (reported in shocking detail in Western newspapers), and later the attack on Pearl Harbor, led to the image of the violent Japanese fanatic, which was only reinforced during the Pacific War. The surprising fall of the American Philippines and British Singapore to Japanese forces made it hard to maintain a belief in Western superiority without attributing unusual characteristics to the Japanese soldiers. Thus, when Benedict set out to explain the Japanese and their culture and character, at the forefront of her mind was the image of the Japanese "fanatic" soldier: emotionless, unconcerned about death and who would never surrender, the opposite to the decent, freedom-loving Americans. Yet, with the Japanese defeat at the dropping of the atom bomb on Hiroshima and Nagasaki, the Americans were surprised to find the Japanese to be charming and helpful, which Benedict could only explain by proposing her image of the Janus-like Japanese character.

The rapid post-war reconstruction of the Japanese economy was also viewed as a surprise in the West – echoing the surprise at its earlier industrialization – especially at its "rebirth" on the international stage, as a modern international country at the Tokyo Olympics. Indeed, in the light of the portrayal of the poor but romantic post-war Japanese in Michener's *Sayonara*, which had been released as a movie just seven years before, the televised images of a modern Tokyo, with its super-fast bullet train, were a surprise to many in the West (see Chapter 6). The contradiction of a new Japan, but still true to its traditions, was played out in the image of the Japanese salaryman. As presented in the James Bond film of 1967, *You Only Live Twice*, the representation of male dominance may have delighted certain Western men, anxious about the developing second-wave feminism in their own society. Yet, soon after, as the Japanese economic miracle led to the loss of Western industries (such as motorcycles, cameras, televisions, shipbuilding and steel), this (surprising) rapid and increasing economic success required explanation. While the secret of the Japanese way of business was sought by some, the image of the "corporate samurai" emerged in the Western media. Just like the image of the fanatical war-time soldier, the corporate samurai now appeared, dedicating his life to the company and using any means to gain a business advantage, with stories of unfair business practices circulating in the West (see Chapter 7). In the British media, to explain the shock of this Japanese economic success (and the failures of its own manufacturing, in a British economy referred to, in the 1970s, as the "sick man of Europe"), there had to be something strange about the Japanese.[1] This weirdness was introduced into the media debates about the effects of Japanese popular culture (such as video games, manga and anime). Now the weird Japanese migrated from the corporate samurai, in the British media, to the dedicated Japanese fan of manga and anime, the otaku, as well.

However, Western anxieties about Japan suddenly dissipated with its shocking economic stagnation (the bursting of the "bubble economy"). Now, initially, schadenfreude entered the Western discourse about the Japanese although, in Britain, the explanation for its economic stagnation and ageing population was also attributed to the weirdness of the Japanese (man), possibly to suggest the reassuring idea that "it could not happen here as we are not like them". However, in the first decade of the 21st century, Western economic anxieties now had a different focus: China; with Japan represented as a reliable ally of the West. In the new internet age, Japan was now the source of popular entertainment that was pervading all areas of Western culture. No longer solely the province of Western youth, Japanese video games and Japanese graphic art were not simply entertainment for children but both reassuringly familiar, and indicative of Japanese innovation and creativity worthy of exhibitions in Western galleries and museums. Now, for many in the West, especially young adults, Japan had become *the* place to visit.

Beyond the national character of the Japanese

What this analysis has shown is that both Western culture and Japanese culture have changed during the nearly 500 years of their intercultural relationship: with the Western representation of the Japanese changing with the changing circumstances of that relationship. The "unexpected" in the cultural other requires explanation and in many instances, particularly those concerning a perception of threat, it has resulted in the attribution of negative characteristics to the Japanese (which have often been employed to maintain a sense of Western superiority). Thus, to consider there to be a *true* "national character" of the Japanese (that Westerners can determine) is a fruitless and academically bankrupt approach to intercultural relations. What members of one culture can observe in another culture are the cultural differences, and the differences to their own normative expectations. While this can lead to character attributions by members of one culture to the members of the other culture (as an explanation of these differences), we need to be aware that these are attributions, and may depend much more on the ideologies of the people making the attributions than on any genuine characteristics of the people being described.

Beyond *The Chrysanthemum and the Sword*

Benedict's *The Chrysanthemum and the Sword* has cast a surprisingly long shadow over the Western view of the Japanese, given its relatively modest sales in the West, and the long-held acceptance in Western anthropology that it is simply a "Benedictian myth" (Ryang, 2004). From the perspective of this current book, Benedict's representation of the Janus-like Japanese can be seen as one of the many accounts of the Japanese in Western culture which reflect the circumstances of its construction in terms of the state of the Western-Japanese relationship; and its attempt to explain the Japanese in terms of a Western ideology of superiority. To Benedict, American society was democratic, freedom-loving (i.e. familiar and "normal"), but the Japanese were alien, locked in their culture of obligation and shame, and suffering for it (suggesting that they were in some way deficient).

Not only do most of the representations presented in this book conflict with Benedict's view (by people who lived in the country and spoke the language) but also these representations reveal how Benedict had to be deliberately selective in her account to construct her representation of the Japanese. For example, while acknowledging that bushido is a relatively new concept, she focused on the concepts of revenge and vendetta as the key feature of it rather than on Nitobe's association of it with the European knightly code of chivalry. To Benedict, the Japanese humane treatment of the Russians after the Japanese victory in the Russo-Japanese war of 1904–5 was because the Russians had not "insulted" them (whereas, she argued, later they viewed the Americans as having done so). Furthermore, the Japanese "lack of mercy" was indicative of their character, rather than a feature of the brutal militarism of the Japanese army during the Pacific War (see Chapter 6). Indeed, Chamberlain (1912) had criticized the use of bushido to support the patriotism, nationalism and militarism of Japanese society at the beginning of the 20th, calling it a modern religion. His criticisms can also be applied to Benedict's historical analysis of Japanese "shame culture", where she uses the actions of the wartime Japanese military as indicative of (an enduring) Japanese culture (and character), rather than acknowledging a diversity of political views in Japan (such as the moderates and liberals, whose voices were suppressed in the 1930s and 1940s). As noted in Chapter 5, Chamberlain argued that, throughout the history of early modern Japan, the samurai had not demonstrated any specific loyalty to their lordly masters or felt any shame in usurping them, contrary to Benedict's view.

Probably the most damning criticism of *The Chrysanthemum and the Sword* came from anthropologist Clifford Geertz (1988). He noted the "candour of her style" (Geertz, 1988, p. 105) in describing Us versus Them, where she presented the strangeness of the other in the context of the familiar. To Benedict, the cultural other (the Japanese) was distinctly alien (and the alienness of the Japanese is emphasized in *The Chrysanthemum and the Sword*). Benedict accounted for the alienness of Them in a style that disturbs the Us, according to Geertz, by presenting the strange in the same straight-forward way as the familiar. In the books, she makes a claim about the Japanese, such as the importance of obligation in their culture, with "the same thing said and resaid until it seems either as undeniable as the laws of motion or as cooked up as a lawyer's brief; only the examples change". Geertz described this as the "hedgehog air of hers of being a truth-teller with only one truth to tell" (Geertz, 1988, p. 110). Characterizing a phase in anthropology that was soon over in the 1950s, to Geertz, the success of Benedict's work lay in her descriptive style: they (the cultural other) are not like us – this is why they are alien (which Benedict's description makes less alien) – so now they are known. By avoiding psychoanalytic methods or other complications, her book became accessible to the lay reader, such as the US military officers in occupied Japan (Geertz, 1988). But what Benedict had done was to represent the Japanese as the extreme cultural other (the "impossible object", Geertz, 1988, p. 116), forever located in their shame culture. Geertz (1988) finished his critique by suggesting that Benedict's work be read in the context of Swift's *Gulliver's Travels*. Hence, we can reject the characterization of the Japanese as the introverted samurai presented (but not seriously) in Chapter 1. Indeed, Geertz argued that the "Western imagination . . . has tended to construct rather different representations for itself of the otherness of others as it has come into practical contact with one or another sort of them" (Geertz, 1988, p. 116). It is these ongoing attempts to explain the differences between the cultures, rather than any fixed idea of character or culture that are illustrated in the present book.

Beyond Orientalism

Said's *Orientalism* (Said, 1978/1995) provided a valuable lesson in how even academics can be influenced in their views of the cultural other by their cultural background and ideological beliefs. But in doing so his characterization of the Orient was in terms of the history of the Christian-Muslim relationship, represented as a "clash of civilizations" in terms of binary differences favouring the West (Adib-Moghaddam, 2010). As Said (1978/1995) argued, in proposing these binary differences (modern versus ancient, familiar versus exotic), the Orientalist is constructing the self (the "us") and also constructing the other (the "them"). To Said, Orientalism has structured the Western discourse about the East (the Orient), creating a representation of it and its inhabitants as inferior, and created a mythology of the Orient that has supported Western imperialism: in objectifying the Oriental as an inferior other, it was employed as a justification for colonialism (Said, 1978/1995, 2014). However, the question arises as to whether this characterization can be applied to Japan, which was not colonized by a European country. Furthermore, the representations of the Japanese illustrated in this book do not always present the Japanese as inferior.

Minear (1980) argued that an Orientalism analysis can be applied to Western representations of the Japanese, but he also acknowledged that the historical relationship between the West and Japan was very different to the clash of cultures described by Said. Minear (1980) gave examples of where Basil Hall Chamberlain (particularly in his book *Things Japanese*) made claims of the superiority of the West over Japan, which also represented the Japanese and the European as distinct "races" with different "mentalities". Minear (1980) also argued that an Orientalist binary distinction is prominent in George Sansom's 1949 book, *The Western World and Japan*, where Sansom, while positing the idea of a unique Japanese civilization, still claimed that "in the basic elements of its growth [*it conformed*] to a general Asiatic pattern" (Sansom, 1950, p. 3). Thus, in one sentence, he shifts from a representation of Japan in terms of its historical and cultural distinctiveness to a generalization that Japan has followed a basic "Asiatic pattern", with the inference that all Asian cultures share common elements.

However, many of the authors cited in this book have not made the sort of binary distinctions characterized by Said. Indeed, Kopf (2000) argued that the application of (a universal idea of) Orientalism ignores the historical differences in different regions of "the Orient". Hence, the approach can homogenize the diversity of the Orient and the diversity of Western representation (of different parts of it). For example, Macfie (2000) argued that the British "Orientalism" in 19th-century India does not fit into the Said characterization. To take a specific example related to Japan, Markley (2003) argued that there is not a consistent historical representation of the West as superior to Japan. Particularly in the 17th century, English writers "did not automatically assume the cultural, economic, or even religious superiority of Christendom" over the Far East (Markley, 2003, p. 495). Markley drew on the example of Heylyn's 1677 *Cosmography* to illustrate his point (see Chapter 4). There is also a distinctive history of the relationship between European countries and Japan, where the Japanese avoided Western colonization. Subsequently, it modernized according to a Western model that led to one European characterization of the country being an emerging "Great Britain of the East" (see Chapter 5). Hence, while it is important to examine how Eurocentric and racial thinking has influenced Western representations of the Japanese, the framework of Orientalism is inadequate for the task of explaining the variety of Western representations of the Japanese discussed in this book.

Beyond stereotypes

It is quite possible to conceive of this current book as a history of Western stereotypes of the Japanese. I have presented the different Western representations of the Japanese and then suggested that these deviate from the Japanese experience. This is also what Matsumoto (2002) did in his book subtitled *Debunking Seven Cultural Stereotypes*, one of which was the Western stereotype of the Japanese salaryman. Indeed, I, too, have done my share of debunking Western stereotypes of the Japanese (Hinton, 2014a), including the British stereotype, in the early 21st century, of the Japanese man (Hinton, 2015). However, my concern here is that the traditional focus on stereotypes is on the characterization of them as erroneous, which tends to ignore how and why they were developed (as a result of a history of intergroup relations) (see Hinton, 2020a). Moscovici (1993, p. 9) made this point by arguing that the traditional stereotyping approach shows an "indifference toward the deep complexion of the social fabric". That is, it tends to ignore the cultural construction of the representation of social groups, and also the change of these representations with the changing intergroup relationship. For example, the 1980s stereotype of the Japanese salaryman is now viewed as old-fashioned, even in the West, and its use in the media is much less common now.

Stereotypes have typically been viewed in Western academic psychology as simplistic and fixed representations of a social group, resulting from a lack of a complex understanding of the group being stereotyped (see Chapter 1). For example, Johnson (1991, p. 163) expressed this common view: "Many of the stereotypes [*of the Japanese*] have their roots in specific events so that one cannot call them entirely erroneous, although like all stereotypes they tend to be one-dimensional". Yet, as Perkins (1979) has argued, this is not the case. In order to make a stereotypical judgement about, say, welfare claimants, a person has to understand the welfare system in their society and make a judgement about whether payments are too generous or too meagre, in terms of their ideological beliefs about the proper use of government funds. As Billig (1985) has shown (see Chapter 1), it is not that one representation is a one-dimensional stereotype (produced by simplistic thinkers) and another an accurate representation (produced by complex thinkers). Rather representations (as stereotypes) differ as a result of different ideologies, such as the different representations of social groups (such as welfare claimants) circulating within the social networks of the supporters of different political parties. For example, the inventor of the stereotype, the journalist Walter Lippmann argued that in the Paris peace talks after the First World War, the French Prime Minister George Clemenceau had an old-fashioned stereotyped view of the Germans (Lippmann, 1922). Yet the reason he claimed this was because he (Lippmann) had an opposing political opinion to Clemenceau. As Pickering (2001) has pointed out, Lippmann's political views were certainly not ones that would have universal agreement on their "accuracy". Indeed, it can be assumed that Clemenceau would have rejected the statement that his views were stereotypes, and Lippmann's views were correct. Thus, it is important to appreciate that the term "stereotype" has been used rhetorically as a label for an ideological viewpoint with which the writer disagrees.

However, if we acknowledge the socio-cultural formation of stereotypes by a social group for their own ideological purposes, then stereotypes cease to be a question of accuracy but one of ideology, and their formation can be examined in terms of the ideological purposes of their construction by that social group about another social group (Hinton, 2020a). Indeed, the ideological significance of stereotypes is clearly demonstrated by the fact that within a culture there will be different stereotypes of different social groups. For example, a representation of the Japanese in Britain (which we might call a stereotype) is different to a British representation of the French (which we might also call a stereotype), as the relationship between the British and the Japanese is different to the relationship between the British and the French. Hence, in order to understand why a representation (a stereotype) has arisen, we need to examine the relationship between the people employing the stereotype and the people being stereotyped – which is an issue of intergroup relations. Hence, to understand why a particular representation of one nationality (such as the Japanese) has emerged in the culture of another nationality (such as British or American culture) at any one time, it is the state of the intercultural relations between the nationalities that should be explored, as argued in this book (see Hinton, 2020a).

Telling stories about the Japanese

As I pointed out in Chapter 1, the psychologist Jerome Bruner (1990), an advocate of cultural psychology, argued that people are meaning-makers (rather than accuracy seekers) in their everyday thinking about the social world, a view that I support. This meaning-making takes place within a culture, because it is within a culture that the meaningful social categories and their definitions are constructed. Indeed, Bruner argued that all categories are cultural constructions, rather than there being "natural" categories (Bruner et al., 1956). In order to negotiate their culture, the members of it need to learn the norms and roles within it, which they do through socialization and living within it. Hence, they develop an understanding of the expectations of behaviour related to the social categories and social roles present in their culture. To put it another way, cultures differ in their "cultural patterning" (see Chapter 1), and the members of it acquire "culture in mind" (Hinton, 2017; Shore, 1996). Moscovici (1998) has argued that not only do known representations within a culture define the cultural categories of social group members but also this common network of representations forms the common cultural understandings of the cultural group members, or as Bruner (1990) puts it, a folk psychology. And, it is within the communication of the culture that new representations are formed and negotiated. In fact, Moscovici (1998) argued that it is within the communication media of a culture that the unfamiliar becomes familiar. In the 1980s, in the United States (for example), very few people would have known what the word "anime" meant, yet through the communication within their culture, it became familiar. So, in 2010, when Peter Griffin, the main character in the popular US cartoon series *Family Guy*, in a drunken state, expresses his confusion about anime, it is assumed that the audience knows what he is talking about.[2]

Crucially, as Bruner argued, this folk psychology is "invested with canonicity". It defines the expected and the usual. Furthermore, "it endows these with legitimacy and authority" (Bruner, 1990, p. 47). This makes living in your own culture generally predictable as you have expectations for everyday life. Bruner (1990) gave the example of a person going into a post-office and behaving "post-office"; that is, you know what to do in the post office (in your culture). We know what to do in ordinary situations and how to behave with people in different social roles, as we have learnt the cultural expectations to guide us. However, breaches of the canonical, by definition, don't make sense. When someone does something unexpected, it calls out for an explanation, to give it meaning. And this is why we tell stories.

For Bruner (1990, pp. 49–50): "The function of the story is to . . . [*make*] . . . comprehensible a deviation from a canonical cultural pattern". When we tell a story to explain the unexpected, it will contain *reasons* (Malle, 2007): such as an attribution of cause, or a justification, or a rationale of some sort. Hence, if we asked a Princeton University student, around 1930, what was the most memorable thing about the Japanese, they might reply with the (surprising) fact that the Japanese had modernized remarkably quickly in the previous fifty years and were now a major world power. (This was unexpected as no other nation had done this so rapidly.) If we then asked them why this happened, they might tell us the following story: "The Japanese were able to rapidly modernize because they are an intelligent and industrious people". This is precisely the outcome that Katz and Braly (1933) found, when they asked Princeton University students to select characteristics of the Japanese. Industrious and intelligent were the most common selections. Except that Katz and Braly referred to it as a fallacious stereotype. While it might be a stereotype, it is not a mistaken belief but an explanation – a story containing a reason. Stereotypes are explanations. Not everyone in a culture will necessarily agree with or condone this explanation (due to their ideological beliefs), but stereotypes are well-known representations as they are shared within a culture.

In conclusion, over the length of time that Westerners have engaged with the Japanese, they have observed cultural differences between themselves and the Japanese.

These differences take place in an intercultural context. In order to make sense of these differences – which are by definition unexpected – they require explanation. In order to provide that explanation, people tell a story. From the first time that Francis Xavier found that the Japanese were interested in a rational argument about religion (a pleasantly unexpected finding in the context of his prior experience), Europeans began to tell stories about the Japanese which they circulated throughout Europe. All the way through the centuries to the (unexpected) collapse of the asset price "bubble", in 1991, in Japan, Westerners have been telling each other stories of the Japanese to make sense of them. Yet these stories are not "fixed" representations (even if we call them stereotypes) but are responsive to the changing intercultural relationship between Westerners and Japanese. As this relationship changes, so will the representation change – of the Japanese in the Western mind.

Notes

1 Rather than contemplating the complacency of British industry and its old-fashioned plant and practices.
2 Series 9, episode 5, entitled "Baby, You Knock Me Out", first broadcast on 14 November 2010.

APPENDIX

Japan at the time of Portuguese trade

Japan is an archipelago to the east of the continental landmass of Asia, stretching 3,000 kilometres (1,900 miles), between Siberian Russia in the north-east and Taiwan in the south-west. It is separated from the Korean, the Chinese North-East (Manchurian) and East Siberian mainland in the north and west by the Sea of Japan. Amongst the thousands of small islands in the archipelago, there are five large ones. Hokkaido (roughly the size of the island of Ireland) in the north was originally only inhabited by the Ainu people but was gradually colonized by the Japanese from the south and fully incorporated into the Japan Empire in the second half of the 19th century. Hokkaido is separated in the south from the main island of Honshu (a little larger than the island of Great Britain) by the Tsugaru Strait, which ranges from twenty-five to forty kilometres wide (fifteen to twenty-five miles). In the south, Honshu partly surrounds the island of Shikoku (roughly the size of Wales), and in the south west, Kyushu (twice the size of Wales[1]) is separated from Honshu by the 700-metre (less than half a mile) Kanmon Straits. The waters between these three islands form the Inland Sea. The north-west of Kyushu is separated from the Korean peninsula on the Asian mainland by the 200 kilometres (120 miles) Korea Strait. The Chinese mainland (of Shanghai and Ningbo) lies nearly 650 kilometres (400 miles) from south-west Kyushu across the East China Sea. Between Kyushu and Taiwan lie the Ryukyu Islands, with the island of Okinawa at its heart. Once a separate kingdom, these islands now form the southernmost part of Japan. Okinawa lies roughly 850 kilometres (over 500 miles) south-west of Kyushu and 750 kilometres (under 500 miles) north-east of Taiwan.

Initially Japanese was not a written language and so the early accounts of the country and its people come from Chinese scholars, such as a 3rd-century CE account of the 倭 people (Wo or Hwa people) at Yamato in Japan (Carr, 1992). Historians locate ancient Yamato in central Japan on the island of Honshu (in the region now known as Kansai). During the 3rd century, the Yamato dynasty (250–587 CE) claimed dominance as rulers of the people we now refer to as the Japanese (Fuqua, 2017). In the 5th century, Chinese authors wrote of the 倭國 (*Wōguó*) to refer to the country of the Wo or Yamato people. However, the Chinese scribes had selected the character 倭 for Wo in their texts, connoting dwarfish and submissive, an example of cultural othering or an "exonymic slur" as Carr (1992, p. 2) put it. When Japanese scholars later adopted and adapted Chinese characters for transcribing their own spoken language, they decided to replace the character 倭 for 和 (harmony, peaceful) which were both pronounced as Wa in the Japanese reading of the character. Now Yamato could be transcribed as 大和 (great harmony) and the name of the Wa-people read as "harmonious people", a positive reading (Carr, 1992). The term "Yamato" became synonymous with "Japanese", as an ethnic epithet, such that the Yamato could be distinguished from the Ainu in the north or the Ryukyuans in the south (see Jinam et al., 2021). In modern Japanese, traditional Japanese things are often distinguished from foreign (typically Western) things by the use of Wa, as in traditional Japanese clothing, such as the kimono, described as *wafuku* (和服 or harmony-clothing) as opposed to Western clothes or *yōfuku* (洋服, or ocean-clothing, that is, across the ocean i.e. foreign).

However, in the 7th century, a new name for Japan appeared in Chinese (and Korean) texts, that of 日本 (read as Nihon or Nippon in Japanese), which translates into English as "the sun's origin". This indicates the direction from which the sun rises from a Chinese perspective; that is, the country or land of the rising sun (日本國). However, it was linked in Japan to the origin myth of a people descending from the sun goddess Amaterasu. Various explanations have been suggested for the new name (such as the dislike of the Wo or Wa terminology), but there is not a definitive agreement on the issue (Carr, 1992). However, it was adopted as the new name for the country and used by Japanese scholars in the 9th-century *Nihon shoki*, an officially commissioned history known as *The Chronicles of Japan*. Thus, 日本 became the agreed name of the country, with 日本國[2] being the country of Japan (pronounced as ni hon koku in Japanese). However, these three characters were read in Chinese as ji-pen-guo (or ri-ben-guo), which can explain why it was termed "Zipangu" or "Cipangu" in the first Western accounts of the country. It is easy to see how this became the source of various European language terms for the country that, in English, became known as Japan.

The Chronicles of Japan (*Nihon shoki*), written in classical Chinese and drawing its influences from Chinese culture, provides a list of Japanese rulers, beginning with the legendary 7th-century BCE Jimmu, the first Emperor of Japan, descended from the sun goddess Amaterasu. As well as his military power, this spiritual heritage gave the emperor religious significance and authority in the native Japanese Shinto worship of deities or spirits (kami). There is little actual evidence of many of the early emperors listed in the text, due to the lack of early written sources or archaeological data (Bentley, 2011). However, much of the history of Japan, from the beginning of the common era to the 9th century CE, involved the coming together of family-based communities into larger regional kinship-based clan groups, owing their allegiance to the emperor, who from 710 CE established an imperial court in Nara, in south-central Honshu, from where he claimed dominance over the various clans in their own domains in different parts of the country.

Buddhism was introduced into Japan from mainland Asia in the 6th century CE (according to the Chronicles of Japan), and soon became influential within the Imperial Court. In 794 CE, the Emperor Kanmu moved the court to Kyoto, and subsequently a large Buddhist monastic and temple complex was built at Enryakuji on Mount Hiei, to the northeast of Kyoto. Over the following centuries, various different Buddhist sects were introduced into the country, such as Shingon Buddhism and Pure Land Buddhism, with their different regulations and practices. Crucially, Buddhism thinkers (such as the monks on Mount Hiei) began to integrate the indigenous nature religion, Shinto, and its gods (*kami*; often spirits of the natural world) into Buddhist practice. Shinto shrines and Buddhist temples (with their Buddha statues) became complementary places of worship, with differences in devotion which, in practice, were not normally a cause of theological dispute (Kasahara, 2001).

In 794 CE, the Emperor Kanmu gave his senior general Ōtomo no Otomaro the title of *seii taishogun* (barbarian-overthrowing general) in leading the war against the Emishi people of northern Honshu (the barbarians of the title). This term was shortened to shogun and continued to be given to the senior general in the war. However, between the 10th and 12th centuries CE, the clan lords called daimyo (great land holders) with their armies of warriors called *bushi*, also known as samurai (followers), gained increasing military power. In 1185 CE, Minamoto no Yoritomo, leader of the Minamoto clan, became the dominant warlord and the Emperor Go-Shirakawa effectively handed over power to him. In 1192, the Emperor Go-Toba named Yoritomo as shogun, which took on a new meaning as the supreme warlord of the country. While still theoretically the pinnacle of the power structure, in reality, the emperor had lost his military power and was now totally reliant on the shogun. The Kamakura shogunate, established by Yoritomo lasted nearly 150 years, during which time (in the later 13th century) two Mongol invasion attempts by ships of Kublai Khan from China were defeated by Japanese forces aided by a typhoon, known as the divine wind or *kamikaze*.

The Emperor Go-Daigo sought to regain power in 1331, only to be defeated by the warlord Ashikaga Takauji who, after five years of upheaval, was established as the new shogun. The Ashikaga shogunate lasted for over 200 years. However, the Onin war of 1467, initiated by a dispute over who would succeed the shogun, brought new disorder. The increased military power of the various daimyo armies meant that no one leader could easily maintain overall dominance and the country descended in the civil war with the powerful clans vying for control. This period, from the second half of the 15th century to the beginning of the 17th century, became known in Japanese history as the *sengoku jidai* (period of civil war or warring states).

Despite the civil war lasting 150 years, for the ordinary agrarian Japanese people, it did not often impinge on their daily lives. Battles, when they occurred, took place between the warrior classes (the samurai) of the different clans. The feudal system placed the local lords, the daimyo, at the head of a domain's hierarchy, with the priests, farmers, peasants, artisans and merchants beneath them, whose everyday lives could remain untouched by the warfare. Each lord's domain could act as an independent state, with its economy based on the production of rice. Lords of small domains might keep out of the warfare except when called upon by a liege lord. In a domain, the family was the key social unit in Japan, with property associated with the family rather than individuals, and duty to the family paramount in social relations. Urbanization occurred around the local castles, creating towns made up of wooden houses, with sliding panels to open the house to let in the breeze in the heat of summer. Wealthy people wore silk *kimono* (literally meaning a thing to wear), but, for less wealthy members of society, the kimono were made of flax or hemp, and later cotton. Manual workers often wore a loincloth to undertake their physical activities. Local markets supplied cooking utensils, pottery, tools and household goods. When possible, most people ate two meals a day, based on rice and vegetables, which were universally eaten using chopsticks. The prevalence of hot springs in Japan led to the development of public baths, allowing people to bathe regularly, with temples providing "charity baths" for the poor. Richer people had bathhouses integrated into their property. Bathing was not only a religious, medicinal and hygienic practice, but the bath also became a place of socializing with friends (Butler, 2005). Hence, in the early modern period (from around 1500 CE, as defined in the West), Japan was a well-organized society that was highly literate and, despite the long-lasting civil war, contained relatively stable local social structures.

In the 16th century, Japan was an essentially agrarian economy based on rice production. Wealth was measured in terms of koku – the amount of land that could produce about 180 litres of rice. Hence a daimyo had few opportunities to increase his wealth except by expanding his domain through war with his neighbours. Thus, for coastal daimyo providing ports for vessels trading with China offered the possibility of a significant increase in wealth. When the Portuguese arrived, their trade would not only bring goods and taxes to a daimyo whose port they traded from, but with their ships and armaments, the Portuguese could prove a useful ally in the constant disputes between rival clans. The first Portuguese factory was established in 1550 on the island of Hirado, just off the coast of Kyushu, which had a history of providing a base for traders with China. Not surprisingly, the daimyo Matsuda Takanobu[3] was willing to allow Francis Xavier to preach when the Jesuits arrived, but this was more as a goodwill gesture than any personal interest in the religion. However, with the Jesuit mission now an adjunct to Portuguese trade, any daimyo in Kyushu seeking to lure the Portuguese traders to his domain needed to take the Jesuits into account (Boxer, 1951/1967).

When the Portuguese arrived in Japan, the country was in the midst of the sengoku jidai, the civil war period lasting nearly a century and a half. The influence of the Portuguese on the progress of this war is debatable, but, arguably, it was not significant in determining the course of the war. It is true that the introduction of

FIGURE BM1 The Main Islands of Japan

(Figure adapted by the author from the map http://d-maps.com/m/asia/japan/japon/japon04.gif, with permission.)

the gun had an effect on specific battles (although later the Japanese gave up the gun) and Portuguese trade did enrich the daimyos whose ports they traded from.

In the 1560s, Oda Nobunaga (1534–1582), daimyo of Owari, a domain in Honshu, expanded his influence by warring against neighbouring domains, becoming the dominant warlord in Japan, and the first of the three "great unifiers". In the following decade, he ended the Ashikaga shogunate. However, in 1582, at Nijo Palace in Kyoto, General Akechi Mitsuhide turned on his lord and forced Nobunaga and his son to commit seppuku. Not long after, Nobunaga was avenged by Toyotomi Hideyoshi (1537–98) defeating Mitsuhide at the Battle of Yamazaki. Hideyoshi now became the pre-eminent warlord, labelled the second of the "great unifiers". Nobunaga had failed to defeat the armed warrior Buddhist monks who threatened his power, so in 1585, Hideyoshi sent an army to defeat the Shingon monks at Negoro, where he confiscated their weapons. In an ongoing action, he forced the monks, including those at Mount Koya (the headquarters of the Shingon Buddhists) to disarm and cease musket production. He supported the Buddhist monks in rebuilding their temples as long as they stuck to their religious activities only. By the early 1590s, Hideyoshi was master of all Japan. However, in 1598, Hideyoshi died, with his five most trusted generals making up a ruling counsel in the name of Hideyoshi's son Hideyori (a boy of five years old).

However, after Hideyoshi's death, Tokugawa Ieyasu (1543–1616), one of the five generals, seized control of the country, and defeated his enemies in the Battle of Sekigahara in 1600. With Ieyasu in control of the country, the sengoku period was over. Tokugawa Ieyasu is described as the third and final of the "great unifiers" of Japan. In 1603, he was named as shogun by the Emperor Go-Yōzei. However, Toyotomi Hideyori, Hideyoshi's son, still lived, and in 1615, Ieyasu destroyed the power of the Toyotomi clan at Osaka Castle, and Hideyori committed seppuku. With all possible challengers defeated, Ieyasu and his descendants established the Tokugawa Shogunate as the unchallenged power in Japan. Amongst the numerous edicts enacted to maintain their dominance and an iron grip on the country was one to avoid a potential fifth column by outlawing Christianity, and a second of removing the risk of European colonization by ejecting the Portuguese (and most other Europeans) from the country and banning the Japanese from travelling overseas. The effects of their actions led Japan to be one of the few Asian countries to avoid European influence, and colonization, during the early modern period. Furthermore, after 150 years of warfare, the Tokugawa Shogunate brought peace to the country for the next 250 years (Mason and Caiger, 1997).

Notes

1 The states in the United States closest in area to main islands of Japan are South Carolina and Hokkaido, Minnesota and Honshu, New Jersey and Shikoku, and Maryland and Kyushu.
2 The character 國 is represented as 国 in modern Japanese and simplified Chinese.
3 In this Appendix, the Japanese name are given in the Japanese order of family name and personal name.

REFERENCES

Abe, T., Shirai, I., & Yuki, T. (2022). Socio-economic activities of former feudal lords in Meiji Japan. *Business History, 64*(2), 405–33.

Abel, J. R. (2012). Japan's sporting diplomacy: The 1964 Tokyo Olympiad. *The International History Review, 34*(2), 203–20.

Adib-Moghaddam, A. (2010). *A metahistory of the clash of civilisations: Us and them beyond orientalism*. Columbia University Press.

Ahler, D. J. (2018). The group theory of parties: Identity politics, party stereotypes, and polarization in the 21st century. *The Forum, 16*(1), 3–22.

Aitken, G., & Delafond, M. (2013). *La collection d'estampes Japonaises de Claude Monet* (Claude Monet's collection of Japanese prints, 3rd ed.). La Biblioteque des Arts.

Ajala, O. A. (2013). African slave trade and maritime transportation. In I. Ness (Ed.), *The encyclopedia of global human migration*. Blackwell Publishing Ltd.

Allport, F. H. (1924). The group fallacy in relation to social science. *American Journal of Sociology, 29*(6), 688–706.

Allport, G. W. (1954). *The nature of prejudice*. Addison-Wesley.

Andrew, D. T. (2013). *Aristocratic vice: The attack on duelling, suicide, adultery, and gambling in eighteenth-century England*. Yale University Press.

Aoki, S., & Zabel, I. (2001). *Fruits*. Phaidon.

Arnold, E. (1891a). Japonica – Second paper – Japanese people. *Scribner's Magazine, 9*(1), 17–30.

Arnold, E. (1891b). Japonica – Fourth paper – Japanese ways and thoughts. *Scribner's Magazine, 9*(3), 321–40.

Ayabe, M. (2007). *Unknown legend of Christ in ancient Japan*. Tankobon. [Japanese edition. Original title. 知られざる古代日本キリスト伝説]

Azuma, H. (2009). *Otaku: Japan's database animals*. University of Minnesota Press.

Babson, A. (2012). 'A Japanese Young Man': British aesthetes turning Japanese in Gilbert's libretto for The Mikado. In N. Falkof & O. Cashman-Brown (Eds.), *On whiteness* (pp. 183–92). Brill.

Ballard, M. E., & Wiest, J. R. (1996). Mortal Kombat: The effect of violent videogame play on males' hostility and cardiovascular responding. *Journal of Applied Social Psychology, 26*(8), 717–30.

Barboza, D. (2010, 15 August). China passes Japan as second-largest economy. *New York Times*. https://www.nytimes.com/2010/08/16/business/global/16yuan.html

Barker, T. W. (2009). Pulling the Spanish out of the 'Christian Century': Re-evaluating Spanish – Japanese relations during the seventeenth century. *Eras*, p. 11. http://www.monash.edu/__data/assets/pdf_file/0007/1667437/tbarker.pdf

Barrett, P., & Eysenck, S. (1984). The assessment of personality factors across 25 countries. *Personality and Individual Differences*, *5*(6), 615–32.

Barry, R. (1995). The development of the Roman Catholic teachings on suicide. *Notre Dame Journal of Law. Ethics & Public Policy*, *9*(2), 449–501.

BBC (2001, 7 December). Japan falls into recession. *BBC*. http://news.bbc.co.uk/1/hi/business/1695282.stm

BBC (2007, 19 November). Japan eyes demographic time bomb. *BBC*. http://news.bbc.co.uk/1/hi/world/asia-pacific/7084749.stm

BBC (2009, 20 November). Deflation returns to the Japanese economy. *BBC*. http://news.bbc.co.uk/1/hi/business/8369767.stm

BBC (2013, 3 December). No sex please, we're Japanese [television programme]. *BBC2*. http://www.bbc.co.uk/programmes/b03fh0bg

Benedict, R. (1947). *The chrysanthemum and the sword: Patterns of Japanese culture*. Secker & Warburg.

Benedict, R. (1959). *Patterns of culture* (Sentry ed.). Honghton Mifflin Company. (Original work published 1934)

Benesch, O. (2014). *Inventing the way of the samurai: Nationalism, internationalism, and bushidō in modern Japan*. Oxford University Press.

Bentley, J. R. (2011). The birth and flowering of Japanese historiography: From chronicles to tales to historical interpretations. In S. Foot & C. F. Robinson (Eds.), *The Oxford history of historical writing: Volume 2: 400–1400* (pp. 58–79). Oxford University Press.

Berggren, C. (1995). Japan as number two: Competitive problems and the future of alliance capitalism after the burst of the bubble boom. *Work, Employment and Society*, *9*(1), 53–95.

Bergreen, L. (2011). *Columbus: The four voyages, 1492–1504*. Viking.

Bernstein, B. J. (1986). A postwar myth: 500,000 US lives saved. *Bulletin of the Atomic Scientists*, *42*(6), 38–40.

Bernstein, B. J. (1999). Reconsidering Truman's claim of 'half a million American lives' saved by the atomic bomb: The construction and deconstruction of a myth. *The Journal of Strategic Studies*, *22*(1), 54–95.

Bernstein, P. (1981, 13 September). Making of a literary shogun. *The New York Times Magazine*. www.nytimes.com/1981/09/13/magazine/making-of-a-literary-shogun.html

Bethune, C. R. D. (Ed.). (1862). *The discoveries of the world, from their first original unto the year of our lord 1555, by Antonio Galvano, governor of Ternate: Corrected, quoted and published in England, by Richard Hakluyt, (1601). Now reprinted, with the original Portuguese text*. The Hakluyt Society.

Billig, M. (1978). *Fascists: A social psychological view of the National Front*. Academic Press.

Billig, M. (1985). Prejudice, categorization and particularization: From a perceptual to a rhetorical approach. *European Journal of Social Psychology*, *15*, 79–103.

Bird, I. L. (1880). *Unbeaten tracks in Japan*, Vol. 1. G. P. Putnam's Sons.

Blakey, M. L. (1999). Scientific racism and the biological concept of race. *Literature and Psychology*, *45*(1–2), 29–43.

Blussé, L., Viallé, C., Remmelink, W., & Van Daalen, I. (2021). *The Deshima diaries: Marginalia 1740–1800*. Brill.

Bodart-Bailey, B. M., & Massarella, D. (1995). *The furthest goal: Engelbert Kaempfer's encounter with Tokugawa Japan*. Routledge.
Boldt, L. G. (1993). *Zen and the art of making a living: A practical guide to creative career design*. Penguin.
Bolitho, H. (1998). Tokugawa Japan: The return of the other? In H. Hardacre (Ed.), *The postwar development of Japanese studies in the United States* (pp. 85–114). Brill.
Boot, W. J. (2013). The transfer of learning: The import of Chinese and Dutch books in Togukawa Japan. *Itinerario*, *37*(3), 188–206.
Borschberg, P. (2011). *Hugo Grotius, the Portuguese, and free trade in the East Indies*. NUS Press.
Boscariol, M. (2021). São Jorge da Mina and Macao: A comparative reappraisal of European encounters. *Journal of the British Academy*, *9*(S4), 32–57.
Boxer, C. R. (1967). *The Christian century in Japan, 1549–1650*. University of California Press. (Original work published 1951)
Boxer, C. R. (1985). A note on the triangular trade between Macao, Manila, and Nagasaki, 1580–1640. *Terrae Incognitae*, *17*(1), 51–9.
Brewer, K. (2015). *Prester John: The legend and its sources*. Ashgate Publishing, Ltd.
Bridge, C. (2011). *William Hughes: Australia*. Haus Publishing.
Bruner, J. S. (1990). *Acts of meaning*. Harvard University Press.
Bruner, J. S., Goodnow, J. J., & Austin, J. G. (1956). *A study of thinking*. Wiley.
Bryce, M., Barber, C., Kelly, J., Kunwar, S., & Plumb, A. (2010). Manga and anime: Fluidity and hybridity in global imagery. *Electronic Journal of Contemporary Japanese Studies*. https://www.japanesestudies.org.uk/articles/2010/Bryce.html
Burges, W. (1862). The international exhibition. *Gentleman's Magazine*, *213*(7), 3–12.
Buruma, I. (2002). The Nanking massacre as a historical symbol. In R. Sabella, F. Li, & D. Liu (Eds.), *Nanking 1937: Memory and healing*. Routledge.
Butler, L. (2005). "Washing off the dust": Baths and bathing in late medieval Japan. *Monumenta Nipponica*, *60*(1), 1–41.
Caldeira, A. M. (2011). Learning the ropes in the Tropics: Slavery and the plantation system on the island of São Tomé. *African Economic History*, *39*(1), 35–71.
Caron, F. (1663). *A true description of the mighty kingdom of Japan and Siam* (R. Manley Trans.). Samuel Brown and John de l'Ecluse. https://quod.lib.umich.edu/e/eebo/A34454.0001.001
Carr, M. (1992). Wa wa lexicography. *International Journal of Lexicography*, *5*(1), 1–31.
Chamberlain, B. H. (1902). *Things Japanese being notes on various subjects connected with Japan for the use of travellers and others*. John Murray.
Chamberlain, B. H. (1912). *The invention of a new religion*. Theophania Publishing.
Chambers, D. (2012). 'Wii play as a family': The rise in family-centred video gaming. *Leisure Studies*, *31*(1), 69–82.
Chang, D. W. W. (2003). The western powers and Japan's aggression in China: The League of Nations and" The Lytton Report". *American Journal of Chinese Studies*, 43–63.
Chang, I. (1997). *The rape of Nanking: The forgotten holocaust of World War II*. Basic Books.
Chen, C. L., & Hall, P. (2011). The impacts of high-speed trains on British economic geography: A study of the UK's InterCity 125/225 and its effects. *Journal of Transport Geography*, *19*(4), 689–704.
Christensen, C. M. (1997). *The innovator's dilemma: When new technologies cause great firms to fail*. Harvard Business School Press.
Christensen C. M., & Raynor M. E. (2003). *The innovator's solution: Creating and sustaining successful growth*. Harvard Business School Press.

Christenson, S., Reschly, A. L., & Wylie, C. (2012). *Handbook of research on student engagement.* Springer.
Cialdini, R. B. (2012). The focus theory of normative conduct. In P. A. M. Van Lange, A. W. Kruglanski, & E. T. Higgins (Eds.), *Handbook of theories of social psychology* (pp. 295–312). Sage.
Cieslik, H. (1954a). Early Jesuit Missionaries in Japan (II): Balthasar Gago and Japanese Christian terminology. *Missionary Bulletin, 8,* 82–90. https://pweb.cc.sophia.ac.jp/britto/xavier/cieslik/ciejmj02.pdf
Cieslik, H. (1954b). *Early Jesuit missionaries in Japan 3: Gaspar Vilela: The Apostle of Miyako.* https://pweb.cc.sophia.ac.jp/britto/xavier/cieslik/ciejmj03.pdf
Cieslik, H. (1954c). *Early missionaries in Japan 6. Soldo Organitino: The architect of the Japanese mission.* https://pweb.cc.sophia.ac.jp/britto/xavier/cieslik/ciejmj06.pdf
Cieslik, H. (1974). The case of Christovão Ferreira. *Monumenta Nipponica, 29*(1), 1–54.
Cliff, N. (2011). *Holy war: How Vasco da Gama's epic voyages turned the tide in a centuries-old clash of civilizations.* Harper Collins.
Clulow, A. (2014). *The Company and the Shogun. The Dutch encounter with Tokugawa Japan.* Columbia University Press.
Coaldrake, K. (2013). Fine arts versus decorative arts: The categorization of Japanese arts at the international expositions in Vienna (1873), Paris (1878) and Chicago (1893). *Japan Forum, 25*(2), 174–90.
Coleridge, H. J. (1872a). *The life and letters of St. Francis Xavier* (Volume the first). Burns and Oates.
Coleridge, H. J. (1872b). *The life and letters of St. Francis Xavier* (Volume the second). Burns and Oates.
Columbus, C. (1893). *The journal of Christopher Columbus (during his First Voyage, 1492–93): And documents relating to the voyages of John Cabot and Gaspar Corte Real.* (C. R. Markham, Trans.) Hakluyt Society.
Conant, M. P. (1908). *The oriental tale in England in the eighteenth century.* The Columbia University Press.
Conte-Helm, M. (2013). *Japan and the north east of England: From 1862 to the present day.* Bloomsbury Academic.
Cooper, M. (1965). *They came to Japan: An anthology of European reports on Japan, 1543–1640.* Centre for Japanese Studies. The University of Michigan.
Cooper, M. (1974). *Rodrigues the interpreter: An early Jesuit in Japan and China.* John Weatherhill Inc.
Cooper, M. (2005). *The Japanese mission to Europe, 1582–1590: The journey of four samurai boys through Portugal, Spain and Italy.* Global Oriental.
Corr, W. (1995). *Adams the pilot: The life and times of Captain William Adams, 1564–1650.* Routledge.
Corrigan, K., van Campen, J., Blyberg, J. C., & Diercks, F. (2015). *Asia in Amsterdam: The culture of luxury in the Golden Age.* Yale University Press.
Cortazzi, H. (2002). *Mitford's Japan: Memories and recollections, 1866–1906.* Routledge.
Cortazzi, H. (2007). Book review: The Japanese mission to Europe, 1582–1590: The Journey of four samurai boys through Portugal, Spain and Italy. *Journal of Interdisciplinary Economics, 18*(4), 370–71.
Cortazzi, H. (2013). *Britain and Japan: Biographical portraits* (Vol. 8). Brill
Crasset, J. (1705). *The history of the Church of Japan. Written originally in French by Monsieur L'Abbe de T. And now translated into English.* [no publisher].

Cravens, H. (2010). What's new in science and race since the 1930s?: Anthropologists and racial essentialism. *The Historian*, 72(2), 299–320.

Crawford, G., & Hancock, D. (2019). *Cosplay and the art of play: Exploring sub-culture through art*. Palgrave Macmillan.

Crewdson, W. (1915). *Japan our ally*. Macmillan.

Cross, G., & Smits, G. (2005). Japan, the US and the globalization of children's consumer Culture. *Journal of Social History*, *38*(4), 873–90.

Cullen, L. M. (2013). Notes: 'Gulliver in Japan'. *Eighteenth-Century Ireland/Iris an dá chultúr*, *28*, 170–76. Eighteenth-Century Ireland Society.

Cummins, J. G. (1992). *The voyage of Christopher Columbus: Columbus' own journal of discovery newly restored and translated*. St Martin's Press.

Darnell, R. (1997). The anthropological concept of culture at the end of the Boasian century. *Social Analysis: The International Journal of Social and Cultural Practice*, *41*(3), 42–54.

Dasgupta, R. (2012). *Re-reading the salaryman in Japan: Crafting masculinities*. Routledge.

Dasgupta, R. (2014). Salaryman anxieties in Tokyo sonata: Shifting discourses of state, family and masculinity in post-bubble Japan. In A. Germer, V. Mackie, & U. Wöhr (Eds.), *Gender, nation and state in modern Japan* (pp. 275–92). Routledge.

De Sousa, L. (2019). *The Portuguese slave trade in early modern Japan: Merchants, Jesuits and Japanese, Chinese, and Korean Slaves*. Brill.

Delgado, M. (2016). "All people have reason and free will". The controversy over the nature of the Indians in the sixteenth century. In F. Klose & M. Thulin (Eds.), *Humanity. A history of European concepts in practice from the sixteenth century to the present* (pp. 91–106). Vandenhoeck & Ruprecht.

Denison, R. (2010). Anime tourism: Discursive construction and reception of the Studio Ghibli Art Museum. *Japan Forum*, *22*(3–4), 545–63.

DeVere Brown, S. (1988). Yasunari Kawabata (1899–1972): Tradition versus Modernity. *World Literature Today*, *62*(3), 375–79.

Dillard, N. R. (1997). Operational leadership: A case study of two extremes during operation watchtower. *Naval War College, Newport RI*. https://apps.dtic.mil/sti/pdfs/ADA307601.pdf.

Dochartaigh, P. Ó., & Schönfeld, C. (2013). *Representing the" Good German" in literature and culture after 1945: Altruism and moral ambiguity*. Camden House.

Dodgson, M. (1995). Review article. The Japanese industrial system. *Prometheus*, *13*(1), 107–18.

Doeff, H. (2003). *Recollections of Japan* (A. M. Doeff, Trans.). Trafford Publishing.

Domínguez, D. C. (2012). Japanese rulers in the Jesuit correspondence, 1573–1605: A case of Public Affairs in the XVI century. *Journal of Asia Pacific Studies*, *2*(3), 294–320.

Döpfert, M. (2022). Christianomachia Japonensis: The Japanese martyr on stage. In H. Oba, A. Watanabe, & F. Schaffenrath (Eds.), *Japan on the Jesuit stage* (pp. 57–83). Brill.

Dower, J. W. (1986). *War without mercy. Race and ower in the Pacific War*. Pantheon Books.

Dower, J. W. (1999). *Embracing defeat: Japan in the wake of World War II*. WW Norton & Company.

Droubie, P. (2011). Phoenix arisen: Japan as peaceful internationalist at the 1964 Tokyo Summer Olympics. *The International Journal of the History of Sport*, *28*(16), 2309–22.

Eason, H. (1984). The pull of protectionism. *Nation's Business*, *72*(5), 53–4.

Elisonas, J. S. A. (2000). The Jesuits, the devil, and pollution in Japan. The context of a syllabus of errors. *Bulletin of Portuguese-Japanese Studies*, *1*, 3–27.

Elisonas, J. S. A. (2007). Journey to the West. *Japanese Journal of Religious Studies*, *34*(1), 27–66.

Elkington, J. (1997). *Cannibals with forks: The triple bottom line of 21st century business*. Capstone.

Ellis, R. R. (2003). "The best thus far discovered": The Japanese in the letters of Francisco Xavier. *Hispanic Review, 71*(2), 155–69.

Embree, J. F. (1939). *Suye mura: A Japanese village.* University of Chicago Press.

Endo, S. (1969). *Silence.* Taplinger Publishing Company.

Envall, H. D. P. (2017). Japan: From passive partner to active ally. In M. Wesley (Ed.), *Global allies: Comparing US alliances in the 21st century.* ANU Press.

Everett, J. E., & Stening, B. W. (1983). Japanese and British managerial colleagues – How they view each other. *Journal of Management Studies, 20*(4), 467–75.

Falchetta, P. (2006). *Fra Mauro's world map.* Brepols.

Farrell, B. (2017). *The defence and fall of Singapore.* Monsoon Books.

Fernandes, N. (2000). Tomb Raider: Looking for St. Francis Xavier. *Transition-Issue, 9*(4), 4–19.

Ferris, J. (1993). "Worthy of Some Better Enemy?": The British estimate of the Imperial Japanese Army 1919–41, and the fall of Singapore. *Canadian Journal of History, 28*(2), 223–56.

Flanagan, D. (2014). *Yukio Mishima.* Reaktion Books.

Flavin, M. (2017). *Disruptive technology enhanced learning: The use and misuse of digital technologies in higher education.* Palgrave Macmillan.

Fleming, I. (1978). *You only live twice.* Triad/Panther Books.

Flint, V. I. J. (1992). *The imaginative landscape of Christopher Columbus.* Princeton University Press.

Francks, P. (2015). *Japanese economic development: Theory and practice.* Routledge.

Fraser, M. C. (1904). *A diplomatist's wife in Japan. Letters from home to home* (4th ed.). Hutchinson & Co.

Fuqua, D. S. (2017). Classical Japan and the continent. In K. Friday (Ed.), *Routledge handbook of premodern Japanese history* (pp. 8–52). Routledge.

Furniture Gazette (1885). Japanese life and industry. *Furniture Gazette, 23,* 56.

Fussell, P. (1981). 'Thank God for the atom bomb'. Hiroshima: A soldier's view. *The New Republic, 185*(8), 26–9.

Geertz, C. (1988). *Works and lives: The anthropologist as author.* Stanford University Press.

Gerster, R. C. (2009). Representations of Asia. In P. Pierce (Ed.), *The Cambridge history of Australian literature* (pp. 303–22). Cambridge University Press.

Ghazanfar, S. M. (2018). Vasco da Gama's voyages to India: Messianism, mercantilism, and sacred exploits. *Journal of Global Initiatives: Policy, Pedagogy, Perspective, 13*(1), 15–40.

Gilbert, G. M. (1951). Stereotype persistence and change among college students. *Journal of Abnormal and Social Psychology, 46,* 245–54.

Goldman, S. D. (2012). *Nomonhan, 1939: The Red Army's victory that shaped world war II.* Naval Institute Press.

Gooday, G., & Low, M. (1998). Technology transfer and cultural exchange: Western scientists and engineers encounter late Tokugawa and Meiji Japan. *Osiris, 13,* 99–128.

Goodman, G. K. (2000). *Japan and the Dutch 1600–1853.* Routledge.

Gordon, B. S. (2014). *The only woman in the room.* University of Chicago Press.

Gripentrog, J. (2010). The transnational pastime: Baseball and American perceptions of Japan in the 1930s. *Diplomatic History, 34*(2), 247–73.

Gualtieri, G. (1586) *Relationi della venuta de gli ambasciatori giaponesi à Roma, fino alla partitadi Lisbona.* Appresso Igiolti.

Gubinskaya, A. A. (2020). AB Mitford as a cultural diplomat and the image of Japan in Victorian England. *История: факты и символы* (History: Facts and Symbols), *3*(24), 112–23.

Gulick, S. L. (1905). *White peril in the Far East.* Fleming H. Revell Company.

Gunter, B. (1998). *The effects of video games on children: The myth unmasked*. A&C Black.

Gutierrez, S. (2019). Comics in action: A reflection of the dominant narrative in World War II. *SMU Journal of Undergraduate Research*, *2*(1), Article 10. https://scholar.smu.edu/jour/vol2/iss1/10/

Hair, P. E. H. (1994). *The founding of the Castelo de São Jorge da Mina: An analysis of sources*. University of Wisconsin Madison African Studies Program.

Hall, E. T. (1959). *The silent language*. Anchor books.

Halloran, R. (1974, 13 March). Soldier's return from 30 years in Jungle stirs Japanese deeply. *The New York Times*. www.nytimes.com/1974/03/13/archives/soldiers-return-from-30-years-in-jungle-stirs-japanese-deeply.html

Hammond, P., & Stirner, P. (1997). Fear and loathing in the British press. In P. Hammond (Ed.), *Cultural difference, media memories. Anglo-American images of Japan*. Cassell.

Harris, M. (1968). *The rise of anthropological theory: A history of theories of culture*. Crowell.

Harrison, C., Wood, P. J., & Gaiger, J. (2000). *Art in theory 1648–1815: An anthology of changing ideas*. Blackwell.

Hashimoto, Y. (2007). White hope or yellow peril?: Bushido, Britain, and the Raj. In J. Steinberg et al. (Eds.), *The Russo-Japanese war in global perspective: world war zero* (Vol. 2, pp. 379–402). Brill.

Haskell, Y., & Garrod, R. (2019). *Changing hearts: Performing Jesuit emotions between Europe, Asia, and the Americas*. Brill.

Havens, T. R. (1987). *Fire across the sea: The Vietnam war and Japan 1965–1975*. Princeton University Press.

Havers, R. P. W. (2003). *Reassessing the Japanese prisoner of war experience: The Changi prisoner of war camp in Singapore, 1942–45*. Routledge.

Haworth, A. (2013, 20 October). Why have young people in Japan stopped having sex? *The Guardian*. http://www.theguardian.com/world/2013/oct/20/young-people-japan-stopped-having-sex

Hazart, C. (1667). *A Church history of the entire world* [original title in Dutch: *Kerckelycke Historie van de Gheheele Wereldt*]. https://digital-archives.sophia.ac.jp/laures-kirishitan-bunko/view/kirishitan_bunko/JL-1667-KB3–492

Hearn, L. (1904). *Japan: An attempt at interpretation*. The Macmillan Company.

Heider, F. (1958). *The psychology of interpersonal relations*. John Wiley & Sons.

Heine, S. J., Buchtel, E. E., & Norenzayan, A. (2008). What do cross-national comparisons of personality traits tell us? The case of conscientiousness. *Psychological Science*, *19*(4), 309–13.

Hendry, J. (2015). The state of anthropology in and of Japan: A review essay. *Japan Forum*, *27*(2), 121–33.

Henning, J. M. (2000). *Outposts of civilization: Race, religion, and the formative years of American-Japanese relations*. NYU Press.

Henrich, J. (2020). *The WEIRDest people in the world: How the West became psychologically peculiar and particularly prosperous*. Penguin.

Henrich, J., Heine, S. J., & Norenzayan, A. (2010). The weirdest people in the world? *Behavioral and Brain Sciences*, *33*(2–3), 61–83.

Hesselink, R. (2002). Memorable Embassies: The secret history of Arnoldus Montanus' Gedenkwaerdige Gesantschappen. *Quaerendo*, *32*(1–2), 99–123.

Heylyn, P. (1677). *Cosmography in four books containing the chorography and history of the whole world and all the principal kingdoms, provinces, seas, and isles thereof* (Vols. I–IV). P. Chetwind, and A. Seile.

Higashibaba, I. (2001). *Christianity in early modern Japan. Kirishitan belief and practice*. Brill.

Hillsborough, R. (2014). *Samurai revolution: The dawn of modern Japan seen through the eyes of the Shogun's last samurai*. Tuttle Publishing.

Hinton, P. R. (2013). Returning in a different fashion: Culture, communication, and changing representations of Lolita in Japan and the West. *International Journal of Communication*, 7, 1582–602. http://ijoc.org/index.php/ijoc/article/view/1333/956

Hinton, P. R. (2014a). Representation or misrepresentation? British media and Japanese popular. *NECSUS. European Journal of Media Studies*, *3*(1), 89–108.

Hinton, P. R. (2014b). The Cultural context and the interpretation of Japanese 'lolita complex' style anime. *Intercultural Communication Studies*, *23*(2). https://web.uri.edu/iaics/files/Perry-R.-Hinton.pdf

Hinton, P. R. (2015). The perverse stereotype of the Japanese man in the British media. *Electronic Journal of Contemporary Japanese Studies*, *15*(2), Article 9. www.japanesestudies.org.uk/ejcjs/vol15/iss2/hinton.html

Hinton, P. R. (2016). The cultural construction of the girl "teen": A cross-cultural analysis of feminine adolescence in popular culture. *Journal of Intercultural Communication Research*. www.tandfonline.com/doi/full/10.1080/17475759.2016.1141309

Hinton, P. R. (2017). Implicit stereotypes and the predictive brain: Cognition and culture in "biased" person perception. *Palgrave Communications*, *3*(1), 1–9.

Hinton, P. R. (2018). Negotiating otaku: A social group, its social representations and the changing cultural context. *Papers on Social Representations*, *28*. http://psr.iscte-iul.pt/index.php/PSR/article/view/474

Hinton, P. R. (2020a). *Stereotypes and the construction of the social world*. Routledge.

Hinton, P. R. (2020b). The dangerous tendency to essentialize cultural categories in academic psychology. *Theory & Psychology*, *30*(3), 383–8.

Hirakawa, S. (2005). *Japan's love-hate relationship with the West*. Brill.

Hirobe, I. (2001). *Japanese pride, American prejudice: Modifying the exclusion clause of the 1924 Immigration Act*. Stanford University Press.

Hoad, P. (2013, 10 July). Akira: the future-Tokyo story that brought anime west. *The Guardian*. https://www.theguardian.com/film/2013/jul/10/akira-anime-japanese-cartoon-manga

Hoey, J. B. (2010). Alessandro Valignano and the restructuring of the Jesuit Mission in Japan, 1579–1582. *Eleutheria*, *1*(1). https://digitalcommons.liberty.edu/eleu/vol1/iss1/4

Hofstede, G. 1980. *Culture's consequences: International differences in work-related values*. Sage Publications.

Holland, C. (1909). *Things seen in Japan*. Seeley and Co. Limited.

Hood, C. (2006). *Shinkansen: From bullet train to symbol of modern Japan*. Routledge.

Houghton, F. (2014). 'To the Kwai and back': Myth, memory and memoirs of the 'Death Railway' 1942–1943, *Journal of War & Culture Studies*, 7(3), 223–35.

House, J. C. (2021). *William Adams' letters – The first decade in Japan*. 明治大学教養論集 *(Meiji University Liberal Arts Collection)*. http://hdl.handle.net/10291/22146.

Huissen, M. J. (1973). England encounters Japan: English knowledge of Japan in the Seventeenth Century. *Terrae Incognitae*, *5*(1), 43–59.

Hurford, E. M. (2009). *Gender and sexuality in shoujo manga: Undoing heteronormative expectations in Utena, Pet Shop of Horrors, and Angel Sanctuary* [Doctoral dissertation, Bowling Green State University].

Hurst, C. C. (1981). Review of 'Learning from Shōgun: Japanese history and western fantasy. Edited by Henry Smith.' *The Journal of Asian Studies*, *41*(1), 158–9.

Hutchings, K. (2003). *Imagining nature: Blake's environmental poetics*. McGill-Queen's Press.

Ibbotson, R. (2020). Revisiting the medievalism of the British arts and crafts movement. In J. Parker & C. Wagner (Eds.), *The Oxford handbook of Victorian medievalism*. Oxford University Press.

Inkeles, A. (2017). *National character: A psycho-social perspective*. Routledge. (Original work published 1997)

Inose, N., & Sato, H. (2012). *Persona: A biography of Yukio Mishima*. Stone Bridge Press.

Itoh, M. (2000). *The Japanese economy reconsidered*. Palgrave Macmillan.

Iwawaki, S., Eysenck, S. B. G., & Eysenck, H. J. (1977). Differences in personality between Japanese and English. *The Journal of Social Psychology, 102*(1), 27–33.

Iwawaki, S., Eysenck, S. B. G., & Eysenck, H. J. (1980). Japanese and English personality structure: A cross-cultural study. *Psychologia: An International Journal of Psychology in the Orient, 23*(4), 195–205.

Jinam, T., Kawai, Y., Kamatani, Y., Sonoda, S., Makisumi, K., Sameshima, H., . . . Saitou, N. (2021). Genome-wide SNP data of Izumo and Makurazaki populations support inner-dual structure model for origin of Yamato people. *Journal of Human Genetics, 66*(7), 681–7

Johnson, S. K. (1991). *The Japanese through American eyes*. Stanford University Press.

Jones, E. E. (2019, 29 October).'So alien! So other!': How western TV gets Japanese culture wrong. *The Guardian*.

Kaempfer, E. (1906). *The history of Japan together with a description of the Kingdom of Siam 1690–92* (J. G. Scheuchzer, Trans., Vols. I–III). The Macmillan Company.

Kangas, S. (2013). First in prowess and faith. The great encounter in twelfth-century crusader narratives. In K. V. Jensen, K. Salonen, & H. Vogt (Eds.), *Cultural encounters during the crusades* (pp. 119–34). University Press of Southern Denmark.

Karlins, M., Coffman, T. L., & Walters, G. (1969). On the fading of social stereotypes: Studies in three generations of college students, *Journal of Personality and Social Psychology, 13*, 1–16.

Kasahara, K. (2001). *A history of Japanese religion* (P. McCarthy & G. Sekimori, Trans.). Kosei Publishing Company.

Kato, R. (1988). National character studies of Japanese. *Mid-American Review of Sociology, 13*(1), 69–78.

Katz, D., & Braly, K. W. (1933). Racial prejudice and racial stereotypes. *Journal of Abnormal and Social Psychology, 30*, 175–93

Kawabata, Y. (1968). Japan, the beautiful and myself. *The Nobel Prize in Literature Lecture*. https://www.nobelprize.org/prizes/literature/1968/kawabata/lecture/

Kawashima, D., Kawamoto, S., Shiraga, K., & Kawano, K. (2019). Is suicide beautiful? Suicide acceptance and related factors in Japan. *Crisis: The Journal of Suicide Prevention, 41*, 114–20.

Kazui, T. (1982). Foreign relations during the Edo period: Sakoku reexamined (S. D. Videen, Trans.). *Journal of Japanese Studies, 8*(2), 283–306.

Keene, D. (1969). Japanese aesthetics. *Philosophy East and West, 19*(3), 293–306.

Keevak, M. (2011). *Becoming yellow: A short history of racial thinking*. Princeton University Press.

Keith, M. E. (2006). *The logistics of power: Tokugawa response to the Shimabara rebellion and power projection in Seventeenth-century Japan* [Doctoral dissertation, Ohio State University]. http://rave.ohiolink.edu/etdc/view?acc_num=osu1164741756

Kerner, A. (2007). Gojira vs Godzilla: Catastrophic allegories. In M. Franko (Ed.), *Ritual and event. Interdisciplinary perspectives* (pp. 119–34). Routledge.

Kerouac, J. (1972). *The dharma bums*. Panther Books Ltd.

Kijewski, L. (2014). The Japanese character and its peculiarity – A study of Carl Peter Thunberg's travel account. *MaRBLe, 6*, 155–74. https://doi.org/10.26481/marble.2014.v6.223

Kim, H. S., & Sherman, D. K. (2007). "Express yourself": Culture and the effect of self-expression on choice. *Journal of Personality and Social Psychology, 92*(1), 1–11.

Kinsella, S. (2000). *Adult manga: Culture and power in contemporary Japanese society*. Curzon Press.

Kipling, R. (1899). *Letters from the East*. The Lovell Company.

Kirk, R. (1993). Natural law and the constitution of the United States. *Notre Dame Law Review, 69*(5), 1035–48.

Kirsh, S. J. (1998). Seeing the world through Mortal Kombat-colored glasses: Violent video games and the development of a short-term hostile attribution bias. *Childhood, 5*(2), 177–84.

Knapp, A. M. (1900). *Feudal and modern Japan* (Vol. 1). L. C. Page & Company.

Kodera, T. (2016). Announcement. *Journal of Japonisme, 1*(1), 151–54.

Koerner, S. (2012). *The strange death of the British motorcycle industry*. Crucible Books

Komroff, M. (1926). Introduction. In M. Komroff (Ed.), *The travels of Marco Polo the Venitian* (W. Marsden, Trans.). Boni and Liveright.

Kondo, D. (2010). Through western eyes: Japanese fashion in the 1980s. *Dress Study, 57*. http://www.kci.or.jp/research/dresstudy/pdf/D57_Kondo_e_Through_Western_Eyes.pdf

Kopf, D. (2000). Hermeneutics versus history. In A. L. Macfie (Ed.), *Orientalism: A reader* (pp. 194–207). NYU Press.

Koppes, C. R., & Black, G. D. (1987). *Hollywood goes to war. How politics and propaganda shaped world war II movies*. The Free Press.

Kowner, R. (2001). Becoming an honorary civilized nation: Remaking Japan's military image during the Russo-Japanese War, 1904-1905. *The Historian, 64*(1), 19–38.

Kowner, R. (2006). *The impact of the Russo-Japanese war*. Routledge.

Kowner, R. (2014). *From white to yellow: The Japanese in European racial thought, 1300–1735*. McGill-Queen's University Press.

Kublin, H. (1959). The evolution of Japanese colonialism. *Comparative Studies in Society and History, 2*(1), 67–84.

Kuhn, A. K. (1933). The Lytton report on the Manchurian crisis. *American Journal of International Law, 27*(1), 96–100.

Kumagai, K. (2013). Floating young men: Globalization and the crisis of masculinity in Japan. *Hagar: Studies in Culture, Polities and Identities, 11*(1), 157–65.

Kumojima, T. (2022). *Victorian women's travel writing on Meiji Japan: Hospitable friendship*. Oxford University Press.

Lambourne, L. (2005). *Japonisme: Cultural crossings between Japan and the West*. Phaidon Press.

Larsonneur, C. (2015). Revisiting Dejima (Japan): From recollections to fiction in David Mitchell's the thousand autumns of Jacob de Zoet. *SubStance, 44*(1), 136–47.

Lavery, G. E. (2019). *Quaint, exquisite: Victorian aesthetics and the idea of Japan*. Princeton University Press.

Law, J. M. (2000). Legacies of imagination: Japan's religious challenges and contributions. *Macalester International, 8*(1), 14, 133–56.

Leckie, R. (1957). *Helmet for my pillow*. Random House.

Lee, H. K. (2011). Cultural consumer and copyright: A case study of anime fansubbing. *Creative Industries Journal, 3*(3), 237–52.

LeVine, R. A. (2001). Culture and personality studies, 1918–1960: Myth and history. *Journal of Personality, 69*(6), 803–18.

Lidin, O. G. (2002). *Tanegashima – The arrival of Europe in Japan*. Nias Press.

Lie, J. (2001). Ruth Benedict's legacy of shame: Orientalism and occidentalism in the study of Japan. *Asian Journal of Social Science, 29*(2), 249–61.

Lindemann, B. W. (2008). *From Rembrandt to Vermeer: Civil values in 17th-century Flemish and Dutch painting: Masterpieces of the Gemäldegalerie in Berlin*. Motta.
Linhart, S. (1988). From industrial to postindustrial society: Changes in Japanese leisure-related values and behavior. *Journal of Japanese Studies, 14*(2), 271–307.
Lippmann, W. (1922). *Public opinion*. Harcourt-Brace.
Littlewood, I. (1996). *The idea of Japan: Western images, Western myths*. Ivan R. Dee.
Lockyer, A. (2001). Japan at the exhibition, 1867–1877: From representation to practice. *Senri Ethnological Studies, 54*, 67–76.
López-Gay, J. (2003). Saint Francis Xavier and the Shimazu Family. *Bulletin of Portuguese-Japanese Studies, 6*, 93–106.
Loti, P. (1905). *Madame Chrysanthème*. Maison Mazarin.
Loureiro, R. M. (2004). Jesuit textual strategies in Japan between 1549 and 1582. *Bulletin of Portuguese-Japanese Studies, 8*, 39–63.
Lynn, L. H. (1998). The commercialization of the transistor radio in Japan: The functioning of an innovation community. *IEEE Transactions on Engineering Management, 45*(3), 220–29.
Lynn, R., & Hampson, S. L. (1975). National differences in extraversion and neuroticism. *British Journal of Social and Clinical Psychology, 14*(3), 223–40.
Lynn, R., & Martin, T. (1995). National differences for thirty-seven nations in extraversion, neuroticism, psychoticism and economic, demographic and other correlates. *Personality and Individual Differences, 19*(3), 403–6.
Macfie, A. L. (2000). *Orientalism: A reader*. NYU Press.
MacMillan, M. (2001). *Peacemakers: The Paris peace conference of 1919 and its attempt to end war*. John Murray.
Madon, S., Guyll, M., Aboufadel, K., Montiel, E., Smith, A., Palumbo, P., & Jussim, L. (2001). Ethnic and national stereotypes: The Princeton trilogy revisited and revised. *Personality and Social Psychology Bulletin, 27*(8), 996–1010
Malle, B. F. (2007). Attributions as behavior explanations: Toward a new theory. In D. Chadee & J. Hunter (Eds.), *Current themes and perspectives in social psychology* (pp. 3–26). St. Augustine: SOCS, The University of the West Indies.
Manning, C. A. (1922). Prester John and Japan. *Journal of the American Oriental Society, 42*, 286–94.
Mantovani, G. (2000). *Exploring borders: Understanding culture and psychology*. Routledge.
Markley, R. (2003). Riches, power, trade and religion: The Far East and the English imagination, 1600–1720. *Renaissance Studies, 17*(3), 494–516.
Markley, R. (2004). Gulliver and the Japanese: The limits of the postcolonial past. *Modern Language Quarterly, 65*(3), 457–79.
Mason, R., & Caiger, J. G. (1997). *History of Japan* (Rev ed.). Tuttle Publishing.
Massarella, D. (2014). Appendix: The Discovery of the missing portrait of Mancio Itō, one of the Japanese Ambassadors. *The Journal of the Hakluyt Society*, 1–3.
Massarella, D., & Farrington, A. (2000). *William Adams and early English enterprise in Japan*. Discussion Paper No. IS/00/394. The Suntory Centre. London School of Economics and Political Science. http://sticerd.lse.ac.uk/dps/is/IS394.pdf
Matanle, P., McCann, L., & Ashmore, D-J. (2008). Men under pressure: Representations of the 'salaryman' and his organization in Japanese manga. *Organization, 15*(5), 639–64.
Matsumoto, D. (2002). *The new Japan: Debunking seven cultural stereotypes*. Intercultural Press.
McCarthy, H. (1996). *The anime! movie guide*. Titan Books.
McDonald, M. (1993). The construction of difference: An anthropological approach to stereotypes. In S. Macdonald (Ed.), *Inside European identities* (pp. 219–36). Routledge.

McLaughlin, J. (2007). “The Japanese Village” and the metropolitan construction of modernity. *Romanticism and Victorianism on the Net, 48*. https://doi.org/10.7202/017441ar.
McLeod, J. (2010). *Beginning postcolonialism* (2nd ed.). Manchester University Press.
McMillan, C. J. (1996). *The Japanese industrial system*. De Gruyter.
McOmie, W. (2005). *Foreign images and experiences of Japan*. Brill.
Mead, M. (1956). The cross-cultural approach to the study of personality. *Revue Internationale de Philosophie, 35*(1), 48–71.
Meehan, J. D. (2014). From alliance to conference: The British Empire, Japan and Pacific multilateralism, 1911–1921. In T. Minohara, T. K. Hon, & E. Dawley (Eds.), *The decade of the Great War: Japan and the wider world in the 1910s* (pp. 45–63). Brill.
Mervart, D. (2015). Republic of letters comes to Nagasaki: Record of a translator's struggle. *The Journal of Transcultural Studies, 6*(2), 8–37.
Mettler, M. W. (2010). Gimcracks, dollar blouses, and transistors: American reactions to imported Japanese products, 1945–1964. *Pacific Historical Review, 79*(2), 202–30.
Mettler, M. W. (2018). *How to reach Japan by subway: America's fascination with Japanese culture, 1945–1965*. University of Nebraska Press.
Meyer, R., & Siwolop, S. (1990). The samurai have landed. *Financial World, 159*(19), 46–50.
Michener, J. A. (1970). *Sayonara*. Fawcett Crest.
Miller, J. G. (1984). Culture and the development of everyday social explanation. *Journal of Personality and Social Psychology, 46*(5), 961–78.
Milner, J. (1822). *A vindication of the end of religious controversy*. Keating and Brown.
Minear, R. H. (1980). Orientalism and the Study of Japan. *The Journal of Asian Studies, 39*(3), 507–17.
Miranda, M. (2022). Majesty and silence: An honorable bald old man called Japan. In In H. Oba, A. Watanabe, & F. Schaffenrath (Eds.), *Japan on the Jesuit stage* (pp. 289–303). Brill.
Miscamble, W. D. (2011). *The most controversial decision: Truman, the atomic bombs, and the defeat of Japan*. Cambridge University Press.
Mitchell, D. (2013). *The basket case sometimes known as Japan*. https://danieljmitchell.wordpress.com/2013/01/15/the-basket-case-sometimes-known-as-japan/
Miyamoto, Y., & Kitayama, S. (2002). Cultural variation in correspondence bias: The critical role of attitude diagnosticity of socially constrained behavior. *Journal of Personality and Social Psychology, 83*(5), 1239–48
Modell, A. (1933). Introduction. In L. Hearn (Trans.), *Stories from Pierre Loti* (pp. v–xi). Hokuseido Press.
Montanus, A. (1670). *Atlas Japannensis: Being remarkable addresses by way of embassy from the East India Company of the United Provinces to the Emperor of Japan* (J. Olgilby, Trans.). The Author.
Mormando, F. (2006). The making of the second Jesuit saint: The campaign for the canonization of Francis Xavier, 1555–1622. In F. Mormando & J. G. Thomas (Eds.), *Francis Xavier and the Jesuit mission in the Far East* (pp. 9–23). The Jesuit Institute of Boston College.
Morris, J. (1895). *Advance Japan. A nation thoroughly in earnest*. W. H. Allen & Co.
Morris, J. (1945). *Traveller from Tokyo*. The Book Club.
Morris, J. H. (2018). *Rethinking the history of conversion to Christianity in Japan, 1549–1644* [Doctoral dissertation, University of St Andrews]. http://hdl.handle.net/10023/15875.
Morris, M. W., & Peng, K. (1994). Culture and cause: American and Chinese attributions for social and physical events. *Journal of Personality and Social Psychology, 67*(6), 949–71.
Morris, N. (2002). Innocence to deviance: The fetishisation of Japanese women in western fiction, 1890s to 1990s. *Intersections: Gender and Sexuality in Asia and the Pacific, 7*. http://intersections.anu.edu.au/issue7/morris.html

Morris, N. (2010). *Japan-bashing: Anti-Japanism since the 1980s*. Routledge.

Moscovici, S. (1993). Introductory address. *Papers on Social Representations, 2*(3), 1–11.

Moscovici, S. (1998). The history and actuality of social representations. In U. Flick (Ed.), *The psychology of the social* (pp. 209–47). Cambridge University Press.

Muldoon, J. (1979). *Popes, lawyers, and infidels: The church and the non-Christian world, 1250–1550*. University of Pennsylvania Press.

Nagata, D. K. (1990). The Japanese-American internment: Perceptions of moral community, fairness, and redress. *Journal of Social Issues, 46*(1), 133–46.

Nagata, K. (2012, 15 May). Exporting culture via 'Cool Japan'. *Japan Times*. www.japantimes.co.jp/news/2012/05/15/reference/exporting-culture-via-cool-japan/

Nakano, Y. (2018). "Wings of the New Japan": Kamikaze, kimonos, and airline branding in postwar Japan. *Verge: Studies in Global Asias, 4*(1), 160–86.

Nelson, E. (2018). Comic cons: Fairy-tale culture and comic conventions: Perpetuating storytelling traditions. In P. Greenhill, J. T. Rudy, N. Hamer, & L. Bosc (Eds.), *The Routledge companion to media and fairy-tale cultures* (pp. 483–91). Routledge.

Nelson, T. (2004). Slavery in medieval Japan. *Monumenta Nipponica, 59*(4), 463–92.

Ngai, M. M. (1999). The architecture of race in American immigration law: A reexamination of the Immigration Act of 1924. *The Journal of American History, 86*(1), 67–92.

Ni, L. (2016). The transformation of the images of Japanese women in America (selected literature from 1853 to 1953). *International Journal of Languages, Literature and Linguistics, 2*(2), 79–85.

Nish, I. (2011). Meiji Japan's ascent towards world power (Discussion Paper IS/11/559). The Suntory Centre, London School of Economics and Political Science. http://eprints.lse.ac.uk/58165/

Nitobe, I. (1907). *Bushido. The soul of Japan* (12th ed.). The Publishing Company.

O'Mahoney, J. (2018). *Denying the spoils of war: The politics of invasion and non-recognition*. Edinburgh University Press.

O'Malley, J. W. (2013). *Saints or devils incarnate?: Studies in Jesuit history*. Brill.

Oba, H., Watanabe, A., & Schaffenrath, F. (2022). *Japan on the Jesuit stage. Transmissions, receptions, and regional contexts*. Brill.

Ohnuki-Tierney, E. (2007). *Kamikaze diaries: Reflections of Japanese student soldiers*. University of Chicago Press.

Okakura, K. (1905). *The awakening of Japan*. The Century Company.

Okakura, K. (1906). *The book of tea*. G. P. Putnam's Sons.

Okakura, Y. (1905). *The Japanese spirit*. James Potts & Co.

Okamoto-MacPhail, A. (2005). Japonism in art. The case of James McNeil Whistler. In E. C. Eoyang (Ed.), *Intercultural Explorations* (pp. 87–94). Brill.

Okie, S. (1990, 21 May). Medicine: Nintendo-related disorders. *The Washington Post*, p. A2.

Peabody, D. (1985). *National characteristics*. Cambridge University Press.

Penick, M. (2017). *Tastemaker: Elizabeth Gordon, house beautiful, and the postwar American home*. Yale University Press.

Pennington, L. E. (1966). Hakluytus posthumus: Samuel Purchas and the promotion of English overseas expansion. *The Emporia State Research Studies, 14*(3), 5–39.

Pepys, S. (1906). *The diary of Samuel Pepys* (Volume I) (E. Rhys, Ed.). J. M. Dent & Sons Ltd.

Perkins, T. E. (1979). Rethinking stereotypes. In M. Barrett, P. Corrigan, A. Kuhn, & J. Wolff (Eds.), *Ideology and cultural production* (pp. 135–59). Croom Helm.

Perry, M. C. (1859). *Japan opened. Compiled chiefly from the narrative of the American expedition to Japan in the years 1852–3–4*. The Religious Tract Society.

Petersen, W. J. (1942). Remember Pearl Harbor. *The Palimpsest, 23*(2), 33–46.

Phillips, C. A., Rolls, S., Rouse, A., & Griffiths, M. D. (1995). Home video game playing in schoolchildren: A study of incidence and patterns of play. *Journal of Adolescence*, *18*(6), 687–91.

Phoenix, W. (2006). *Plastic culture: How Japanese toys conquered the world*. Kodansha International.

Pickering, M. (2001). *Stereotyping: The politics of representation*. Palgrave.

Pinto, F. M. (1989). *The travels of Mendes Pinto* (R. D. Catz, Ed. and Trans.). University of Chicago Press.

Polo, M. (1958). *The travels of Marco Polo* (R. E. Latham, Trans.). Penguin Books.

Pombo, P., & Cardoso, H. C. (2020). Shining a spotlight on the history of Diu. *Asian Review of World Histories*, *8*(2), 203–6.

Powell, M. A. (2000). The Magi as Kings: An adventure in reader-response criticism. *The Catholic Biblical Quarterly*, *62*(3), 459–80.

Prak, M. (2005). *The Dutch Republic in the seventeenth century*. Cambridge University Press.

Prohl, I. (2014). California 'Zen': Buddhist spirituality made in America. *Amerikastudien/American Studies*, *59*(2), 193–206.

Prothro, E. T., & Melikian, L. H. (1955). Studies in stereotypes: V. Familiarity and the kernel of truth hypothesis. *The Journal of Social Psychology*, *41*(1), 3–10.

Pyle, K. B. (1969). *The new generation in Meiji Japan: problems of cultural identity, 1885–1895*. Stanford University Press.

Pyle, K. C., & Cunningham, S. (2014). *Bad for you: Exposing the war on fun!*. Henry Holt and Company BYR Paperbacks.

Raepple, E. M. (2008). Divan Japonais: Toulouse-Lautrec and Japanese art. *Philosophy Scholarship* (Paper 1). http://dc.cod.edu/philosophypub/1

Rani, A. (2013, 24 October). *The Japanese men who prefer virtual girlfriends to sex*. www.bbc.co.uk/news/magazine-24614830

Rattan, S. (1972). The Yap controversy and its significance. *The Journal of Pacific History*, 7(1), 124–36.

Ravenstein, E. G. (1898). *A journal of the first voyage of Vasco da Gama, 1497–1499*. Hakluyt Society.

Renteln, A. D. (1995). A psychohistorical analysis of the Japanese American internment. *Human Rights Quarterly*, 17(4), 618–48.

Robertson, J. (2005). Introduction: Putting and keeping Japan in anthropology. In J. Roberson (Ed.), *A companion to the anthropology of Japan* (pp. 3–16). Blackwell Publishing Ltd.

Rosenberg, E. S. (2003). *A date which will live: Pearl Harbor in American memory*. Duke University Press.

Rosenstone, R. A. (1980). Learning from those "imitative" Japanese: Another side of the American experience in the Mikado's Empire. *The American Historical Review*, *85*(3), 572–95.

Ross, L. D. (1977). The intuitive psychologist and his shortcomings: Distortions in the attribution process. In L. Berkowitz (Ed.), *Advances in experimental social psychology* (Vol. 10, pp. 173–220). Academic Press.

Rundall, T. (1850). *Memorials of the Empire of Japon: In the XVI and XVII Centuries*. The Hakluyt Society.

Russell, P. E. (1997). A quest too far: Henry the navigator and Prester John. In I. Macpherson & R. J. Penny (Eds.), *The medieval mind: Hispanic studies in honour of Alan Deyermond* (pp. 401–16). Tamesis Book Limited.

Russell, R., Metraux, D., & Tohen, M. (2017). Cultural influences on suicide in Japan. *Psychiatry and Clinical Neurosciences*, *71*(1), 2–5.

Russell-Wood, A. J. R. (1978). Iberian expansion and the issue of black slavery: Changing Portuguese attitudes, 1440–1770. *The American Historical Review*, *83*(1), 16–42.

Ryang, S. (2002). Chrysanthemum's strange life: Ruth Benedict in postwar Japan. *Asian Anthropology*, *1*(1), 87–116.

Ryang, S. (2004). *Japan and national anthropology: A critique*. Routledge.

Ryang, S. (2020). Toward a New Anthropology of Japan. *Transnational Asia*, *4*(1). https://doi.org/10.25615/VRJ9-RX55

Said, E. W. (1995). *Orientalism: Western conceptions of the orient*. Penguin. (Original work published 1978)

Said, E. W. (2014). Orientalism reconsidered. In B. Moore-Gilbert, G. Stanton, & W. Maley (Eds.), *Postcolonial criticism* (pp. 126–44). Routledge.

Saito, K. (2014). Magic, shōjo, and metamorphosis: Magical girl anime and the challenges of changing gender identities in Japanese society. *The Journal of Asian Studies*, *73*(1), 143–64.

Sandberg, J. (1964). 'Japonisme' and Whistler. *Sandberg*, *106*(740), 500–07.

Sansom, G. B. (1950). *The western world and Japan*. Charles E. Tuttle Company Inc.

Sanyal, S. R. R. (2019). Orient: The cultural other. In S. A. Beg & S. Bandyapadhya (Eds.), *Pursuits of philosophical thought* (Vol. II). PAIOLCK.

Schodt, F. L. (1983). *Manga! manga!. The world of Japanese comics*. Kodansha International.

Schodt, F. L. (1996). *Dreamland Japan: Writings on modern manga*. Stone Bridge Press.

Schodt, F. L. (2007). *The astro boy essays: Osamu Tezuka, mighty Atom, and the manga/anime revolution*. Stone Bridge Press.

Schrijvers, P. (2010). *Bloody Pacific: American soldiers at war with Japan*. Palgrave Macmillan.

Schwemmer, P. R. (2022). Found in translation: The Jesuit Japan letters as a source of early modern European images of Japan. In H. Oba, A. Watanabe, & F. Schaffenrath (Eds.), *Japan on the Jesuit Stage* (pp. 35–56). Brill.

Scidmore, E. R. (1891). *Jinrikisha days in Japan*. Harper & Brothers.

Screech, T. (2002). Dressing Samuel Pepys: Japanese garments and international diplomacy in the Edo period. *Orientations*, *33*(2), 50–7.

Screech, T. (2005). *Japan extolled and decried: Carl Peter Thunberg's Travels in Japan 1775–1776*. Routledge.

Screech, T. (2012). The English and the control of Christianity in the early Edo period. *Japan Review*, 3–40.

Seago, D. W. (1947). Stereotypes: Before Pearl Harbor and after. *The Journal of Psychology*, *23*(1), 55–63.

Semin, G. (1980). A gloss on attribution theory. *British Journal of Social and Clinical Psychology*, *19*, 291–300.

Sheff, D. (1993). *Game over. How Nintendo zapped an American industry, captured your dollars, and enslaved your children*. Random House.

Sherif, M. (1936). *The psychology of social norms*. Harper.

Shi, F. D. (2019). The yellow peril as a travelling discourse: A comparative study of Wang Lixiong's China Tidal Wave. *Comparative Critical Studies*, *16*(1), 7–30.

Shibusawa, N. (2006). *America's geisha ally. Reimagining the Japanese enemy*. Harvard University Press.

Shimada, T. (2008). *Japan in eighteenth-century English satirical writing*. Edition Synapse.

Shimazu, N. (1989). The Japanese attempt to secure racial equality in 1919. *Japan Forum*, 1(1), 93–100.

Shi-xu, & Feng-Bing. (2013). Contemporary Chinese communication made understandable: A cultural psychological perspective. *Culture & Psychology*, *19*(1), 3–19.

Shi-xu. (1995). Cultural perceptions: Exploiting the unexpected of the other. *Culture & Psychology*, *1*(3), 315–42.

Shore, B. (1996). *Culture in mind: Cognition, culture, and the problem of meaning*. Oxford University Press.

Short, M. B., Black, L., Smith, A. H., Wetterneck, C. T., & Wells, D. E. (2012). A review of Internet pornography use research: Methodology and content from the past 10 years. *Cyberpsychology, Behavior, and Social Networking, 15*(1), 13–23.

Shufelt, J. (2005). The trickster as an instrument of enlightenment: George Psalmanazar and the writings of Jonathan Swift. *History of European Ideas, 31*(2), 147–71.

Sibey, D. J. (2012). *The Boxer Rebellion and the great game in China*. Hill and Wang.

Siebold, J. (2015). *Behaim Globe*. https://myoldmaps.com/late-medieval-maps-1300/258-martin-behaims-globe/258-behaim.pdf

Sindemann, K. K. (2001). Japanese Buddhism in the 16th century. Letters of the Jesuit Missionaries. *Bulletin of Portuguese-Japanese Studies, 2*, 111–33.

Sledge, E. B. (1981). *With the old breed: At Peleliu and Okinawa*. Presidio Press.

Smith, H. (1980). *Learning from Shōgun: Japanese history and western fantasy* (Program in Asian Studies), University of California.

Smith, H. L. (2014). *The British women's suffrage campaign 1866–1928* (2nd ed.). Routledge.

Southern, R. W. (1962). *Western views of Islam in the middle ages*. Harvard University Press.

Spalding, W. L. (1952). Review of the Christian Century in Japan, 1549–1650, by C. R. Boxer. *The Hispanic American Historical Review, 32*(3), 399–401.

Spencer-Oatey, H., & Kádár, D. Z. (2021). *Intercultural politeness: Managing relations across cultures*. Cambridge University Press.

Steele, M. W., & Caiger, J. G. (1993). On ignorant whalers and Japan's 'shell and repel' edict of 1825. *International Journal of Maritime History, 5*(2), 31–56.

Steinberg, J. W., Menning, B. W., Van der Oye, D. S., Wolff, D., &Yokote, S. (2005). *The Russo-Japanese war in global perspective. World war zero* (Vol. 1). Brill.

Stigler, J. W., Shweder, R. A., & Herdt, G. E. (1990). *Cultural psychology: Essays on comparative human development*. Cambridge University Press.

Stone, E. W. (2021). *Captives of conquest: Slavery in the early modern Spanish Caribbean*. University of Pennsylvania Press.

Storrs, D. (2000). Like a bamboo: Representations of a Japanese war bride. *Frontiers: A Journal of Women Studies, 21*(1–2), 194–224.

Strausz, M. (2019). *Help (not) wanted: Immigration politics in Japan*. SUNY Press.

Stuckey, C. F. (1985). *Monet. A retrospective*. Hugh Lauter Levin Associates.

Sue, S., & Kitano, H. H. (1973). Stereotypes as a measure of success. *Journal of Social Issues, 29*(2), 83–98.

Syring, J. J. (2018). *Zen and the art of fly fishing*. lulu.com.

Takao, M. H. (2018). We are not Jesuits: Reassessing relations between Protestantism, French Catholicism, and the Society of Jesus. In J. Cañizares-Esguerra, R. A. Maryks, & R. P. C. Hsia (Eds.), *Late Tokugawa to early Shōwa Japan. In encounters between Jesuits and protestants in Asia and the Americas* (pp. 17–44). Brill.

Terracciano, A., Abdel-Khalek, A. M., Adam, N., Adamovová, L., Ahn, C. K., Ahn, H. N., . . . McCrae, R. R. (2005). National character does not reflect mean personality trait levels in 49 cultures. *Science, 310*(5745), 96–100.

Thomas, J. L. (1897). *Journeys among the gentle Japs: In the summer of 1895; with a special chapter on the religions of Japan*. Sampson Low, Marston & Company Limited.

Tierney, R. K. (2007). From popular performance to national sport: The 'Nationalization' of sumo. In W. W. Kelly & A. Sugimoto (Eds.), *This sporting life: Sports and body culture in modern Japan*. Council on East Asian Studies at Yale University.

Timenes Jr, N. (1970). *Defense against kamikaze attacks in World War 2 and its relevance to anti-shipmissile defense. Volume 1. An analytical history of kamikaze attacks against ships of the United*

States Navy during World War 2. Alexandra VA: Center for Naval Analyses, Operations Evaluation Group. https://apps.dtic.mil/sti/pdfs/AD0725163.pdf

Tipton, F. B. (2007). *Asian firms: History, institutions and management*. Edward Elgar Publishing Inc.

Titsingh, I. (1822). *Illustrations of Japan*. (F. Shoberi, Trans.). R. Ackerman.

Towle, P. A. (1975). Japanese treatment of prisoners in 1904–1905–foreign officers' reports. *Military Affairs, 39*(3), 115–8.

Trani, E. P. (2014). *The Treaty of Portsmouth: An adventure in American diplomacy*. University of Kentucky Press.

Trefalt, B. (2004). Fanaticism, Japanese soldiers and the Pacific War, 1937–45. In M. Hughes & G. Johnson (Eds.), *Fanaticism and conflict in the modern age* (pp. 45–59). Routledge.

Vadakkekara, B. (1995). *Origin of India's St. Thomas Christians: A historiographical critique*. Media House.

Valignano, A., & Braga, J. M. (1942). The panegyric of Alexander Valignano, SJ. *Monumenta Nipponica, 5*(2), 523–35.

Vallance, A. (1897). *The art of William Morris: With reproductions from designs and fabrics printed in the colours of the originals . . . and many other illustrations*. George Bell & Sons.

Van den Berghe, P. L. (1997). Rehabilitating stereotypes. *Ethnic and Racial Studies, 20*(1), 1–16.

Van Eeghen, I. H. (1972). Arnoldus Montanus's book on Japan. *Quaerendo, 2*(4), 250–72.

Van Wolferen, K. G. (1986). The Japan problem. *Foreign Affairs, 65*(2), 288–303.

Velleman, J. D. (2001). The genesis of shame. *Philosophy & Public Affairs, 30*(1), 27–52.

Venning, T. (2015). *A chronology of the crusades*. Routledge.

Verberckmoes, J. (2020). Cornelius Hazart and a connected history of executed Christian Japanese children. *Journal of the Northern Renaissance, 11*, 1–20.

Vitkus, D. J. (1999). Early modern orientalism: representations of Islam in sixteenth-and seventeenth-century Europe. In D. R. Blanks & M. Frassetto (Eds.), *Western views of Islam in medieval and early modern Europe: Perception of other* (pp. 207–30). Palgrave Macmillan.

Vogel, E. F. (1971). *Japan's new middle class* (2nd ed.). University of California Press.

Vogel, E. F. (1979). *Japan as number one: Lessons for America*. Harvard University Press.

Von Siebold, P. F. (1841). *Manners and customs of the Japanese, in the nineteenth century*. John Murray.

Waisberg, T. (2017). The treaty of Tordesillas and the (re)invention of international law in the age of discovery. *Meridiano 47 – Journal of Global Studies, 18*, e18003.

Walker, J. S. (2004). *Prompt and utter destruction: Truman and the use of atomic bombs against Japan*. UNC Press.

Wallach, S. (1952). *China Seas and Japan under the command of Commodore M. C. Perry United States Navy*. Macdonald & Co.

Ward, H. N. (2006). Jesuits, too: Jesuits, women catechists, and Jezebels in Christian-century Japan. In J. M. O'Malley, G. A. Bailey, S. J. Harris, & T. F. Kennedy (Eds.), *The Jesuits II: Cultures, sciences, and the arts, 1540–1773* (pp. 638–57). University of Toronto Press.

Ward, R. E., & Sakamoto, Y. (1987). *Democratizing Japan: The allied occupation*. University of Hawaii Press.

Watt, W. M. (1991). *Muslim-Christian encounters: Perceptions and misperceptions*. Routledge.

Watts, A. W. (1957). *The way of Zen*. Pantheon Books Inc.

Watts, A. W. (1973). *This is it and other essays on Zen and spiritual experience*. Vintage Books.

Weinstein, F. (1980). *The dynamics of Nazism: leadership, ideology, and the holocaust*. Elsevier.

West, M. I. (2008). *The Japanification of children's popular culture: From Godzilla to Miyazaki*. Scarecrow Press.

Westney, D. E. (1987). *Imitation and innovation: The transfer of Western organizational patterns to Meiji Japan*. Harvard University Press.

White, J. (1860). Lord Elgin's mission to China and Japan. *Blackwood's Edinburgh Magazine, 87*, 533, 255–277.

Wilde, O. (1894). The decay of lying. In *Intentions* (pp. 1–55). Osgood, McIlvaine and Company.

Wildes, H. E. (1954). The war for the mind of Japan. *The Annals of the American Academy of Political and Social Science, 294*(1), 1–7.

Williams, L., & Clark, S. (2017). Isabella Bird, Victorian globalism, and Unbeaten Tracks in Japan (1880). *Studies in Travel Writing, 21*(1), 1–16.

Willis, C. (2012). Captain Jorge Álvares and Father Luís Fróis SJ: Two early Portuguese descriptions of Japan and the Japanese. *Journal of the Royal Asiatic Society, 22*(2), 391–438.

Windrum, P., Haynes, M., & Thompson, P. (2019). "Breaking the mirror": Interface innovation and market capture by Japanese professional camera firms, 1955–1974. *Industrial and Corporate Change, 28*(5), 1029–56.

Wittner, D. G. (2007). *Technology and the culture of progress in Meiji Japan*. Routledge.

Woo, B., Johnson, B., Beaty, B., & Campbell, M. (2020). Theorizing comic cons. *Journal of Fandom Studies, 8*(1), 9–31.

Wood, E. E. (1916). *A bachelor in Japan*. T. Fisher Unwin Ltd.

Woronoff, J. (1990). *Japan as – Anything but – Number one*. Palgrave Macmillan.

Woronoff, J. (2001). *The 'no-nonsense' guide to doing business in Japan* (2nd ed.). Palgrave Macmillan.

Wu, F. H. (2002). Profiling in the wake of September 11: The precedent of the Japanese American internment. *Criminal Justice, 17*(2), 52–60.

Yasunori, A. (1988). *Kinsei Nihon to Higashi Ajia* (Early modern Japan and East Asia), University of Tokyo Press.

Yoffie, D. B. (1983). *Power and protectionism: Strategies of the newly industrializing countries*. Columbia University Press.

Yokoyama, T. (1987). *Japan in the Victorian mind: A study of stereotyped images of a nation, 1850–80*. Springer. Macmillan.

Yuill, K. (2021). "America must remain American": The liberal contribution to race restrictions in the 1924 Immigration Act. *Federal History, 13*. www.shfg.org/resources/Documents/04 – Yuill _America must remain American_.pdf

Zurndorfer, H. (2018). Encounter and coexistence: Portugal and Ming China 1511–1610: Rethinking the dynamics of a century of global-local relations. In M. P. García & L. de Sousa (Eds.), *Global history and new policentric approaches: Europe, Asia and the Americas in a world network system* (pp. 37–52). Palgrave Studies in Comparative Global History.

INDEX

For Product Safety Concerns and Information please contact our EU representative GPSR@taylorandfrancis.com
Taylor & Francis Verlag GmbH, Kaufingerstraße 24, 80331 München, Germany

www.ingramcontent.com/pod-product-compliance
Ingram Content Group UK Ltd.
Pitfield, Milton Keynes, MK11 3LW, UK
UKHW020002200926
475702UK00015B/2442

* 9 7 8 0 3 6 7 5 3 4 6 7 7 *